Network Operating Systems

S0-BZJ-561

Data Communications and Networks Series
Consulting Editor: Dr C. Smythe, University of Sheffield

Selected titles

Network Operating Systems
Making the Right Choices

Philip Hunter

 Addison-Wesley Publishing Company
Wokingham, England • Reading, Massachusetts • Menlo Park, California • New York
Don Mills, Ontario • Amsterdam • Bonn • Sydney • Singapore • Tokyo • Madrid
San Juan • Milan • Paris • Mexico City • Seoul • Taipei

©1995 Addison-Wesley Publishers Ltd.
©1995 Addison-Wesley Publishing Company Inc.

All rights reserved. No part of this publication may be reproduced, stored in a retrieval system, or transmitted in any form or by any means, electronic, mechanical, photocopying, recording or otherwise, without prior written permission of the publisher.

Many of the designations used by manufacturers and sellers to distinguish their products are claimed as trademarks. Addison-Wesley has made every attempt to supply trademark information about manufacturers and their products mentioned in this book. A list of trademark designations and their owners appears below.

Cover designed by Designers & Partners of Oxford and printed by The Riverside Printing Co. (Reading) Ltd.
Typeset by Colset Pte Ltd, Singapore in Plantin
Printed in Great Britain at University Press, Cambridge

First printed 1994. Reprinted 1995.

ISBN 0-201-62766-3

British Library Cataloguing in Publication Data
A catalogue record for this book is available from the British Library.

Library of Congress Cataloging in Publication Data applied for

Trademark notice
IBM™, DB2™, LAN Server™, System Network Architecture™, NetView™, OS/2™ and Presentation Manager™ are trademarks of International Business Machines Corporation
Apple™, Appleshare™, AppleTalk™, Macintosh™ and Mac™ are trademarks of Apple Computer, Incorporated
Oracle® is a registered trademark and Oracle 7™, Oracle Glue™, Oracle Office™ and OracleWare™ are trademarks of Oracle Corporation UK Ltd
DEC™, PathWorks™, VAX™ and VMS™ are trademarks of Digital Equipment Corporation
Ingres™ is a trademark of Ingres Corporation
Lotus-123® and Lotus Notes® are registered trademarks of Lotus Development Corporation
Microsoft® is a registered trademark and Windows™, Win32™, Windows NT™, Windows for Workgroups™, Xenix™, Hermes™, LAN Manager™ and NT Server™ are trademarks of Microsoft Corporation
Sparcstation™ and Sun View™ are trademarks of Sun Microsystems Incorporated
Sybase™ and Replication Server™ are trademarks of Sybase Incorporated
UNIX™, OpenLook™ and OpenView™ are trademarks of AT&T
100VG-Anylan™ is a trademark of Hewlett-Packard
LANtastic™ is a trademark of Artisoft
Motif™ is a trademark of Open Software Foundation Incorporated
NetWare™, HubCon™, Personal NetWare™, UnixWare™, SNA Gateway™, AppWare™, DOS Requester™ and IPX™, are trademarks of Novell Incorporated
PowerLAN™ is a trademark of Performance Technology
Sequent™ is a trademark of Sequent Computer Systems Incorporated
WordPerfect® is a registered trademark and WordPerfect Office™ a trademark of WordPerfect Corporation
Vines™ is a trademark of Banyan Systems Incorporated
10Net™ is a trademark of Sitka

Preface

Network operating systems (NOSs) are required whenever two computers cooperate on a single task. The most common example is in local area networks (LANs), where desktop PCs typically make use of shared machines, usually called servers, for accessing common resources such as printers and data files.

NOSs handle the underlying processes required for sharing resources such as printers and databases across a network. Increasingly, they also provide facilities that allow complex networks to be managed, with support for security along with monitoring of faults and data traffic levels.

This book provides a business perspective on the issues involved in selecting a network operating system, and how it relates to the surrounding information technology issues such as security and systems management. It is aimed particularly at small- and medium-sized organizations, or workgroups within them, that either do not have a NOS installed or are not yet familiar with some of the key issues, but it also addresses some of the issues that arise in linking LANs into large-scale enterprise networks. The role of the NOS in this is covered in Chapter 6, which will be of interest to departments in larger companies that want to integrate LANs with existing computing facilities based around proprietary operating systems.

The book attempts to cut through the web of jargon that shrouds the NOS field and identify the key issues that need to be considered when selecting and installing a NOS and managing the network. Among such issues are on-going technical and market developments, which may need to be tracked to ensure your network takes advantage of advances in the field. The history of IT (information technology) is littered with extinct products and technologies that have left users stranded and with no option other than to invest afresh in new systems. The goal is an IT platform that is itself constantly evolving, and that can take aboard new products and technologies at a steady pace as they emerge.

Philip Hunter
October, 1994

Contents

8 What are application programming interfaces and how are they supported in the NOS?   195

9 What is network computing and what is the role of the NOS in this?   211

10 How is the NOS likely to evolve?   221

Case study: Bass plc   245

Introduction

The major information technology trend during the 1990s is the growth of networking, and especially of local area networking. Associated with this is a change in the way software applications are organized, with increased cooperation between different computer systems across a network. When desktop personal computers (PCs) began to be used in businesses in the early 1980s, there was initially no connection with existing mainstream data-processing applications running on larger systems. At first, PCs were little more than useful office tools for personal productivity as a natural successor to electric typewriters and pocket calculators.

Nowadays, PCs are running mainstream applications in many organizations and this has introduced new requirements. Such applications include word processing, accounting, desktop publishing, marketing and sales order processing. However, resources and data need to be shared and this requires a means of controlling access to systems from PCs. The network operating system (NOS) emerged as the solution for sharing resources and data across a local area network (LAN). Initially, in the mid 1980s, this was done simply by allowing PCs to share printers and data files but the role of NOSs has since extended to embrace management of the resources, the file servers and printers that they control, and to link up with other systems outside their control, for example wide area networks and remote mainframe computers.

Another important trend is the integration of the NOS with desktop operating systems, which can be seen in the emergence of products such as Microsoft's Windows NT operating system. NT runs on a variety of different computer systems, including desktop PCs, but incorporates features from Microsoft's NOS, which was originally called LAN Manager. Another product highlighting this trend is UnixWare, developed by Univel, which is now a subsidiary of Novell. UnixWare is a version of UNIX for desktop operating systems offering close links with NetWare.

The traditional network operating system, as typified by different versions of Novell's NetWare from the mid 1980s, relied on a central dedicated server machine holding common data files and providing access to shared resources, such as printers. A better name in the case of NetWare might have been server operating system. The NOS controlled the server and the resources directly attached to it, while PCs were under the direction of a second operating system, such as DOS. The server was linked to PCs via a LAN, yielding an overall network of the type illustrated in Figure I.1. A key component of the NOS in this arrangement was the shell that ran in the PC to intercept calls between applications and the PC operating system and to route them to the server. The basic function of the NOS shell is shown in Figure I.2.

A NOS that emerged slightly later was the peer-to-peer type. This still required a server to hold common data files and provide access to a shared printer but the server did not need to be dedicated. The server could also function as a desktop PC in a network of the sort illustrated in Figure I.3. One major advantage of peer-to-peer operation was that a separate PC dedicated to server operation became unnecessary. A small business could run the same applications with one less computer, although this did not generally apply when large amounts of data needed to be shared by a number of users: in that situation, a dedicated server was easier to manage and provided superior protection against data corruption or unauthorized access.

The relationship between the NOS and desktop operating system did not change with the advent of peer-to-peer operation. The desktop operating system was still unaware that it accessed shared resources that were not directly attached to it. The NOS had to mimic the file commands expected by the desktop operating system. The desktop operating system was not 'network aware', leaving the NOS to make the network appear to reside within the PC.

A more recent development has been desktop operating systems that are 'network aware'. These have been designed with the requirements of networking in mind, providing facilities such as support for protocols that facilitate

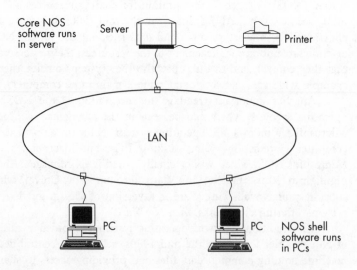

Figure I.1 Basic function of a NOS in a simple LAN.

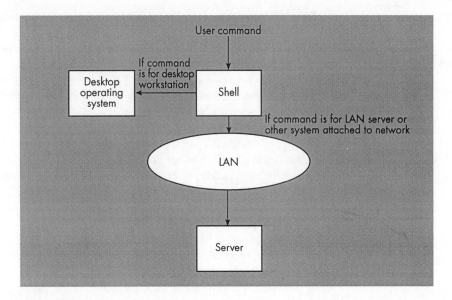

Figure 1.2 Function of a NOS shell.

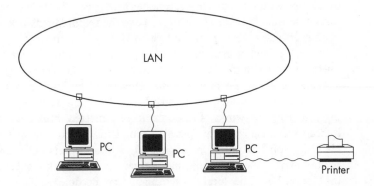

Figure 1.3 Peer-to-peer network. There is no dedicated server. All machines can, in principle, run user's desktop applications although some may be configured to operate as servers on behalf of users and some may have printers attached.

cooperation with other computers across a network. This removes the need for a NOS that has to pander to the requirements of specific desktop operating systems. Now, different operating systems can interwork across a network in peer-to-peer fashion; to do this, each operating system must support relevant protocols that enable them to understand commands issued by other operating systems on different systems.

An important point is that this development does not spell the death knell of the NOS – it does not change the fundamental structure of networked computer applications, which operate in some form of client/server fashion. Client/server computing, as it is often called, can work in myriad ways on a wide variety of networking platforms, and is discussed in detail in Chapter 9.

In all cases, client/server computing involves the division of applications into client and server parts, with each being processed on computers most suited to them. On typical LANs controlled by a NOS, desktop PCs are the clients running the presentational part of applications, while servers handle file and database management and print services. The client application issues a request to the server, which returns a result or provides a service to the client. The client then concentrates on parts of the overall application that are specific to a particular user, including control and presentation of the screen. The server handles tasks required by different users and applications; these are most commonly the control of access to shared resources, files and databases.

As already noted, LANs can operate in peer-to-peer mode with some PCs functioning simultaneously as servers and clients. In this case, major components of the NOS will run in the same computer as the PC operating system. Here the argument for integrating desktop and server operating systems is particularly strong, as they both reside in the same computer. The goal is to make PCs themselves 'network ready' so that they can automatically be attached to a LAN without requiring additional products. The operating system alone cannot do this: the PCs also need to have the required network interfaces built in. Nevertheless, the operating system is a key component.

As Chapter 9 explains, there are many different shades of client/server operation of which the classic LAN situation of desktop clients clustered around a single server is just one example. However, the NOS is not only involved in relatively straightforward isolated LANs serving a single workgroup; increasingly in large networks, LANs are interconnected with each other and also linked to larger host computers providing a multi-tiered client/server structure. Here desktop PCs might be connected to local servers and subsequently to a remote mainframe as the ultimate server, in a network similar to that shown in Figure I.4. The local server may then become a client of the remote mainframe. This could happen, for example, when a PC application requests some data from the local server. If the local server has the required data, it will return this to the desktop client, but if not it may submit a request to the remote mainframe. In this case it becomes the client, because it is now taking control by initiating a request to another machine functioning as the server.

The role of the NOS now becomes crucial, because it sits in the middle connecting the desktop PC with the remote systems. Increasingly, leading NOSs such as NetWare are providing the functions needed to support operations such as relevant communication protocols and links to various network management systems. The role of the NOS in expanded enterprise wide networks is explained in Chapter 6.

NOS vendors can therefore be seen to be moving in two directions in an attempt to expand their share of the overall operating system market: on the

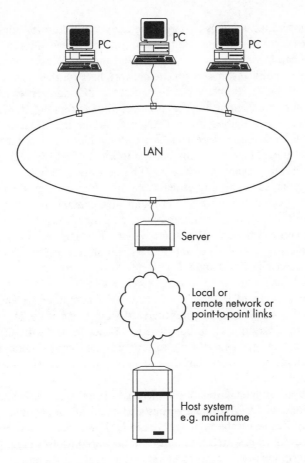

Figure I.4 A LAN providing access to larger remote systems, which may function as the ultimate server, acting perhaps as a repository for corporate data.

one hand, they are vying for the desktop market with operating systems and related products that support complete LAN applications; on the other, they are attempting to expand their realm into larger-scale networks providing increasingly sophisticated security and management features, and tighter integration with operating systems for large computers.

From the point of view of network users, it is more constructive to regard the NOS as a set of functions required to support client/server operation across a LAN, and to provide a type of glue that binds larger networks together. These functions may be provided in traditional form in a server-based product or be part of overall networking software packages for implementation across a LAN. The distinction between the NOS and other operating systems is fading. For this reason, this book does not confine its attention to traditional NOSs but covers other operating aspects of a LAN. This incorporates sophisticated desktop operating systems that provide networking features, along with other desirable qualities including multi-tasking, which is the ability to run more than one application simultaneously, and a GUI (graphical user interface). Both of these have significant impact on the network because they tend to increase the amount of data traffic between client desktop PCs and server machines, so it is becoming more important that the operating system on the server performs as efficiently as possible. For a LAN, this means the NOS.

The NOS is therefore just part of the wider network picture, albeit an important one. The aim of this book is to set the NOS in this larger context, drawing in all relevant components. The network as a whole comprises a set of computers, each running at least one operating system. There may also be networking components which, although they contain computer processors in their own right, do not require an operating system because they serve a single function controlled from some other system. This includes LAN internetworking products such as bridges and routers, whose role and relationship with the NOS is described in Chapter 6.

No book on operating systems can ignore UNIX, which is unique in that there are versions of it capable of running on computer systems of all sizes, from notebook PCs to supercomputers. Most versions of UNIX offer considerable networking support, although it is distinct from the traditional NOS in that it is not designed specifically to support client/server operation on a LAN. The relationship between UNIX and networked applications is described in Chapters 3 and 6.

A basic understanding of the physical structure of LANs and how devices such as PCs connect to the network is a prerequisite for any discussion of NOS operation. Readers unfamiliar with basic LAN technology will find an outline of the relevant topics such as cabling and network interface cards (NICs), along with descriptions of key protocols and standards, in the appendices.

What is a NOS and when do I need one?

CHAPTER OBJECTIVES:

- To define what a NOS is, and to describe its major functions
- To set the scene for Chapter 2, where leading NOSs are compared on the basis of these functions, and subsequent chapters, where the functions are dealt with in more detail when dealing with key issues for users and purchasers of NOSs

☐ 1.1   Introduction

A computer's operating system is the software platform needed to support applications so that they can access the various resources available. On a PC this will include screen, keyboard, disk drive and central processing unit (CPU). A traditional computer operating system, such as MS-DOS for PCs, controls access to and use of such resources on a single computer. A network operating system, on the other hand, allows an application on one computer to access resources on another to which it is attached via a network.

Network operating systems can take various forms. They can be distributed across two or more computers, or even all computers on a network, in which case they may control resources on several machines. Alternatively, they may control just a single computer but allow applications on other computers to access the resources. In the latter case, the network operating system (NOS) will cooperate with other operating systems in other computers on the network.

The best-known NOSs, which essentially control file or database servers on a LAN and provide shared access to printers, are of this latter type. For many people these are the definitive NOSs, well-known examples being NetWare, LAN Manager and LANtastic. However the scope of this book is broader than this, encompassing other operating systems such as UNIX and Windows NT that provide extensive facilities for operating across a network.

In the rest of this chapter, the features of a network operating system will be defined more clearly, before proceeding to establish the situations where one is needed. First, though, it is necessary to define the fundamental principles of all operating systems, whether for networks or not. Readers familiar with basic operating system principles can skip to Section 1.3.

☐ 1.2　What is an operating system?

Operating systems were originally developed for large mainframe computers, in order to provide a common set of instructions for applications to control the underlying hardware resources. Subsequently they have been refined and extended to progressively smaller computers as they evolved – first mini-computers and then desktop PCs. But the purpose of the operating system remained the same – to control the computer's hardware resources. For a desktop PC or workstation, such resources typically include screen, keyboard, CPU, RAM (random access memory), magnetic disk drive and communication ports. The basic function of the operating system is shown schematically in Figure 1.1. The operating system provides a common platform for applications to exploit the various hardware resources of the computer.

1.2.1　Why have an operating system?

A major reason for having an operating system is to provide a common base for software applications to build on, which is independent of the underlying hardware. For example, an operating system provides a Print statement that will write formatted information to a printer without the application software having to specify any details of the device's operation. Any printer that supports industry-standard protocols can then be used. Operating systems also provide

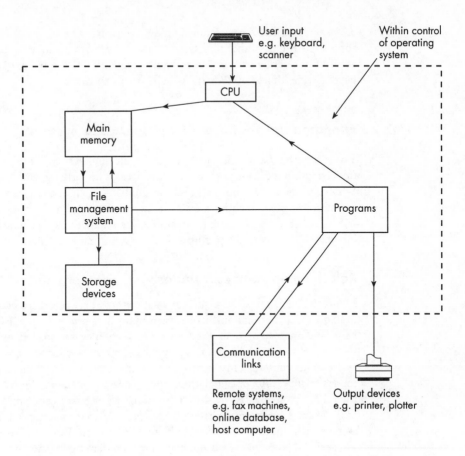

Figure 1.1 Basic operating system functions, shown schematically.

some important higher-level functions above the underlying hardware, the most significant being file management. This allows application programs to read and write data without having to know what device it is stored on or how it is physically organized on that device. In the case of a PC, this device would normally be a fixed magnetic disk drive.

Without an operating system, programmers would have to write different software for each type of computer, and would also have to provide options for a variety of associated devices such as printers. As it is, application software written for a particular operating system should be able to run on any computer that supports that operating system. This situation is still far from ideal, because there are so many operating systems. There is as yet no universal operating system for all computers, the nearest being UNIX, which unfortunately, until recently at least, has been bedevilled by the many different versions that are not completely compatible with each other.

However, for desktop PCs the MS-DOS operating system has become the *de facto* standard. Apart from Apple Macs, virtually all major desktop PCs support MS-DOS, and this has led to the growth of a huge base of such applications. The result is that software companies have a big market and users have a wide choice of PCs on which to run them.

1.2.2 Fundamental features of an operating system

To grasp the basic functions of an operating system, it is necessary to understand the relationship between the various underlying hardware resources. We have taken desktop PCs as our model – with larger systems, such as mainframes, the principles are the same but there are differences in scale and in some of the components: for example, the CPUs of PCs generally use single integrated circuits (ICs) or chips, whereas mainframe CPUs use multiple ICs.

Relationship between underlying components

Figure 1.2 illustrates the principal relationships between these components in desktop PCs; the relationship between main memory and the CPU is an intimate and important one. Programs and data files are loaded into the main memory as they are being run, under the control of the operating system. Then, instructions contained in the program are passed to the CPU for execution, any intermediate results of calculations being stored in memory. Main memory and the CPU are connected by the PC's input/output bus, as shown in Figure 1.2.

Main memory, often called RAM (random access memory), is a temporary storage medium that is constantly being overwritten. PCs also have permanent memory called ROM (read only memory) containing instructions that enable the computer to start up correctly. These instructions have the generic title BIOS (basic input/output system) and provide a vital underlying platform for the operating system, as explained later in this section.

Main memory then is just a temporary storage medium. Programs and data are stored in some permanent location, usually a hard disk drive, which is connected to the main memory and CPU as shown in Figure 1.2. Most PCs also have a floppy disk drive, enabling new software and data to be introduced to the hard disk drive, or existing files to be copied. Unlike permanent memory, hard and floppy disk drives can be overwritten but differ from main memory in that data is semi-permanent – it can be deleted by the user or an application but it is not erased when the PC is switched off.

The other major component is the screen or VDU (visual display unit), which receives output from applications via the CPU. The screen can also be fed directly from the keyboard, or from remote applications via communications ports. The communications ports link a PC to external devices, which can be local peripherals such as printers, or devices such as modems to access remote systems. Typical PCs have two types of port, serial and parallel, which are connected to the PC's internal communications bus. Usually there is just one parallel port, used chiefly for printers, and two serial ports. The latter can also

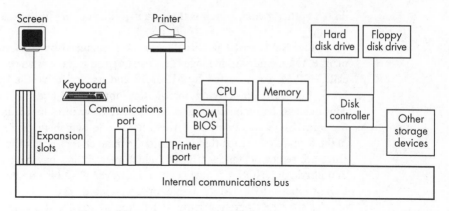

Figure 1.2 How a PC's components are connected (not in correct order).

be used by printers but are mainly intended for other external devices attached to the PC. These ports allow the PC to communicate via its CPU with external devices that do not come packaged with the PC.

There is also another well-known component of PCs: the expansion slots. Expansion cards available for these slots provide a variety of functions not available on the PC's own system board housing the CPU. Examples of expansion boards include internal modems for dial-up communications and, of most relevance for this book, network interface cards (NICs), which enable PCs and servers to be attached to LANs. NICs and the issues involved in selecting them are discussed in Appendix 7.

Interactions between the PC's components require low-level machine code specific to the particular CPU. For most PCs, the CPUs are all compatible with the standard originally developed for Intel processors; this means that PCs from a variety of manufacturers can all be controlled with the same machine code. However each application would have to come with its own package of machine code to control the computer's basic functions, which would waste a lot of time that could otherwise be spent on providing higher-level features for users. This is where the operating system comes in – by providing a command set allowing both applications and users directly to manipulate the computer's underlying resources. The operating system itself may be written using machine code, or it may use a standard higher-level computer language that in turn compiles the instructions into low-level machine code that the computer can understand.

Role of BIOS (basic input/output system) in PCs

Early PCs in the late 1970s consisted of primitive operating systems permanently encoded in ROM, providing basic instructions to control the devices. There were no facilities to manage storage and retrieval of data files on magnetic disks or other media, which is the core ingredient of any fully fledged operating system.

The ROM-based facilities were soon enhanced by software loaded into main RAM memory to manage files. First on the scene was an operating system called CP/M, soon ousted by MS-DOS and its derivative for IBM PCs, PC-DOS, but basic underlying instructions for controlling the PC's resources continued to be embedded in ROM. When IBM introduced its PC in 1982, the term BIOS was coined for this set of code, which in current PCs comes in the form of two chips that plug into the main chassis or 'motherboard'. These chips are typically standard ROM, which means that they have to be replaced to upgrade the BIOS to a new version. However, BIOS is implemented in some PCs in Flash EPROM (erasable programmable read only memory), which enables it to be upgraded without needing to replace the chips.

The BIOS provides the basic link between the operating system and the underlying hardware resources. It is the machine-dependent part of the overall operating system, but has become standard across the whole range of industry-standard PCs based on the CPUs developed by Intel (some of which are now also supplied by Advanced Micro Devices).

Other features of operating systems

The main feature provided by operating systems like MS-DOS is comprehensive file-handling facilities. This enables users or applications to store data or programs in files, and organize them in directories. These files are usually held on hard disk drives built into the computer. Typically desktop PC hard disk drives have capacities in the range 80 Mbytes to 500 Mbytes, or roughly 80 million to 500 million characters of information. Files can also be copied to floppy disks inserted into a floppy disk drive. Nowadays, floppy disks are 90 mm (3½ inches) across and hold up to 2 Mbytes of data.

Taking MS-DOS as an example, hard disks need to be formatted when the operating system is first loaded into the computer. This structures the disk in such a way that MS-DOS can find and write data on it. Data can then be collected in files, for example a list of names and addresses, and then stored on the hard disk. The names of files are held in directories, which also specify the file size in bytes and the date and time it was last updated. The great majority of features that MS-DOS provides are concerned with creating, editing, deleting and manipulating files and directories.

Another important facility is the ability to reconfigure the PC when new devices are added: as the operating system controls the PC's resources, it must be able to recognize all of them. Internal devices that are built into or come with the computer, such as keyboard, screen and primary hard disk drive, are specified in the BIOS; external devices such as printers, modems and mice that do not come boxed with the PC and therefore can vary, need to be specified by device drivers. These are special programs that are part of the operating system and allow it to recognize particular devices. With MS-DOS there is also a device driver which instructs the PC to look for networking software.

Another essential function of the operating system is to control the execution of programs, and support the linking of different software components within a given application. Typically, programs written in a high-level language such as C are compiled into a so-called object file, containing low-level binary instructions which the computer's CPU can understand and process.

1.2.3 Limitations of MS-DOS and the development of network and multi-tasking operating systems

MS-DOS was tailor made for early PCs, which because of their limited processing power and memory could only handle one task at a time, and were not connected to other computers. MS-DOS is therefore 'single user and single task' (although Microsoft eventually added the ability to share files with the 'Share' command, as discussed further in Section 3.7.1). MS-DOS was also limited in that it could only support 640 Kbytes of memory. None of these limitations was important when MS-DOS was first implemented in the early 1980s but became so with the advent of LANs, and as the power and memory of PCs increased. This led to developments on two fronts: for LANs, so-called network operating systems were developed enabling PCs to share resources, in particular printers and a file server across the network. Secondly, operating systems capable of handling more than one task at a time were developed, and which could handle larger amounts of main memory; OS/2 is a well-known example of a multi-tasking operating system.

OS/2 was originally designed as a successor to MS-DOS for industry-standard PCs in commercial applications. Meanwhile, progress with CPU and main memory technology took single-user machines in a different direction, leading to more sophisticated computers called workstations. These in general have more main memory and faster CPUs than do standard PCs, although perhaps the main distinction is that they tend to have larger and higher resolution monitors suitable for graphics applications. Workstations also tend to incorporate RISC (reduced instruction set computer) CPUs to achieve extra speed on a number of routine calculations.

These workstations do not run the MS-DOS operating system, because of the limitations already mentioned. In general, they run a version of the UNIX operating system, which is capable of supporting both multiple users and tasks. Furthermore, some versions of UNIX have been extended to provide networking support. This enables UNIX to function more like a network operating system, providing the facilities necessary for computers to cooperate across a network. We shall define more clearly what features a network operating system should have later in this chapter. Then in Chapter 2 we shall look in more detail at UNIX along with other network operating systems.

Another development was the advent of so-called network operating systems (NOSs), initially as extensions to MS-DOS supporting operation of a complete LAN rather than just a single-user PC. In Chapters 8–10 we shall examine further the relationship between different types of operating system across the network, concluding in Chapter 10 with a discussion about likely future trends.

□ 1.3 How and why did network operating systems evolve?

The original motive for installing a LAN was to share resources such as disk drives and printers. However MS-DOS assumed all resources to be the exclusive preserve of each PC and had no facilities for sharing resources between two or more users. Clearly for resource sharing to work, requests for access to shared devices such as printers would have to be channelled through some common computer processing device. Without this, there would be no way of handling tasks such as printer queuing, needed for more than one user to share a single printer. Also, there needed to be some mechanism for making all resources appear local to the PC's operating system. It had to appear to each PC that shared resources like printers were attached directly to it and not shared with others.

   The solution that emerged most strongly was the network operating system running on a single PC on the LAN, called the file server, or simply the server. We shall refer to it as the server throughout the rest of this book. The server became the vehicle for sharing all LAN resources, not just shared files residing in the server's own disk drive but also other devices, for example printers attached to the LAN. The principle is illustrated in Figure 1.3, which

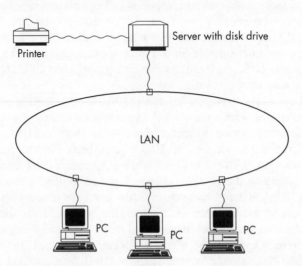

Figure 1.3 Typical simple LAN workgroup with dedicated server and printer attached.

shows a server with its own disk storage for shared data and a printer attached, supporting individual desktop PCs each with their own data.

Therefore each PC can still have its own personal data, and access a shared pool of data residing in a common server computer. The server also manages queuing for one or more printers attached to the network. Leading network operating systems are described in detail in Chapter 2, while the basic principles of operation are covered in Section 1.4.

Note that LANs are not confined to PCs and PC-based servers. They can additionally be used to attach PCs and terminals to larger systems such as mainframe computers. The role of the NOS in supporting links with larger systems is covered in Chapter 6.

□ 1.4 Basic principles of a network operating system

The NOS originally had to fulfil two fundamental requirements: to allow resources to be shared across a LAN; and to enable existing PC operating systems like MS-DOS to continue working in each PC without change. Subsequently, other requirements have emerged, for example security, network management and integration with other types of computer system. Such features are described briefly later in this chapter, and expanded on in subsequent chapters.

To fulfil the two fundamental requirements, a NOS needs two components. The major component controls the operation of the server and manages the files stored there. To do this it needs the features of a PC operating system like MS-DOS but with the difference that there are now multiple users contending for its resources across a network, instead of just one user. Furthermore, not all the users of a LAN will necessarily want to do the same things: one may want to print a letter, while another may want to access data. Hence the server component of the LAN needs to support multiple users and tasks.

The second NOS component is software running in client systems, enabling them to access the network and the resources on it. Clients in this context are systems running applications for users, typically desktop PCs or workstations. These clients access resources and services provided by servers, which are usually larger systems dedicated to their task.

Various NOSs have emerged to provide these facilities in ways that differ in detail but essentially all require at least one shared server that is accessed by all users on a LAN. This server provides access to data files and also to shared hardware resources, typically one or more printers.

The differences between individual NOSs are described in Chapter 2. Some NOSs require a dedicated server that solely handles shared tasks like accessing files on behalf of all users. A dedicated server does not run specific applications such as word processing. Other NOSs support non-dedicated servers that combine the functions of server and desktop PC; in these cases a desktop PC can also function as a server. Figure 1.4 shows two LANs, one with a single dedicated server and the other where one user's PC is designated as a non-dedicated server, providing shared access to its disk drive and also its printer.

LANs with non-dedicated servers are sometimes called peer-to-peer LANs and can provide an ideal solution for small businesses because the expense of an additional server computer is avoided. NOSs that support peer-to-peer operation and provide low-cost network solutions are described in Chapter 3.

In all cases a NOS must cooperate with the operating system of each desktop PC or workstation on the LAN, often referred to collectively as clients. In this book we shall sometimes refer to desktop systems attached to a LAN as clients.

As they control the server but not the PCs on the LAN, NOSs are sometimes described as server operating systems – this is particularly true of the major versions of Novell's NetWare NOS. NetWare was designed to provide efficient shared access to files and printing facilities across a LAN, and its success on these two counts is the main reason for it becoming the dominant NOS in the PC LAN arena. However in addition to managing servers, a NOS has to provide a transport mechanism for data to be transmitted between the server and desktop PCs.

We will now restate the basic requirements of a NOS: it must provide facilities for sharing resources and be able to resolve conflicts between requests for such resources from multiple users. The NOS must therefore be able to load and unload the appropriate resources requested by users. To do this, it usually incorporates a server operating system dedicated to supporting multiple users and tasks. Hence a mechanism exists for the server to interact with the operating system of each PC, in order to intercept calls from applications that want to access data or a resource on the network. The NOS must also provide or support a communications protocol that enables data to be transported across the LAN. To fulfil these requirements, a NOS needs two essential components: a full operating system running on the server(s); and software running in each PC or desktop workstation to interact with the client operating system and provide a protocol for communication with the server across the LAN.

1.4.1 Components of NOSs running in the desktop or client system

In the case of NetWare, the software running in each desktop PC is called a shell, which has two components. The first is a mechanism by which the PC liaises with its network interface card (NIC), which enables the PC to communicate with other devices on the LAN. On most NetWare LANs the method used

(a)

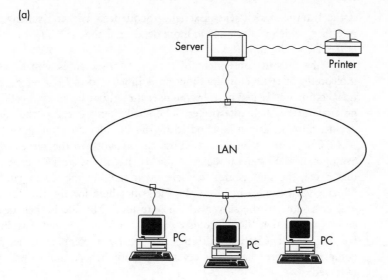

(b)

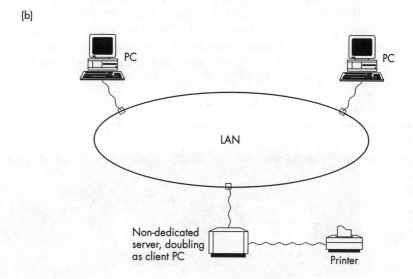

Figure 1.4 (a) Classic LAN with dedicated server; (b) peer-to-peer LAN, where one PC functions as server while also running client applications.

is the Internetwork Packet Exchange/Sequenced Packet Exchange (IPX/SPX) interface, which is discussed in more detail in Chapter 2. The function of NICs is described in Appendix 7.

The second component of the NetWare shell is sometimes called the interpreter or redirector. Its function is illustrated in Figure 1.5, which shows how commands issued both by the user directly or by an application in the PC go first to the shell interpreter. The shell then interprets the command and decides whether it can be handled by the PC's local operating system, such as MS-DOS, or must be passed across the network to the server. Suppose, for example, a user wants to delete a file. If that file is stored locally on the PC's disk drive, the shell routes the delete command to the local operating system, which then executes it; but if the file is not held locally, the delete command will be routed to the server where it resides. The file is then deleted on the server, unless that file is protected against deletion by that particular user. As we shall see in Chapter 5, things become more complex on larger networks comprising more than one server, especially where more than one NOS is involved.

Other NOSs operate on similar principles, although there are differences in technical detail. All need a mechanism for determining whether an instruction can be executed locally in the PC or whether it needs routing to another computer on the network. Also all need to be able to communicate with the NIC so that commands and data can be transmitted to and received from the network. In order to communicate with the network in this way, many NOSs use an interface called NetBIOS, which we now describe.

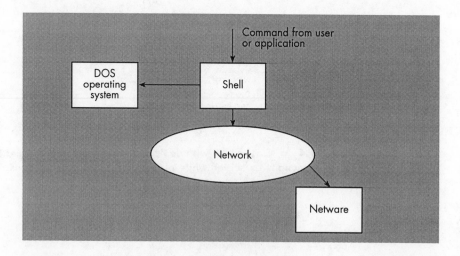

Figure 1.5 Function of netware shell. Shell interprets commands and decides whether to route them to DOS, or to the NetWare server via the network.

Role of NetBIOS

NetBIOS, as the name suggests, was developed as an extension of BIOS (see Section 1.2) to cope with resources distributed across the network rather than just those local to the PC. Recall that BIOS provides the link between the PC's operating system and resources such as disk drive, screen, keyboard and serial communications port.

NetBIOS was developed first as a specific link between the components of a network operating system running in each PC or device attached to a LAN and the network itself. Just as BIOS provides the underlying software link between a PC's operating system and the underlying hardware, so NetBIOS links the NOS or shell software in a client system to the underlying network hardware; the difference is that a network's hardware resources may be physically separated by a length of cable from a PC accessing them. The only network hardware directly attached to the PC or server is the network interface card (NIC), the hardware link between the computer and the LAN. NetBIOS was developed as a software link between the operating system in the PC attached to the LAN and the NIC, initially for DOS 3.1, which at that time was IBM's version of MS-DOS. IBM published the specifications and it quickly became the *de facto* standard, supported by other PC and server operating systems. Subsequently more sophisticated alternatives to NetBIOS were developed, such as Microsoft's Win32, described in Chapter 8. NetBIOS is also an API (application programming interface) in that it can be used directly by applications as well as the operating system to access network resources. However, as is explained in Chapter 8, other APIs provide more sophisticated and easier-to-use facilities for cooperation and communication between applications and operating systems across a network.

The basic operation of NetBIOS is shown in Figure 1.6. If commands from a user application cannot be executed locally in the PC or workstation, they are routed towards the network by a redirector, which is part of the NOS. The redirector transfers the command to NetBIOS, which performs the necessary protocol packaging to forward it to the NIC for transmission onto the network.

In NetWare, Novell implemented the functions of NetBIOS in its own shell, as can be seen by referring back to Figure 1.5. However Novell subsequently added a NetBIOS interface to NetWare because a number of PC applications had been written to take direct advantage of this interface. The NetBIOS part of the NetWare shell is optional and should not be loaded for applications that do not require it.

The shell components of the best-known NOSs are discussed further in Chapter 2.

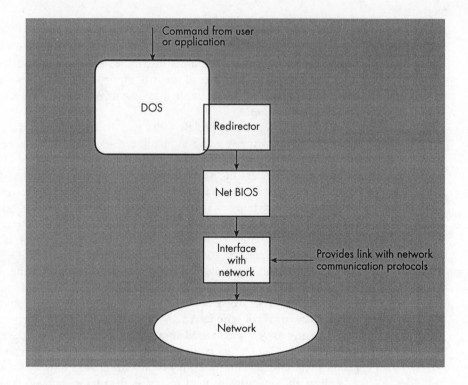

Figure 1.6 Function of NetBIOS. Redirector that overlaps with DOS intercepts network commands and routes them to the network.

1.4.2 Server component of NOSs

Although NOSs differ in their function and structure, all are based to some extent on the concept of clients and servers. On typical LANs, clients are desktop PCs or workstations running applications for users; servers are more variable in type. On many LANs there is a single dedicated server, which is a powerful PC, committed to delivering file and print services to users attached to the LAN. However it is also possible to have client desktop PCs doubling up as non-dedicated servers, and there may be more than one server on a LAN, each being either dedicated or non-dedicated.

Whatever the exact configuration, in all PC LANs there is a NOS server component that manages the services provided to client workstations, and this comprises most of the NOS. Whereas the shell only has to route commands and data between client PCs and workstations across the LAN, the server component has to provide the functions of a complete operating system in addition to managing communications across the LAN.

However, not all NOSs provide all the components needed to control a server; in practice most are built on top of an underlying operating system designed to handle just single machines. For example, Microsoft's NT Server (formerly LAN Manager) was originally built on top of the OS/2 operating system, and has since been extended to work on top of other operating systems such as UNIX and Microsoft's own Windows NT. NetWare is an example of a network operating system built from scratch to manage the operation of servers and the surrounding LAN.

It makes little difference to users on the LAN whether the NOS controls the server or requires an underlying operating system; for example, users of older LAN Manager LANs did not need to know there was an operating system like OS/2 underlying the NOS. So although, strictly speaking, many server functions such as file handling may be provided primarily by an underlying operating system, we will consider them as NOS functions. These can be identified under four broad headings: file handling, print serving, management of communications across the network and security. The way in which leading NOSs tackle these functions will be explained in Chapter 2 and detail will also be given in subsequent chapters, such as Chapter 7 which deals with network management. In this chapter we shall give only some general detail on each of these four areas.

File handling

On PC LANs, servers are the central points of control, acting as gateways to shared resources. The most important shared resource is probably the data, including applications software for loading across the network into desktop PCs. The server component of the NOS manages the storage, updating and access to that data. The NOS is responsible for ensuring that updates are made consistently, with support for locking techniques that prevent two users from making simultaneous changes to a given piece of data, and that data is accessed as efficiently as possible. Although the performance of the LAN as a whole depends on several factors, including the basic transmission capacity of the network and the power of both servers and client PCs, the NOS plays a crucial role. Methods used by several individual NOSs to speed up access to data on the server are described in Chapter 2.

As with operating systems like the DOS family for computers serving just one user, the NOS in the server provides a common file structure for applications that is independent of the underlying hardware. This is essential if applications are to be written that allow the use of any server on which the NOS is running. However the fact that a NOS needs to support more than one user on different PCs on a LAN imposes two key additional requirements:

(1) it must be able to understand commands from different desktop operating systems and support the associated filing systems;

(2) it must support simultaneous requests to access data (and also other resources such as printers, discussed later) from more than one user.

Understanding commands from the desktop operating system and supporting the associated filing system

As explained earlier, each PC has a component, sometimes called a shell, which intercepts calls from applications to the normal PC operating system. If such calls require action from resources located on the LAN, they are routed to the server. These calls emulate filing protocols specific to the desktop operating system, therefore the central part of the NOS running in the server has to emulate the relevant filing protocol. In particular, it must support the file and directory structures of each desktop operating system it supports. By so doing, the NOS enables the network's file server to appear to all PC users as part of their system. The file and directory structures of the most popular desktop operating system (the DOS family) are described in Appendix 6.

For some smaller low-cost NOSs, support for different desktop operating systems is not essential. Some, for example, are designed just for PCs running MS-DOS but clearly such products restrict freedom of choice, and are not likely to appeal for larger networks where there may already be a range of desktop operating systems within the organization.

Supporting simultaneous requests to access data from more than one user

Not all data stored on the server is for sharing. For example, each user may have a private electronic mailbox on the server for storing messages; although other users can send messages into this mailbox, they are not allowed to access files stored in it. Most NOSs provide some facilities to stop users accessing files they are not authorized to see. In some cases, users may be allowed to access a file but not to alter it. Generally, the NOS allows files to be flagged as read only or read/write. Leading NOSs also allow permission to update a file to be restricted to a specified list of individuals, or even just one person.

NOSs also allow files to be shared by a number of people, some of whom might attempt to access them simultaneously. As well as individual files, servers may hold whole databases, containing sets of related files, shared among a number of users. This introduces more complex requirements for sharing data, because actions taken on one item might have knock-on effects on others. For example, a customer database might have one file listing customer addresses and another listing products each customer has purchased in the past. If a customer is deleted, the relevant records in both files need to be deleted. The subject of database management and its relationship with the NOS is discussed further in Chapter 9.

Print serving

One of the original motives for developing LANs was the desire to allow a number of PC users easy access to one or more printers. The NOS typically allows printers to be shared via a file server, in an arrangement similar to that shown in Figure 1.4. Jobs to be printed are routed from a PC to the file server, which holds them in a queue. The file server takes over responsibility for printing the jobs as soon as the correct printer becomes available. However the printers themselves do not need to be physically attached to the file server: they can be attached to another PC or workstation on the LAN or directly to the network without an intermediate computer. Methods of attaching printers to the LAN are discussed further after the next subsection.

Print queuing and spooling

Print spooling (the word spool is an acronym for simultaneous peripheral operation on line) is the fundamental mechanism that allows a printer to be shared across a network. When a PC wants to print, it issues a request via the network to the print server. The server then 'spools' the print job onto its hard disk, where there may also be other jobs queued up for printing. The server then retrieves print files one at a time from the hard disk into its main memory, according to priority, and prints them.

Spooling solves two problems: it enables the server to print files larger than can be accommodated in its main memory, but above all it enables the network to take the burden of managing print queues away from each PC. Without spooling, each PC would have to negotiate directly with the printer, and wait for it to become free before transmitting the print file across the network. As many desktop PCs cannot handle more than one task at a time, this would frustrate users, who would need constantly to check if the printer was free.

Queuing mechanisms determine the order in which print jobs are 'despooled' off the hard disk and printed. NOSs vary in their precise arrangements for queuing print jobs. Typically there are multiple queues with different priorities, and various options for deciding in which order to pick jobs from the various queues. Consideration of two typical situations will demonstrate how queuing operates. One common situation is where a single printer handles all jobs but is reconfigured from time to time to produce different types of output. Suppose, for example, a printer is used to produce letters on standard A4 paper, and also to print self-adhesive address labels. Obviously it cannot print both in a single run, because it needs to be loaded with different paper for each. It therefore makes sense to pick jobs that require the paper currently loaded, even if there are others with higher priority but requiring a different paper. In this example, all letters could be printed first, followed by the labels needed to address them. Of course if there are two printers, then the letters can be printed on one while the corresponding address labels are printed in parallel on the other.

Another fairly typical situation for a larger network is where there are three printers: two laser and one dot matrix for producing rough drafts. A suitable arrangement might be to arrange jobs in three queues, one for rough drafts, one for low-priority long slow jobs, and one for high-priority short fast jobs. The way the queues could be matched to the three printers is shown in Figure 1.7. The first queue, comprising draft jobs, is matched solely to the dot

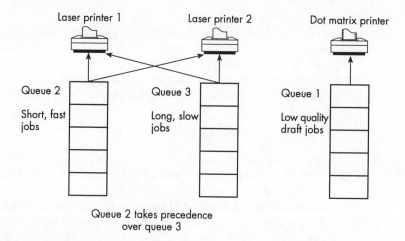

Figure 1.7 Example of the use of print queues.

matrix printer, because the quality of the more expensive laser printers is not required. The other two queues would be shared between the two laser printers, with the second queue, comprising the short fast jobs, taking precedence over the third queue, the long slow jobs. However when the second queue is empty, jobs from the third queue could print on both laser printers. Then when a small urgent job re-enters the second queue, it would print on either laser printer 1 or 2 as soon as one had finished printing its job from the first queue. In some cases it may be possible to configure the queuing system so that an urgent job interrupts a long slow job.

Methods of attaching a printer to a network

Essentially there are three ways of attaching a printer to a LAN, as illustrated in Figure 1.8. Jobs are always routed to a printer via a file server but it is not always convenient or desirable to locate printers next to the file server. The file server may be located some distance away or locked in a secure area, while the best place for a printer is close to the users whose output will be produced on it. It may be desirable to provide communal access to printers attached to individual users' PCs. When printers are not attached to a file server, they can either be attached via another PC functioning as a print server or connected directly. The function of a print server, which is software running in a PC or NIC, is to control the link between the printer and the file server handling the spooling of print jobs. Its function is depicted schematically in Figure 1.9. The print server function is slightly confusing, because sometimes it can be provided by the main file server, while at other times it is implemented in one or more PCs or printers.

For direct network attachment, the printer must either incorporate its own network interface card (NIC) or alternatively be connected via an external

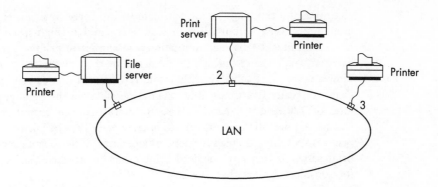

Figure 1.8 Three ways of attaching a printer to a LAN: (1) printer attached via file server; (2) printer attached via dedicated print server; (3) printer attached directly.

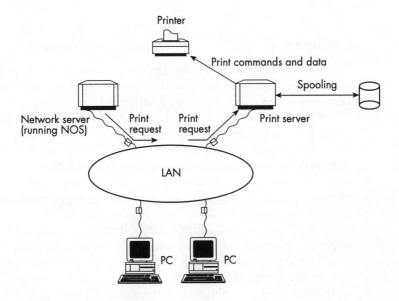

Figure 1.9 Function of a print server.

black box. Either the NIC or the external box then provides the print server function: each option has advantages and disadvantages. Printers with their own NIC provide higher performance than printers attached via external modules or, for that matter, printers attached via PCs or file servers. Normally, printers designed for PCs (as opposed to larger centralized computers) attach via either a serial or parallel port. In the former case, data is transmitted bit by bit at a speed of $9600 \, \text{bit s}^{-1}$. Printers attached via the parallel port receive data eight bits at a time, and can accept data two to three times faster, at typically around 23 Kbit s^{-1}, but are still slow compared to high-speed printers for large computers. This same limitation also applies to printers attached via an external box, because they are still attached by their own serial or parallel port. However, being attached directly via an NIC, the printer can accept data much faster, typically five times faster than is possible via the parallel port, at data rates of 120 Kbit s^{-1}. Modern laser printers that can output at 16 pages a minute require this performance to operate at full speed but this does require printers specially designed for network operation. The advantage of an external print server is that any standard printer can be attached via its parallel port for considerably less than the cost of a PC.

Apart from allowing the use of printers located anywhere on the network, having print server functions separated from the file server can confer other performance advantages. Heavily used printers impose a considerable load on the server's CPU, memory and disk drives. Much of this can be freed for other applications by distributing print jobs to separate servers across the network.

Management of communications and network

The role of the NOS is to manage and control access to shared resources. Apart from computing devices and data, this includes the physical network itself. The basic cabling structure of a LAN, described in Appendix 4, is independent of the NOS, as is the mechanism used for transmitting data packets across the LAN. With reference to the universal OSI seven-layer model for computer networking, described in Appendix 3, the physical cabling is included in layer one, while the data transmission is handled in layer two. The role of the NOS begins at layer one at the level where NICs physically attach systems to the network. Then in layer two, the NICs communicate on a packet-by-packet basis using the underlying LAN protocol, such as Ethernet or token ring. In layer three, the NOS provides a link between devices for streams of data to flow, using the disjointed packet-by-packet transmission service provided by layer two. There are a number of independent network management products to manage the bottom two layers, which, as explained in Chapter 7, are increasingly being integrated with facilities provided by the NOS. However the main role of the NOS is in layers three upwards, to transmit data and control sessions between PCs and servers. A session is defined as a continuous period during which a PC is logged onto a server, and can therefore issue requests to it and receive data from it.

Some NOSs, such as NetWare, provide their own protocol stack (IPX/SPX) to handle data transport, while others use industry-standard protocol stacks such as TCP/IP. Various relevant protocol stacks are defined in Appendix 2. Essentially, these protocol stacks provide a framework for data to be transmitted between devices on a LAN, using the basic communications facilities of layers one and two. They also provide the basis for wider communication with other remote LANs, or with different types of computer system such as mainframes.

Leading NOSs provide routing facilities that allow multiple LANs to be interconnected to form what is sometimes called an internet. Products for interconnecting LANs are described in Chapter 6 and touched on elsewhere in the book where relevant. The major NOSs, such as NetWare and LAN Manager, also provide gateways for accessing other computing environments such as IBM SNA (system network architecture) networks; these are also described in Chapter 6. In essence, gateways enable PCs on a LAN to access data and applications held on a larger computer system that supports different protocols. Gateways also allow two dissimilar networks to be interconnected.

Security

As LANs become larger and provide increasing access to different sources of information, the need for security grows substantially. The phenomenon of down-sizing, in which applications that previously ran on large centralized computers are implemented on LANs with PC servers, has also increased the need for security. Large computers are protected by sophisticated security procedures, including physical measures to prevent unauthorized people from accessing the machine and data, along with technical measures like multiple levels of passwords and biometric devices. In contrast, LANs began as inherently insecure systems, with their file servers being physically unprotected and offering only limited password protection. Another key weakness is that data is usually transmitted on LANs via external cables, which potential hackers can readily tap into, to eavesdrop with relatively simple monitoring devices.

The provision of adequate security on LANs is the responsibility of the NOS. Chapter 2 looks at the security features of leading NOSs, while Chapter 7 gives a more detailed discussion of the overall security problem, indicating which aspects are tackled by NOSs in general. Fundamentally there are two goals: to prevent data or network resources being accessed by unauthorized people; and to prevent data being lost or corrupted. The latter can be the result of deliberate abuse or tampering, or caused by faults in hardware or software.

The NOS plays a significant role in meeting both these objectives, although protecting data against failures of individual communications links or system components comes down to good overall design of the network to avoid, whenever possible, single points of failure. However, the NOS plays a key role in providing automatic data backup services for data located in servers. Most NOSs also provide links with uninterruptible power supplies, so that users can be warned to finish what they are doing and the network can be shut down in an orderly fashion in the event of a power failure.

The other major role of the NOS as far as security is concerned is in controlling access to the server, and in some cases encrypting data as it passes across the network. In particular, NOSs are becoming responsible for ensuring that users cannot obtain access to unauthorized data files and resources such as specialist printers that may be restricted to a few specified individuals. With NetWare, for example, each file on the server can be associated with a list of users authorized to access it; users not on this list are denied access to the file.

☐ SUMMARY

Now that its role and basic functions have been described, it should be apparent that the NOS is an essential component of any LAN because it manages and controls access to shared resources and data. NetWare, the first popular NOS and now the market leader with its various versions, evolved as an operating system to control single dedicated file servers that also provided access to printers. Many other possibilities have evolved, ranging from large networks with multiple servers to small LANs without a dedicated server, where data is distributed across just a few desktop PCs. NOSs have been developed to cope with these different configurations, as explained in Chapters 2 to 4. In Chapter 6 we shall examine how the NOS helps to integrate LANs with larger-scale computing environments like IBM SNA networks. Then in Chapter 10 we shall describe important new developments, such as the evolution of the NOS into complete networked systems comprising the operating system for desktop PCs and workstations as well as servers.

2

The main types of NOS and how they differ

CHAPTER OBJECTIVES:

- To describe all the main NOSs, except those used mainly on small networks, which are covered in Chapter 3
- To compare the leading NOSs on the basis of key functions

☐ 2.1   Introduction

In this chapter the main NOSs are described and compared on the basis of their support for the functions outlined in Chapter 1. This in turn lays a base for Chapter 4, which considers the choice of a suitable NOS for a network. While Chapter 3 focuses on NOSs suitable for small networks, including some less well-known products, in this chapter we shall confine our attention to the leading NOSs.

A major theme of this book is the increasing integration between the

29

traditional NOS function of controlling the operation of servers, and desktop operating systems. An important aspect of this chapter is therefore an assessment of how the major NOSs are providing better links to desktop operating systems. The way this is handled is an important differentiator between NOSs. This leads on to the UNIX operating system which, although not strictly a NOS, does include support for networked operation. The differences between UNIX and traditional NOSs will be clarified.

Further important aspects of a NOS are the strength of its supplier and the commitment to future enhancement and support. On this assessment the three strongest suppliers of traditional NOSs are Novell, Microsoft and IBM. The following are discussed in detail:

(1) The versions of Novell NetWare, which include NetWare 4.x, NetWare 3.1, UnixWare and Personal NetWare. However the latter, being designed for smaller networks, is dealt with more fully in Chapter 3. The older NetWare 286 is touched on, although this is now being phased out. The activities of Novell in linking NetWare with desktop operating systems are also discussed.

(2) The derivatives of the original LAN Manager developed by IBM and Microsoft, which was based on the OS/2 operating system. This leads to IBM's LAN Server and Digital Equipment's Pathworks, as well as to Microsoft's implementations of LAN Manager, where the focus is very much on integration with the desktop operating system. For example, Windows 3.11 combines Microsoft's desktop Windows operating system based on MS-DOS with LAN Manager. At the high end, Microsoft's current NOS derived from the original LAN Manager is called NT Server, which has become the main competitor to NetWare for larger networks.

(3) Banyan's Vines, which established a niche in large networks by providing comprehensive directory and electronic mail facilities while supporting links with other NOSs and operating systems.

(4) UNIX, which fits into the NOS scene from various angles. It can run as a desktop operating system, accessing servers controlled by traditional NOSs; alternatively, at the other end of the scale it may control powerful host computers capable of supporting up to 1000 users, where the NOS may provide a focal point of access from desktop PCs. UNIX may also be used as a server operating system, to control servers on a LAN. It is in this latter guise where UNIX is closest in function to a traditional NOS such as NetWare.

Another twist to the UNIX story came when Novell acquired UNIX System Laboratories (USL) from AT&T. This followed the launch by Novell in 1992 of Univel, a joint partnership with USL, to develop Unix-Ware, integrating UNIX with NetWare into a single operating environment and so combining the advantages of both operating systems. Its acquisition of USL therefore gave Novell full control of Univel, and turned it at a stroke into a complete operating system company like Microsoft, rather than just a NOS vendor. The fundamental principles of UnixWare are described later in this chapter, while further implications are discussed in subsequent chapters. However, by late 1994 UnixWare had failed to make a significant impact on the market, even though other versions of UNIX, without NetWare, were still doing well.

□ 2.2   The NetWare collection

Under the NetWare banner are several related products for different types and sizes of network. In all cases there are essentially two components:

(1) Software running in desktop client PCs to control access to the network and its resources. This software has been called the NetWare shell but, with NetWare 4, Novell introduced a new type of client software called the DOS Requester. This is described in Section 2.2.4.

(2) The main network operating system running in one or more servers and managing and controlling access to the data and resources of the network. Later in this section we shall describe the different versions of NetWare but first we outline the operation of the shell and the core NOS.

2.2.1   The NetWare shell

The relationship between the NetWare shell and the network is illustrated schematically in Figure 2.1. As the figure indicates, the shell has two related functions:

(1) To link up with applications and the desktop operating system. This is necessary because data required from the applications might reside either locally on the desktop PC or remotely on a file server on the network. The shell decides whether to pass commands to the local operating system, such as DOS, or to route it across the network to a NetWare server.

(2) To communicate with the network interface card (NIC), which provides the hardware interface with the LAN. This enables commands or data to be packaged in such a way that they can be transmitted to and received from a standard LAN like Ethernet or token ring. To handle the communication process between applications and the NIC, and onwards across the network, Novell developed a protocol called IPX (internet packet exchange).

IPX is in fact an end-to-end communication protocol for transmitting data between nodes on a network, such as client PCs and servers. At each end, on both clients and servers, the NIC functions as the door into the network: all

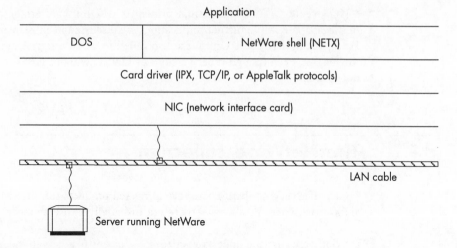

Figure 2.1 Function of NetWare shell depicted schematically.

communication across the network is handled in a standard way using layer two protocols from NIC to NIC. IPX in conjunction with the shell software allows applications designed only for a desktop PC to direct requests to the server via the NIC. At the server end, the NetWare software also uses IPX to communicate with the server's NIC. Note that Novell now also has shells that support protocols other than its own IPX. This enables applications written for other protocols such as TCP/IP to run unchanged across NetWare networks.

Readers unfamiliar with the structure of communication protocols and how they are split into seven layers should refer to Appendix 3, while IPX is described in more detail in Appendix 2.

Although the bulk of the NetWare software is located in the server, the shell is a vital ingredient because it provides the link between users' applications and both the network and desktop operating system. The overall performance of the network therefore hinges almost as much on the shell as on the server component of NetWare. The shell needs to be tuned both to the desktop operating system and the server part of NOS in order to provide efficient transmission of instructions and data across the network.

Accordingly Novell has introduced new and revised shells, not just for emerging versions of NetWare but also to exploit advances in the desktop operating system; for example, revised shells are released to accompany major new versions of DOS.

Novell had to take particular care in designing shells to support Microsoft's Windows. Windows 3.1 and preceding versions are tightly coupled with the DOS operating system and manipulate some of the internal DOS data files. At the same time the NetWare shell shares some of the DOS tasks, as it intercepts commands from applications, some of which are then processed as DOS commands. It is therefore important that Windows can also manipulate some of the internal data files of the NetWare shell. If this cannot happen, Windows applications would be unable to work in this way when there is a NetWare shell present.

A further development in 1990 was a new version of the shell, which would load into expanded and extended PC memory, instead of having to reside in the standard DOS memory. The role of expanded and extended memory is described briefly in Appendix 8. Essentially, this move left more immediate memory available for DOS applications.

2.2.2 The core NetWare operating system

The core NetWare has become a distributed operating system for multiple LAN servers. It has evolved from a single server file system to embrace multiple LANs, and also to provide a range of associated functions, in particular network management and global directory services. The scope of NetWare is described in more detail in the following sections, starting with a potted history.

2.2.3 How NetWare has evolved

NetWare is the great success of the NOS world, as MS-DOS and Windows 3.1 have been for the desktop. It is unique among the major NOSs in having been built from scratch as a LAN operating system. Other NOSs require a conventional computer operating system as base – for example, LAN Manager was originally built on OS/2.

When the first version of NetWare was introduced in 1983, it was designed purely to control small LANs comprising a single file server. Since then NetWare has grown steadily in sophistication, and evolved into several related but distinct product lines to handle increasingly diverse networking requirements. Six major trends shaping the evolution of NOSs in general, and NetWare in particular, can be identified:

(1) Computers, and especially the PCs commonly used as LAN file servers, have become much more powerful, reliable and versatile.

(2) The maximum size of LANs has increased steadily, with some large single-site NetWare networks now having over 1000 users.

(3) LANs can now be interconnected by telecommunications links and can provide access to remote host computers.

(4) LANs have been used for increasingly critical applications where failure or breach of security is expensive.

(5) A counter trend to the others: the cost of LANs has fallen to the point where they are being implemented by small businesses that previously could not afford a network.

(6) There are increasing requirements for integration of desktop operating systems with the NOS.

It soon became clear to Novell that these diverse requirements could not be met in practice by a single product. However, although the product range has diverged, the central focus remains what it always was – the provision of a file server system that is fast and reliable. This turns a PC LAN into a flexible multi-user computer system that has increasingly eaten into the market traditionally held by larger centralized host computers driven by dumb terminals.

The product that first lifted Novell to NOS fame was NetWare/286 released in 1985, designed to take advantage of Intel's then new 80286 microprocessor's improved power and functionality. In particular it exploited the protected mode of the 80286, which is described in Appendix 8 where microprocessor developments relevant to the NOS field are dealt with.

The release of version 2.0 of Advanced NetWare in 1986 made further progress by allowing two LANs to interoperate, either being linked to a common file server or via an external bridge. These two possibilities, which are still relevant, are shown in Figure 2.2.

However, LANs could never be used for serious applications previously implemented on larger centralized computers unless they offered comparable levels of resilience against hardware and software failures. Novell was the first NOS vendor to start toughening LANs up, with the release of the system fault tolerant (SFT) version of NetWare in 1986. This first version of SFT introduced Novell's hotfix utility, which provides protection against defective regions of the file server's hard disk. The next version of fault-tolerant NetWare, SFT NetWare Level II released at the end of 1986, introduced disk duplexing and transaction tracking. Disk duplexing, as illustrated in Figure 2.3, protects against failure of disk drives and their controllers by writing data simultaneously to two disk drives. Note the distinction, shown in the figure, between disk mirroring and full disk duplexing. The latter protects against failure of the disk controller as well as the drive itself. The transaction tracking system helps maintain the integrity of a database by ensuring that the sequence of updates to data generated by transactions is performed consistently.

Subsequently, additional fault-tolerant features have been introduced, culminating in server mirroring with NetWare 4.0 introduced in 1993. As Figure 2.4 illustrates, server mirroring protects against complete failure of a server by duplicating all actions on a physically separate computer.

Since the introduction of SFT NetWare, fault-tolerant features have filtered down into standard versions of NetWare; for example, hotfix and disk mirroring are both standard across all versions of NetWare, except for Personal NetWare. Fault tolerance on LANs in general is discussed further in Chapter 7.

The SFT developments chiefly address item (4) on the above list of six trends that shaped the development of LANs. Novell has pushed equally on all six fronts, as can be summarized as follows:

(a)

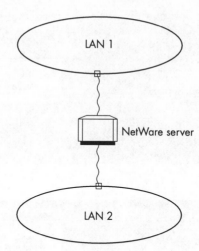

(b)

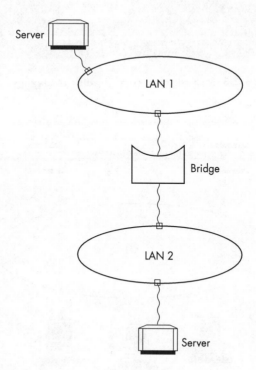

Figure 2.2 Showing how advanced netware first allowed two LANs to interoperate in 1986: (a) LANs interconnected by server; (b) LANs interconnected by external bridge each with its own server.

(a)

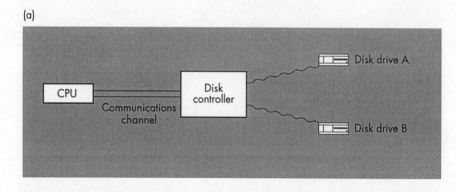

(b)

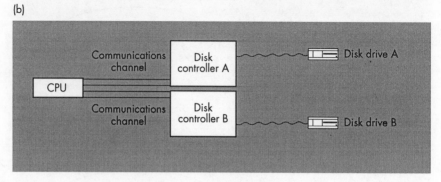

Figure 2.3 (a) Disk mirroring; (b) disk duplexing.

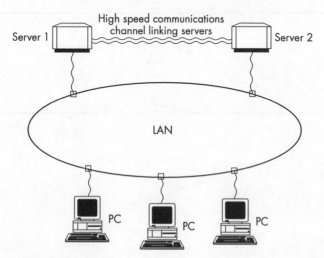

Figure 2.4 Server mirroring. Server 2 shadows server 1 during normal operation and takes over if it fails.

- Point (1) was addressed initially by NetWare/386 version 3.0 released in September 1989, to exploit the additional power and facilities of Intel's 386 and subsequently 486 ranges of microprocessors. This also tackled point (2), establishing the foundation for larger LANs supporting greater numbers of concurrent users.

- Novell tackled the first part of point (3) by introducing support for bridges and routers, which enable LANs to be interconnected both locally and remotely by telecommunication links. Routers, bridges and the interconnection of LANs are discussed in Chapter 6; however the role of these devices in overall network management is discussed in Chapter 7. It is important to note here that bridges and routers provide only a foundation for large networks of interconnected LANs. Ideally, a large network should appear to its users as a single coherent system providing transparent access to data and resources wherever they are located. As the NOS controls access to data and resources on LANs, it has a significant role to play on virtually all large networks, given that LANs have become established as the platform for local workgroup computing. To accomplish this, various facilities must be provided at a higher level than bridging and routing, such as support for distributed directories and network management. Novell introduced these facilities in 1993 with NetWare 4.0, which was designed specifically for large networks comprising multiple servers.

- Novell has also addressed the second part of point (3), the requirement for access to remote networks and host systems, in various ways; for example, it introduced the NetWare SNA Gateway, which allows DOS PCs on a NetWare network to access an IBM SNA network. Novell also acquired an X.25 gateway from Eicon Technology, allowing NetWare LANs to communicate with remote systems via a packet-switched X.25 network.

- With regard to point (5), the move downscale to smaller networks, Novell's first attempt at this came in 1987 when NetWare ELS (entry level solution) was introduced. Aimed at small networks, this initially supported just four concurrent users and also allowed servers to operate in non-dedicated mode. This made significant savings possible for small network users, because it avoided the need to purchase an additional computer for the server. However it was primarily aimed at dedicated server operation, and it was not until the introduction of NetWare Lite (later combined with DR-DOS and renamed Personal NetWare) in 1991 that Novell offered a product designed specifically for non-dedicated servers.

- Finally, Novell is addressing point (6) from two directions. Firstly, its acquisition of Digital Research in 1991 took Novell into the DOS market with DR-DOS. Novell then bundled DR-DOS with NetWare Lite, later renaming the combined package Personal NetWare, to provide a complete operating system package incorporating both desktop and server for small networks. Secondly, Novell is tackling the desktop UNIX market through Univel, a company set up jointly in December 1991 with UNIX System Laboratories (USL), which is now itself a subsidiary of Novell. The fruit of this partnership is UnixWare, a version of UNIX for standard desktop PCs providing seamless integration with NetWare servers.

2.2.4 The various versions of NetWare

Novell's product portfolio now includes three major versions of NetWare. In addition, for industry-standard desktop PCs there are two operating systems: the version of DOS called DR-DOS and, from its subsidiary Univel company, UnixWare. The company does not provide operating systems for Apple Macs, or other desktop PCs not based on the standard x86 range of microprocessors available from Intel or Advanced Micro Devices (AMD). However these machines can still participate in NetWare networks, and in any case Novell is now porting NetWare to other hardware platforms.

The primary focus in this chapter is NetWare itself. The three major versions are: Personal NetWare for small networks with non-dedicated servers; NetWare 3.1 for larger networks but ideally without more than a handful of servers; and NetWare 4.1 for large distributed networks comprising many servers. NetWare 3.1 and 4.1 overlap to some extent, the main distinction being that the latter has additional features for multi-server networks. As Personal NetWare is intended for smaller networks, we shall postpone a description of that until Chapter 3, which deals with lower-cost, less sophisticated NOSs. There is a further version, NetWare 2.2, which we shall also describe as it still has users. However, Novell's development focus is on the more powerful 3.12 and 4.1 products, and the company's strategy involves migrating users away from 2.2.

Can the different versions of NetWare work together?

All versions of NetWare can co-exist on the same network and are interoperable in the sense that file servers under the different regimes can be connected and exchange data, but mixing different flavours of NetWare presents a variety of problems and limits the overall range of functions available.

NetWare 2.2

Like most software vendors, Novell prefers its customers to use the latest versions of its products. This reduces the number of different versions that need to be supported and generally makes life easier for the vendor. Nevertheless, users do not necessarily need the latest technology and are often reluctant to upgrade just for the sake of it if an existing product is still working satisfactorily. NetWare 2.2 furnishes a classic example of this syndrome: Novell wanted it to wither rapidly in favour of the more powerful 3.1 and latterly 4.x, but some of its customers dug their heels in and insisted that the product enjoyed continued support.

The fact is that NetWare 2.2 is a stable mature product, coming at the end of a line of enhancements for the 286 version. However it is limited in its potential to support large networks, because of restrictions on the size of server and the number of users it can support. Table 2.1 summarizes the main features of NetWare 2.2. The principal features of NetWare 2.2 relating to performance, reliability and security are also described later in this chapter under NetWare 3.1, where they are gathered together for convenience.

Value-added processes (VAP)

The value of a NOS can be enhanced if it can be tailored to specific networking environments by adding functions as appropriate. For a NOS to provide all conceivable functions it would have to occupy more memory than is available on a file server, and its performance would be abysmal. Therefore the approach adopted by Novell and some other NOS vendors is to supply a core that handles essential server-operating functions, and then provide hooks for additional applications. For NetWare 2.2 these hooks, or more correctly the applications built using these hooks, are generically referred to as VAPs (value-added processes): some were developed by Novell itself while others came from third parties. A wide variety of VAPs are available for functions such as communications services, gateways to other networks, additional support for printing on a network and offloading processing from the server to other workstations on the network.

Against the positive benefits of VAPs are some negative factors relating to network performance and reliability. VAPs can consume large amounts of server memory and, if several are running, the response of the network can slow down significantly. Also, if they are not properly installed, VAPs can crash the file server with possible loss of critical data. However, as we shall see, most of these problems have been resolved in NetWare Loadable Modules (NLMs), which are Novell's sequel to VAPs for NetWare 3.1 and 4.1, running on servers with at least a 386 processor.

Table 2.1 Key features of NetWare 2.2.

Limited to a maximum of 100 users.

Support for server-based applications in the form of VAPs that could not be loaded and unloaded dynamically on the fly.

Ability to run in non-dedicated mode, although Novell did not recommend this for larger networks.

Support for disk mirroring and disk duplexing.

Maximum file size 255 Mbytes (raised to 2 Gbytes in NetWare 3.11).

Maximum of 1000 concurrently open files (raised to 100 000 in NetWare 3.11).

NetWare 3.1

Novell paved the way for a new generation of more sophisticated LANs capable of running serious business applications with the launch of NetWare/386 version 3.0 in 1989. This version evolved during 1990 into NetWare 3.1, which until early 1993 was Novell's top-end version of the NOS. NetWare 3.1 runs only on PCs with at least a 386 processor, enabling it to support larger LANs and provide various more sophisticated facilities, which include NetWare Loadable Modules (NLMs), described below. The additional features of NetWare 3.1 not found in NetWare 2.2 are summarized in Table 2.2.

A key point about NetWare 3.1 is that Novell did not make the mistake of simply modifying NetWare 2.2. Instead the company completely redesigned the operating system with a new 32-bit architecture to exploit the greater potential for performance available with the 386 and 486 Intel processors. The benefits this delivered to users can be summarized under four headings: performance, reliability, security and support for open networking protocols other than Novell's IPX.

Performance

As already indicated, the performance improvement sprang from three factors: the greater power of the 386 and 486 processors; the rewriting of the operating system, with a 32-bit architecture, to exploit this power; and the use of dynamically loadable NLMs, which are described in the next section. This led to improved response times for almost any application requiring action on the part of the server.

NetWare 3.1 also has a variety of other performance features for the

---

Table 2.2 Additional features of NetWare 3.1 not found in NetWare 2.2.

Support for NLMs (but no longer for VAPS).

Files up to 4 Gbytes now supported.

Up to 100 000 concurrently open files allowed.

Support for disk volumes up to 32 Terabytes (32 million million bytes).

Up to 250 concurrent users supported, with licences for 5, 10, 20, 50, 100 and 250.

Non-dedicated peer-to-peer operation no longer supported.

Additional performance features to speed up disk operation.

Support NFS (Network File System), enabling NetWare users to access UNIX applications.

Support for TCP/IP and OSI protocols in addition to Novell's own IPX.

Support for IPX tunnelling over TCP/IP, allowing NetWare LANs to be interconnected via TCP/IP networks.

---

file server system, some of which were already available in NetWare 2.2 and these will now be described briefly.

1. *Turbo file allocation tables (FAT) indexing*

Files are not necessarily stored as contiguous blocks of data on hard disk drives, as this would quickly create numerous fragments of unused disk space, which would greatly impair the amount of available storage capacity. Instead, files are written in disjointed fragments on the disk, with the disk head jumping from one free block of space to the next, and then writing as much of that file as it can before encountering a block of data. This makes efficient use of space but slows down the time taken to read and write files, because the disk head has to jump from fragment to fragment. Each file has a FAT table listing the physical addresses of the blocks containing each of its fragments on the disk. For large files, this table may itself be of significant size. Turbo FAT indexing speeds up the process of searching for the FAT table of large files, by storing the tables in an index. Otherwise NetWare would need to scan all FAT tables when searching for the specific table relating to a file it needs to access but, with FAT indexing, NetWare can jump straight to the required FAT entry, so speeding up both disk reads and writes. In NetWare 2.2, FAT indexing was an option only recommended for large files, for which it was activated through use of the 'FLAG' command. However it is automatically performed on all files in NetWare 3.1 and NetWare 4.x.

2. *Directory caching*

This also relates to the directory entry of each file. By caching these entries, which means storing them in the computer's main memory rather than on disk, the directory entry of each file can be found much faster, speeding up the time taken to read or search files. RAM is much faster to access than the hard disk drive, thus leaving the disk drive, access to which can become a bottleneck, free to work on reading and writing data rather than accessing directories.

3. *File caching*

This also speeds up the process of reading data files by retaining the most recently accessed portions in RAM. It exploits the fact that the more recently data has been accessed, the more likely on average it is to be accessed again in the near future. In many cases the proportion of file reads or writes that only require access to cache rather than the disk drive is 85 per cent or more. Therefore this technique can increase performance significantly.

4. *Directory hashing*

This is a technique that shortens the time taken to locate a file name in the file directory held on the server. Whenever a file is updated, its directory entry is looked up. There may be several thousand files held on a NetWare server, so the process of locating the name in the directory can take a significant amount of time on a heavily used network. Directory hashing is a technique that shortens the time taken to locate file names in the directory. Essentially, each file name is converted by the hashing algorithm into a number, which identifies the location of the directory entry. Searching for a file name involves simply determining its hash number and then accessing the physical location in the directory table identified by that number.

5. *Elevator seeking*

This is so called because it works in a similar way to elevators (or 'lifts' for UK readers). When you summon an elevator or lift, it does not necessarily come straight away but may stop to pick up someone on another floor, even if that person pressed the button after you. This process increases the time you have to wait in this instance, but in the long run improves the efficiency of the lift, because it reduces the number of times it changes direction. Similarly, elevator seeking on a LAN server allows the disk read/write head to pick up fragments of files as it travels across the disk, irrespective of the order in which requests to do so were submitted by an application. Only when the head reaches the end of the disk will it reverse direction, reading or writing newly requested file fragments on the way back. To make elevator seeking work efficiently, NetWare collects several requests and acts on them together, rather than handling each one on a first-come first-served basis. This improves average disk access time significantly, because the head travels less, and does not continually change direction; it also reduces wear on disk components, so prolonging the life of the disk drive.

6. *Data scattering*

This allows NetWare to spread data efficiently over multiple disk drives, reducing the time taken to access and write data. If the fragments of a file are distributed across more than one disk, some of them can be accessed simultaneously, reducing the overall access time. In theory, if a file is distributed across three disk drives rather than one, three times the number of input/output operations can be performed in a given time. The same applies to complete disk volumes, which are regions of disk drives defined for a specific purpose, such as for a given set of users. Volumes are described in more detail in Appendix 9, which covers key aspects of disk drive technology.

7. *Multi-tasking*

This allows NetWare to handle many requests simultaneously, up to 1000 or more per second, so increasing overall network performance.

8. *Split seeks*

These only apply to network servers with duplex disk drives, as described in the next section on reliability. All blocks of data are held on both disk drives and, as there are also two controllers, there is a choice of access route. The idea is that if one of the disk channels is busy at any time, data can be accessed via the other channel. NetWare monitors the status of each channel continuously and decides which of the disk drives will be able to respond faster to each request.

Reliability

On reliability, NetWare 3.1 added one major new feature – support for mirrored servers – although this was not actually made available until two years after the announcement. The way mirrored servers work is shown in Figure 2.4.

Having a completely redundant standby server is not always necessary but for critical applications the cost of having an extra server may be insignificant compared with the cost incurred in terms of lost time and the impact of a server failure on business. With two mirrored servers, the network is protected against failure of either one or the other. Furthermore, it may be possible to locate the servers some distance apart within a site, providing some protection against localized disasters such as a fire. However for mirrored servers to work, they must be interconnected by a link of significantly higher speed than the LAN itself. For example, if the servers were attached to an Ethernet LAN running at $10 \, \text{Mbit s}^{-1}$, the link connecting the servers directly should probably run at $80 \, \text{Mbit s}^{-1}$ or more. In some cases the servers might be linked by a common high-speed backbone network interconnecting a number of LANs across a large site such as a university campus.

Apart from mirrored serving, NetWare 3.1 retained the reliability features already introduced into NetWare 2.2: these include disk mirroring and disk duplexing, which are both illustrated in Figure 2.3, and transaction tracking.

Novell's collective term for reliability features is system fault tolerance (SFT). Other key components of SFT, which were mostly introduced in NetWare 2.2, can be summed up as follows:

1. *Redundant directory structures*
There are two copies of directory entries and FAT tables, each held on different cylinders of the disk drive to reduce the risk of a disk drive fault destroying both.

2. *Automatic directory management*
When a failure occurs in a sector holding the file directory, NetWare automatically switches to the redundant directory.

3. *Read-after-write verification*
NetWare automatically reads all data as soon as it has been written to ensure that it is legible on the disk, so that it can be read subsequently as required. In conjunction with hotfix, this provides powerful protection against loss of data as a result of local faults developing on the disk drive.

4. *Hotfix*
It is quite common for isolated faults to occur in a disk drive, introducing the risk of data corruption and loss. Some of these faults manifest themselves as soon as there is an attempt to write data to that part of the disk, while others

develop with wear. Network file servers are especially prone to faults that develop with wear and tear, given that the rate of usage is much higher than for standalone workstations. If NetWare finds that an area is bad, it labels it as such so that no future attempt is made to write data there.

However if the error manifests itself during a read operation, the data in that space is probably unrecoverable. Unless disk mirroring or duplexing is in operation, the data is lost, although at least with hotfix the area is labelled as bad and not used in future.

5. *Error detection and correction*

Sometimes data can be recovered from areas of disk drives where errors are only beginning to occur. However NetWare reduces the incidence of disk errors by rewriting data to good areas if a faulty area is discovered during a read, write or read-after-write verification.

6. *Disk mirroring and duplexing*

Disk mirroring protects against failure of disk drives, while disk duplexing also shields the network from the failures of associated hardware such as controllers, interfaces and power supplies. These were described earlier in this section.

7. *UPS (uninterruptible power supply) monitoring function*

A UPS can provide a server with protection against power fluctuations and in some cases against complete power failures. NetWare monitors the UPS status and responds to users' requests. In particular, it can tell users that a power failure has occurred, so that the network can be shut down smoothly without loss of data. The role of UPSs in LANs is described more fully in Section 7.2.10.

8. *Retrieval and salvage of deleted files*

Sooner or later we all delete a file in error. Many users of DOS are familiar with the Norton utilities that allow recently deleted files to be salvaged. NetWare provides a similar utility called Salvage, except that this contains additional facilities which are desirable for a file server shared by a number of users rather than just one. For example, it allows the system administrator to set a minimum time during which a deleted file should be kept before it is physically overwritten on the disk, after which point it becomes irretrievable.

9. *Transaction tracking system (TTS)*

This maintains the integrity of a database by ensuring that transactions are either finished or aborted, and cannot be left hung with some updates completed and others not. Suppose, for example, a transaction entails updating a customer's address and telephone number. If the network crashed after updating the address but before updating the associated telephone number, the database would be inconsistent. TTS ensures that if the network crashes, or if the transaction is not completed for some other reason, both the address and telephone number are as they were before the update began. NetWare 3.1 can track up to 25 000 transactions that are under way at any one time.

Security

NetWare provides four security layers, all, some or none of which can be activated to provide varying levels of control over unauthorized access to resources and data. These layers are authentication, authorization, accounting and administration. Many of the security features are provided by the SysCon utility, described below.

Authentication is the process of identifying who the user is, which then allows the network to decide whether to allow that user to perform the tasks or access the data requested. Authentication takes place during the login process, through user names and passwords. It is the latter which provides the real protection and therefore Novell has taken steps to ensure that passwords cannot easily be discovered by potential hackers. For example, passwords are stored in encrypted form both in client workstations and in the server, and are never transmitted across the network; instead, the server and client negotiate using codes generated from a combination of the encrypted password and the user's identifier.

This leads on to authorization, which is the control of access to data and resources based on the user's identity. Individual restrictions can be imposed on both directories and individual files. Restrictions include read only, read and write, create, erase, modify, scan and full supervisor rights. The latter includes the ability to change both the restrictions on each particular file and the rights of each user, so it is important to guard supervisor rights closely.

Accounting fulfils two functions: to monitor usage of the network; and for capacity planning to manage on-going network growth and change. The aim of the former could be to charge for network services, or to discourage their profligate use. Users can be billed in various ways, including by connection time, by the number of requests issued by their workstations or by the amount of disk storage consumed on the server. The different usage parameters can be combined to yield an overall billing formula. For capacity planning, use of resources by different individuals and workgroups can be tracked to provide early warning of bottlenecks or saturated resources. Action can then be taken to remedy potential problems before they occur, maintaining consistent network performance in the face of traffic growth and changing usage patterns.

Security administration embraces the management of the overall NetWare security system. This task subdivides into three areas: console security, account restrictions and login restrictions. The first helps ensure that only those authorized to do so can access the server console and therefore load software and edit data on the server itself. With servers commonly now running critical applications, this role is vital to prevent key data and software being tampered with or destroyed either accidentally or deliberately. The server can be physically locked away, and its keyboard can have a logical lock imposed which prevents keystrokes from being acted on until the correct password has been entered. Account restrictions allow administrators to impose good housekeeping rules on users, such as compelling them to change passwords periodically to reduce the risk of their being guessed or accessed by eavesdropping. Login restrictions allow access for some users to be restricted to certain locations and/or times of day; for example, users may be allowed to log in only from the PCs on their own desks and only during normal office hours. This reduces the risks both of hacking from an uncontrolled location during the day and of breaking into an office to hack from a user's own PC out of hours.

NLMs (NetWare loadable modules)

Like VAPs, the idea of NLMs is that they behave as an integral part of the overall NetWare operating system, providing additional functions. Users are unaware of any difference between VAPs and NLMs: both provide functions that are available as if they were part of the core NetWare system. However NLMs are technically superior to VAPs, in that they make more efficient use of the file server's resources. This means either that NLMs will provide better response times to users or that equivalent performance can be delivered at a lower cost in terms of file server resources, or both.

The reason for the improved performance is that NLMs are only loaded into the file server's main memory when they are needed. VAPs are loaded all the time, even when their function is not needed, and as already noted can slow down the machine significantly. NLMs, in contrast, can be loaded and unloaded as and when the user's application requests the function they provide. Before they are loaded, and after they are unloaded, they do not take up any memory or consume any processing resources.

While an NLM is loaded, its status can be checked using resource-tracking features built into NetWare 3.1; furthermore, the Monitor utility can be used to determine which network resources the NLM is using. These NLM tracking and monitoring facilities are particularly important in a large distributed network, where they help identify and manage all the resources used by server-based applications. They also make it possible for different NLMs to cooperate in a distributed network by synchronizing their use of services.

NLMs are also easier to program than VAPs. However, the NetWare environment does not provide the same level of sophistication and support for applications development as does the UNIX operating system. This was one reason for Novell's acquisition of UNIX System Laboratories early in 1993. As discussed in Chapter 6, this enabled Novell to offer its customers a combined UNIX/NetWare environment, with the application development facilities of the former and the networking functions of the latter.

SysCon

SysCon is a utility providing some of the facilities required to manage and administer a LAN, particularly with regard to controlling access to the network's resources. For example, SysCon can be used to force users to change their passwords at regular intervals, and can control the amount of server disk space that they are allowed to fill with their own files. Some of NetWare's extensive range of security and access control features are described above. For more comprehensive coverage, there are numerous specialist books on NetWare both from Novell and independent authors.

SysCon also provides options from a menu which allows supervisors to tailor the configuration of the network on a user-by-user basis.

Hub management interface (HMI)

Structured cabling in star-shaped networks based on centralized wiring hubs is rapidly replacing traditional bus and ring-shaped networks that have no physical centre. Figure 2.5 shows the principle. Novell in 1991 introduced its hub management interface (HMI) to allow hubs to be managed from NetWare servers. Included in HMI is a management utility called HubCon, which allows a hub to be managed either locally from a console attached to the server, or remotely using the SNMP (simple network management protocol). The hub will often be a separate unit but for smaller networks HMI brings the possibility of incorporating the hub functions into the server on a hub interface card, as illustrated in Figure 2.6. This is an elegant solution, in that the server which is the logical centre of a small network also becomes the physical hub. However on larger networks all the expansion slots on the hub may be needed for network applications; furthermore, this solution has limited scope for network growth and is recommended only for single networks with at most around 30 users. An alternative option is to turn things around and have a product designed primarily as a hub functioning as a server with the addition of appropriate cards or modules. This may offer greater expansion potential but also limits the flexibility of the network. IBM and LANoptics are among vendors offering such hub/servers.

Apart from HubCon for hub management, which works similarly to SysCon for other server management utilities, there are two other components

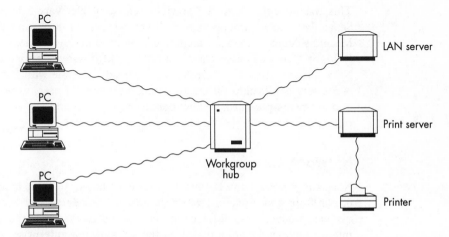

Figure 2.5 LAN based on star-shaped structured cabling system.

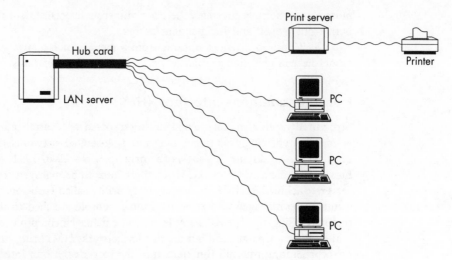

Figure 2.6 Cabling hub on a card in the server.

to HMI: one is the interface itself, providing a standard specification for developing the relevant software drivers; and the other is the SNMP agent software, which facilitates management of the hub via remote SNMP consoles.

HMI is part of Novell's overall product set for network management called NMS (NetWare management system). As this has become a major contender in the network management arena in its own right, it is described fully in Chapter 7, which is dedicated to that field.

NetWare 3.12

This was an upgrade to the previous release of NetWare 3.1, introduced in September 1993. Among new facilities were improved support for Apple Macintosh clients, enabling them to exploit most of the functions that standard DOS- or Windows-based clients can. Also added was the option to install the NOS software from CD-ROMs, as was already possible with NetWare 4, but of greatest significance for most existing NetWare 3.1 users were performance improvements provided by new caching algorithms and the ability for applications to run multiple transactions against the same file.

NetWare 4.x

Normally new versions of software supplant the old but this is not quite true of NetWare 4.x. Novell's strategy is now to provide several overlapping but distinct products for different sectors of the market. All the products are interoperable and can be mixed on the same overall enterprise-wide network, but each has different strengths and weaknesses.

NetWare 4.0 was released in early 1993 as an enterprise-wide network operating system aimed at large installations with multiple servers, often spread over more than one site. The purpose was to capture a share of the growing market for software needed to control a large network beyond single LANs, and to compete with companies already established in that field, such as Banyan Systems. Banyan's Vines is described in Section 2.7. NetWare 3.1 was already moving in that direction with features such as NetWare communications services, which allow LANs to be interconnected with each other and with remote hosts and services, but missing in NetWare 3.1 were facilities such as distributed global directory services, which are needed on a large-scale network of multiple servers. Such facilities were introduced in NetWare 4.0. However, as already indicated, NetWare 3.1 is not being phased out and will continue to be enhanced, but with the emphasis now primarily on networks with one or at most a few servers. In borderline cases, where both products meet current requirements, the better choice will depend on whether there are plans to extend the network substantially. If this is the case, then NetWare 4.x will be the better choice, especially if global coverage spanning servers in different countries is required. Even networks with two to four servers, which constitute the majority of NetWare sites, will derive some benefit from NetWare 4.x.

Enhancements to NetWare implemented in version 4.x but not 3.1 can be summarized under six headings: directory services, storage management, imaging, internationalization of the product, improvements to the core NetWare product, and at the client end a new way of accessing the network called the DOS Requester.

1. *Directory services*

Novell implemented a distributed directory based on the international X.500 standard with the aim of making a global network of multiple servers perform as far as possible like a single LAN as far as its users are concerned. The basic principle of operation is shown in Figure 2.7, which depicts five servers linked by a distributed directory. Each server has a directory of the information it holds and also a list of other adjacent servers. In Figure 2.7, servers adjacent to A are B and C, while servers adjacent to C are A, D and E. Suppose a user's application running on a PC attached to LAN A requests data held on server D. The request is first handled by server A, which fails to elicit the required information. Server A then informs the PC that it does not have the information, and lists all the adjacent servers, in this case those attached to LANs B and C. The PC transmits the request to the adjacent servers simultaneously, although in this case they do not hold the information either. Servers B and C each transmit lists of servers adjacent to them back to the PC via server A. This list cites servers D and E, to each of which the PC issues requests. Server D eventually locates the information and transmits it back to the PC on LAN A via LANs D, C and finally A.

An important aspect of Novell's distributed directory services is support for redundancy, to avoid any single point of failure. The larger the network, the greater the probability of at least one server failing during a given time,

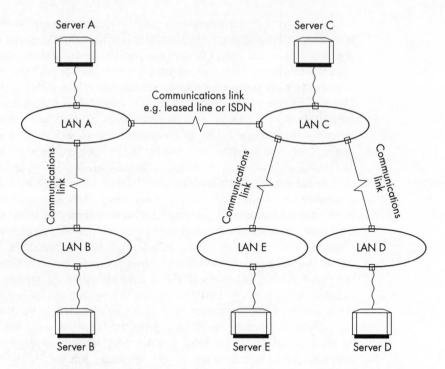

Figure 2.7 A network of five servers linked by remote communication lines, via Novell's distributed directory service.

so it is increasingly important to ensure that this does not corrupt or disable the whole distributed directory structure. Novell guarantees that, if its distributed directory service is correctly implemented, all information held on the network can be found somewhere should any single server fails. This is made possible through replication of all directory entries – no single server contains the complete directory for its locality, and all directory entries and the associated information are held on two servers.

Apart from protection against failure, this replication facility provides an improved response for users who travel widely and need to access information from different countries, because having the information distributed across the network reduces the average time taken to access it from remote locations.

Another feature provided is browsing, which allows users to scan the whole distributed directory under Microsoft Windows. As browsing proceeds, information flows to the user's workstation from whichever server holds it, irrespective of its location on the network.

Improved software tools to help build distributed directories were included in NetWare 4.1, the first major new version of NetWare 4.

2. *Storage management*

There are two objectives here: to bring mainframe storage technology down to the PC network level; and to provide a single interface for software developers to utilize the new facilities. In the past, Novell has upgraded the NetWare file system a number of times, which has brought improvements but also compelled third parties to redevelop their products to exploit the new facilities. Subsequent enhancements introduced by Novell will not alter the interface with software provided by external suppliers, which is good news both for users and software developers.

In addition to this, the new storage management facilities provide three tangible benefits for users:

- More efficient use of disk storage enables files two to three times as big to be stored in a given disk space. Users can therefore delay having to increase the disk storage capacity of their server.
- Introduction of hierarchical data storage of the kind available on large centralized computers makes it easier to manage large databases and provides more efficient use of different grades of storage media.
- New, more efficient data compression saves further on disk space and improves network performance.

The first of these three benefits follows from the more efficient use of data blocks. Blocks are the storage units on the disk drive used when files are written and under previous versions of NetWare, no one block could hold the contents of more than one file. Thus a file comprising three and a half blocks of data would be written into the first three empty blocks that the disk head encountered and then into half of the fourth. The remainder of the fourth block would be left empty but could not be used to store any other file, so it would be wasted space. Given that files very rarely fill an exact number of blocks, this is an extravagant use of disk resources, particularly where there are large numbers of relatively small files occupying less than one block. Yet this has been the method used on PCs and LAN servers to date. However with NetWare 4.0 Novell introduced the concept of suballocation, which allows the final bits of two or three files to be stored in a single block. This means that there is less empty space left in blocks, and Novell estimates it increases the amount of information a disk can hold by two to three times for a typical network.

In addition, NetWare 4.0 allows variable block sizes, ranging from 2 Kbytes to 64 Kbytes in multiples of 2, which allows the server to be tuned to the application; for example, larger block sizes are more efficient for big files because the disk head has fewer hops to make each time each file is read or written to, which means access times are faster. However, if most files are smaller even than a minimum-sized 2K block, there is no performance gain by having larger blocks than this, and even with suballocation, bigger blocks are wasteful of space when storing small files.

The second benefit follows from the introduction of mainframe-like hierarchical storage management. This exploits the fact that there are several grades of storage media with costs proportional to performance. The principle is to hold the most frequently accessed data in high-performance expensive media, with data that is accessed only occasionally being stored in low-performance low-cost media. The four most important types of storage media for LANs are, in descending order of cost and performance: solid state memory, as used for disk caching; the disk drive itself; optical disks; and tapes. The latter are used for backing up data and, with NetWare 4.0, to archive data that has not been accessed for a set period of time. Optical storage can be used for backup, or as an alternative to disk drives where high performance is not required.

Cache is used to hold data that has been most frequently accessed, in order to increase performance – essentially it is a fast buffer between the CPU and the disk drive subsystem. Depending on the relationship between the amount of cache and disk drive capacity, 96–99 per cent of all data-access operations can be executed in cache, without involving the slower disk drive. Meanwhile the cache communicates with the disk drive as a background task to pass on updates, without noticeable impact on performance of the network.

The third benefit follows from Novell's development of a new data-compression algorithm designed specifically for the NetWare environment; other methods are just as effective at compressing data, but Novell's scores for NetWare by handling the processing as a background task. This means that the benefit of compression, packing more data into a given amount of disk space, can be obtained without a corresponding sacrifice in performance.

3. *Imaging*

Document image processing (DIP) is an application area of steadily growing importance because of its great potential for cost savings and improvements in productivity by reducing paperwork. Companies in the finance sector, particularly insurance, have already moved into DIP to reduce the costs of processing claims, for example. Claims forms are digitized by scanners and stored electronically so that they can be retrieved quickly from a desktop workstation: paper storage space is saved, the cost of managing the information is reduced, document retrieval time is cut and the same document image can be used simultaneously by more than one person without the need to make photocopies.

With DIP applications figuring increasingly on PC LANs, Novell decided to exploit the market opportunity by introducing comprehensive support for imaging in NetWare 4.0. Lacking expertise in image manipulation, Novell collaborated with Kodak, which provided the algorithm needed to compress the image data. Images produce a large amount of raw data but much of this can be eliminated by exploiting the fact that most of a typical image, such as the background of a paper document, comprises identical picture elements. However, the techniques needed to compress the images are different from the ones Novell itself developed for conventional coded data such as text – hence the need for Kodak's involvement. In addition, Kodak provided the software tools needed to manipulate images, so that they could be accessed and displayed efficiently without impairing performance of the overall network more than was necessary.

Novell, for its part, developed the techniques for storing images on the server and manipulating them within the actual network services. At this level, Novell did not have to take account of the peculiarities of image data so much, but had to be aware of the amount of data generated and the applications in which it was being used.

4. *Internationalization of the product*

Novell found that the inability of NetWare to present itself to users in any language other than English was a growing disadvantage in several major markets, especially Japan. Furthermore, major competitors were introducing multilingual support into their products. Hitherto Novell's efforts had extended only to translating a few manuals into German and French, so internationalization of NetWare 4.0 became a major priority.

Novell has introduced code into NetWare 4.x that permits different character sets to be supported. This, in conjunction with a development kit, enables the product to be translated into other languages, including those like Japanese that have radically different character sets from the Roman alphabet. Translations performed by Novell directly, with the aid of native speakers of the language, are Japanese, Italian, French, German and Spanish, these currently being the five major languages of the industrial world, apart from English. Translations into other languages are left to third parties.

Note that a given server can support more than one language – this is because each translation is handled by an NLM, of which a number can run simultaneously. These NLMs can be activated by each user's identifier, therefore users can be presented on the screen with messages in their own language after they have logged on.

5. *Improvements to the core NetWare product*

The objective here was to make NetWare a more robust operating environment in line with its growth in scale to embrace larger multi-server networks. The major change was to allow NLMs to run in protected mode of the server's processor; up to that time, NLMs had to run in unprotected mode. Applications run more slowly in protected mode but if they crash because of a bug in the software, they are much less likely to corrupt other processes going on simultaneously.

The core operating system always runs in unprotected mode, known as ring 0, to maximize performance. Novell considers that because network services are part of the network operating system as far as users are concerned, they should run in unprotected mode; however, the counter-argument, espoused by the developers of the OS/2 operating system for example, is that whereas the core operating system code is relatively stable, network services such as NLMs are continuously being developed by a variety of third parties and some are less stable than others; there is thus a greater risk of unforeseen bugs impairing the reliability of the overall network. Network services should therefore, according to the counter-argument, be run in protected mode or ring 3 (rings 1 and 2 offer progressively greater levels of protection against software bugs).

Novell has embraced part of this argument for the first time, and has come up with a compromise: while under development, NLMs can and perhaps should run in protected mode, then when the developer is confident the product is mature enough and that all serious bugs have been eradicated, the code can be transferred to ring 0, unprotected mode. Furthermore, users themselves may feel happier 'running new NLMs in' in protected mode until they feel confident that the products are stable enough to be transferred to unprotected mode. In effect Novell has conceded that, especially on large networks, immature NLMs can cause other applications to crash, with the risk of lost data and disruption of business.

6. *DOS Requester and VLMs (virtual loadable modules)*

Novell launched DOS Requester 1.0 with NetWare 4.0 in April 1993. Since then it has undergone various upgrades, primarily to improve performance.

The DOS Requester performs an equivalent function to the NetWare shell but more efficiently, and there is also a fundamental difference in the way both interact with the underlying DOS operating system. The shell, as described in Section 2.2.1, operates in front of DOS, intercepting commands from applications and passing them to DOS only after ascertaining that they are not destined for the network. DOS Requester, on the other hand, operates behind DOS, in effect only acting on DOS's leftovers. This exploits the DOS Redirector Interface, which allows DOS to recognize foreign file systems – a facility unavailable when Novell originally designed its shell software. Now DOS passes commands to one or more redirectors if it determines that it does not have the requested resource, such as a file or a printer, locally.

With the DOS Requester, Novell introduced the concept of virtual loadable modules (VLMs): programs providing functions that are logically grouped together. A typical example is the group of transport-related functions associated with sending a data packet from a client PC across a LAN and receiving a packet back from the LAN.

The DOS Requester architecture comprises four types or layers of VLM: VLM Manager, multiplexor VLMs, child VLMs and standard VLMs. The VLM Manager coordinates the other VLMs, then a multiplexor VLM provides a common API (application programming interface, see Chapter 8) to child VLMs, which in turn provide the required communication functions. Standard VLMs provide some additional functions, such as the ability to reconnect to a network automatically.

Failure of NetWare 4.0 to match expectations

By mid 1994, 15 months after the product's launch, sales of NetWare 4.x were still below Novell's hopes and expectations, accounting for about 10 per cent of the company's total sales. The attitude of the Bass group, featured in the Case Study later in this book, is typical of a number of large Novell sites that did not believe the benefits of upgrading to NetWare 4.x justified the effort. Novell's efforts to break out of the workgroup LAN market into enterprise networks had been largely unsuccessful for several reasons:

(1) It took time for Novell to acquire the expertise in dealing with senior staff responsible for major strategic IT investment decisions.

(2) NetWare 4.0 needed time to stabilize and was less mature than established large-scale computer operating systems such as Digital's VMS with which it was starting to compete.

(3) Many large organizations did not perceive Novell as a serious player outside the LAN workgroup.

(4) The emergence of alternative operating systems, notably Microsoft's Windows NT, delayed many purchasing decisions.

(5) Novell initially failed to provide adequate tools to help users migrate from NetWare 3.1 to NetWare 4.x.

2.2.5 UnixWare

UnixWare is a version of the UNIX operating system designed for LANs, complete with a graphical user interface (GUI), software development tools and facilities for integrating with other UNIX applications. In particular, it allows applications written for the UNIX operating system to run on NetWare networks, combining the best of both environments. Before giving more details, let us consider its *raison d'être*.

Why Novell moved into UNIX

For Novell, the development of UnixWare sprang from both technical and commercial motives. The commercial motive was provided by arch rival Microsoft, which was threatening Novell on two fronts. Firstly, many users of NetWare servers also run Microsoft's Windows 3 operating system on the desktop as a front end to their DOS- and NetWare-based applications. In 1992 and 1993, Microsoft tried to oust Novell from these sites by offering unlimited user licences for LAN Manager relatively cheaply, working out at typically a third of the price of an equivalent NetWare configuration. Furthermore, Microsoft started offering NetWare shell software, threatening to expunge Novell's influence from the desktop even at those sites that retained their NetWare servers. This weakened Novell's hold over the accounts, and in turn made a switch to Microsoft for server software as well more likely in the future. Also, for new sites Microsoft could set up its stall as a supplier of complete networking software embracing both the client and server.

Novell badly needed to compete with a similar complete LAN package. One move was the acquisition of Digital Research, whose version of DOS, called DR-DOS, was then bundled in with Personal NetWare. However this was only for small LANs, and in any case did not include a Windows-like GUI. One option was for Novell to develop its own GUI to compete with Windows, but this would have been a substantial investment and unlikely to succeed given the ever-strengthening hold on the desktop software market by Microsoft. The only alternative was to go for the UNIX environment, for which there were already GUIs available. A move into UNIX was also attractive because it would enable Novell to exploit the large existing base of applications and software development tools already available for that operating system. Furthermore, UNIX was becoming a threat to leading NOS vendors, especially Novell, as a server-based operating system. By acquiring UNIX System Laboratories, Novell ensured that it could control this threat and derive revenue from it.

This leads on to the technical reasons for Novell's move into UNIX. Novell had aims of becoming a supplier of global networking solutions, which required network services considerably more sophisticated than had hitherto been developed for NetWare servers. Essentially, NetWare lacked software development tools of the sophistication and power required to build some of the large-scale applications that would be needed, in network management and distributed security services for example.

UNIX, on the other hand, had evolved into an applications development environment based around the core operating system with all the facilities needed for developing large-scale applications serving multiple users. Unix-Ware was conceived as a way of having the best of both worlds, combining NetWare's strengths as a LAN server operating system providing high performance and local security with the application development facilities of UNIX. As Microsoft was already gunning for UNIX with Windows NT, then still under development, Novell's introduction of UnixWare was set to heighten competition between the two companies.

However, UnixWare was not pitched solely at Microsoft – Novell was also hoping to win business from traditional vendors of large-scale UNIX systems such as Pyramid, Sequent and Sequoia. Novell hoped that UnixWare would allow large-scale UNIX applications of the sort that had already been established on big UNIX systems to run on PC LAN servers. The theory was that PC LAN systems would be cheaper than these companies' UNIX systems. Previously, such UNIX systems had themselves been introduced as lower-cost alternatives to traditional mainframe computers from leading manufacturers such as IBM and ICL, therefore Novell was also hoping to win business from users of mainframes looking to reduce costs by offloading at least some applications onto less expensive computing platforms.

As will be discussed in Chapters 6 and 7, it does not follow automatically that LANs work out cheaper in the long run than centralized host systems just because the hardware and operating software costs less. Management and other costs also need to be considered. Novell lacked the resources internally to develop a major version of UNIX unaided, therefore it sought and found the ideal partner, UNIX Systems International (USL), which was then part of AT&T and responsible for the development of System V, the most important version of the operating system. The two companies set up a joint venture called Univel, which then developed UnixWare, with shipments starting during the first quarter of 1993. At this time Novell took advantage of AT&T's desire to wean itself from direct involvement in UNIX development and acquired USL

for an undisclosed sum, reputed to be around $300 million. Novell then became
the sole owner of UNIX and now had effective control of its destiny: combined with NetWare it was an ideal base for its increasingly bitter war with
Microsoft. However, Microsoft is still the larger company, even after Novell's
acquisition of WordPerfect; furthermore, as we shall see, there is such
momentum behind the Windows family of products, with Windows NT having
been one of the most eagerly awaited software products ever, that Novell will
have to fight just to maintain its share of the basic NOS market. Note that
Novell's customer base is under fire not just from Microsoft itself but also from
several other notable computer vendors that sell LAN Manager under OEM
agreements – including Digital Equipment (DEC), NCR and SCO (Santa Cruz
Organisation).

What is UnixWare?

UnixWare has three components to support modular growth, from a single-user
desktop operating system to a complete networking environment embracing
both UNIX and NetWare. The component for desktop PCs is UnixWare
Personal Edition, which is a version of UNIX that can be used on its own; it
incorporates a GUI based on the X Windows standard widely used within
UNIX environments as a basis for providing graphical displays and windows
in UNIX applications, so users of Personal Edition could run standalone
applications in their PC and access them directly via the UnixWare GUI.
However, the product is rather an overkill if this is the only requirement, as
none of the networking features built into the product would be exploited. Such
features include enterprise-wide administration capabilities which are part of
UNIX System V.4 upon which UnixWare is based, along with point-and-click
facilities for accessing NetWare file, print and electronic mail services.

To access NetWare services, the product supports Novell's IPX transport
protocol. Clearly then the product is intended to be used in conjunction with
the second component of UnixWare, the Application Server. UnixWare Application Server provides all the features of the Personal Edition, with the addition
of facilities required to support access to network services by multiple users.
Such services are of four kinds: UNIX applications running on the UnixWare
server itself; NetWare applications running on a NetWare server connected to
the UnixWare server; existing UNIX applications running on another UNIX
system to which access can be gained via a UnixWare server; and non-UNIX
applications running on other host systems. These four possibilities are illustrated in Figure 2.8. In this guise the UnixWare server appears as a universal
communications server providing users with access to the applications they need
wherever they are on the network. To some extent NetWare itself already
provided these capabilities, although there are two important differences.
Firstly, UnixWare provides much more seamless and efficient access to UNIX
applications for desktop clients. Secondly, UnixWare itself is capable of running
UNIX applications and has development tools enabling such applications to be
written. Therefore the view of the world according to Novell is that UnixWare

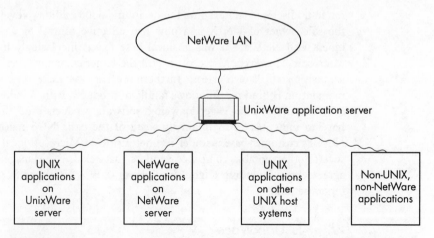

Figure 2.8 The four types of service provided by Novell's UnixWare server.

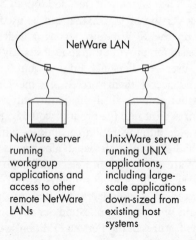

Figure 2.9 Novell's view of how the computing world ought to be.

servers provide access to existing host systems which are then gradually phased out, so that ultimately Figure 2.8 is replaced with Figure 2.9. This is unlikely to happen as a general rule, if only because most users are reluctant to stake everything on one vendor for all critical operating software. Indeed, UnixWare can co-exist with operating software from rival vendors, including Microsoft Windows and other versions of UNIX, and it is binary compatible with Xenix, SCO UNIX and Interactive UNIX, as well as System V itself. Therefore applications written for these versions of UNIX should run on UnixWare servers, or on client PCs under Personal Edition.

The third component of UnixWare is slightly different, and not actually a core part of the operating system – the software development toolkit (SDK), which is a set of utilities and documentation to help developers build applications in the UnixWare environment. The role of these can be understood better with reference to the structure of UNIX, which is described in Section 2.5.2. SDK includes tools to support development of graphical applications running under Personal Edition, adhering to the 'look and feel' of either Motif or Open Look – these being two well-known graphical front ends enabling users to manipulate data and applications through windows on their screens. SDK also includes application programming interfaces (APIs) facilitating development of client/server applications with components on both desktop client workstations and servers.

□ 2.3   The LAN Manager family

The story of LAN Manager is more complex and convoluted than that of NetWare. Although there are now four different versions of NetWare, they are all completely under the control of one company and have a common origin as an operating system designed specifically to run on LAN servers, along with shell components enabling client workstations to participate in the network. LAN Manager, on the other hand, was built initially on top of the OS/2 operating system, which was developed jointly by IBM and Microsoft as an intended sequel to DOS, but events have not proceeded as originally envisaged by the two companies.

The theory was that, as an operating system supporting just a single user at any one time, OS/2 could not function on its own as a NOS, which needs the ability to handle simultaneous requests for data and network services from all users on a LAN. However, being, unlike DOS, a multi-tasking operating system capable of handling a number of processes at once, it was an ideal base for a NOS. LAN Manager was written as an OS/2 application, providing the file and print-handling facilities required of a NOS. Originally the product was called OS/2 LAN Manager and available in almost identical forms from both IBM and through Microsoft's resellers such as 3Com.

Around 1990, IBM and Microsoft went through a much publicized divorce – partly on account of the success Microsoft was having with its Windows 3 system based on DOS. Windows made DOS more like the Apple Macintosh operating system, replacing command lines with point-and-click operations using icons and pull-down menus, and also introduced a limited multi-tasking ability, so that for example word-processing software allowed users to put several documents on screen and work on them all simultaneously (although such facilities can also be provided by the applications software, as in WordPerfect 6.0 for DOS).

OS/2, in contrast, had a different windowing system called Presentation

Manager, which Microsoft had been offering, although the success of Windows 3 directed the firm onto a different course: it decided to sever links with IBM over OS/2, and to use its huge installed Windows 3 base as a springboard for a new multi-tasking operating system, complete with graphical user interface and in-built support for networking, called Windows NT (New Technology). We shall look at Windows NT in detail later in this section. Although Microsoft was left with LAN Manager running over OS/2 after parting company with IBM, this has subsequently been reshaped to run on UNIX also, and now parts of it have been incorporated into Windows NT. For larger networks Microsoft developed enhanced NOS features, building on the base provided by LAN Manager, in its NT Server NOS. Microsoft also produced a stripped-down version of LAN Manager called Windows for Workgroups, which we shall discuss in Chapter 3. Windows for Workgroups was subsequently bundled in with Windows 3.11.

IBM also inherited LAN Manager after its split with Microsoft, and the product evolved into the IBM LAN Server; both retain similarities but the principal differences are indicated in Section 2.4.

IBM continued alone with the development of OS/2, announcing version 2 of the operating system in April 1992, and version 3 in late 1994. OS/2 version 2, also described later in this chapter, was designed partly as a base for future IBM network operating systems evolving from LAN Server.

2.3.1 Microsoft LAN Manager

LAN Manager compared with NetWare

Microsoft's own version of LAN Manager was the best-known member of the family before the launch of Windows for Workgroups and NT Server, and it still serves to illustrate the core features of the operating system. When first released, LAN Manager could not match the performance or reliability of its principal and well-established competitor NetWare, which Microsoft hoped it would eventually overtake, but it did have some advantages, a major one being its impartiality with regard to transport protocols across the LAN. NetWare was designed with its own transport protocol stack, IPX/SPX, which helped achieve high performance but had to be converted to other protocols to allow NetWare networks to access different systems. LAN Manager also scored over NetWare by allowing groups of servers on different LANs to be organized into what were termed domains. Users could access all servers in a domain via a single password, and all servers could be managed from a single point.

However these differences have lessened as both Novell and Microsoft have chased each other's tails with successive releases of their software. NetWare 4.x, for example, supports multiple servers, while, following the launch of Windows NT and more especially NT Server, Microsoft now has a complete network operating system that does not rely on an underlying operating system such as OS/2 or UNIX.

Another disappearing historical difference between NetWare and LAN Manager is over support for protected-mode operation, which can increase the overall reliability of a large complex network. Until NetWare 4.0, Novell did not support protected-mode operation for its NLMs (see section on NetWare 4.x) but protected mode has always been supported for LAN Manager applications, being an integral part of OS/2.

The early versions of LAN Manager lagged behind NetWare as far as performance was concerned but in 1990 Microsoft caught up dramatically with the introduction of an improved file system – LAN Manager 2.0. Benchmarks conducted by the US LANQuest Laboratories in 1991 showed that version 2.1 of LAN Manager was equal to NetWare 3.1 in terms of file retrievals and saves.

Having pointed out that NetWare and LAN Manager are converging to some extent, we should emphasize that many organizations, particularly smaller businesses, will not be using the latest versions of the products and therefore some of the distinctions will still apply. Microsoft LAN Manager 2.2 differs from NetWare 3.1 in the following:

- centralized domains
- designed from outset for both peer-to-peer and client/server operation
- requires OS/2
- protected-mode operation.

Key features of LAN Manager

LAN Manager supports all the fundamental NOS features described in Chapter 1, in particular file sharing, printer and peripheral services, and server management; its strengths lie in security, ability to interoperate with other systems and networks, and the combination of support for peer-to-peer networking with centralized administration of multiple servers. Microsoft also makes much of the fact that LAN Manager is well integrated with its Windows 3 desktop operating system, although this is somewhat disingenuous, given that Microsoft also promotes Windows 3 as a *de facto* standard, which therefore should be open to other vendors to link their products into. Indeed, as Windows has been taking over from DOS as the dominant desktop operating environment on industry-standard PCs, other NOS vendors are forced to support it; for example, Novell in March 1993 announced full Windows support for its Personal NetWare peer-to-peer NOS. Microsoft, however, as we have already pointed out, is increasingly bundling the NOS functions of LAN Manager in its desktop environment.

Technical design of LAN Manager

LAN Manager was designed from the outset for client/server applications, which are defined in Appendix 11. Earlier versions embodied a server operating system based on OS/2, with client components based either on OS/2 or

Microsoft's own Windows environment. On the server, OS/2 was designed specifically to support multi-tasking in protected mode, meaning that more than one application could safely run simultaneously without risk of any one corrupting any other. The principle of protected-mode operation is shown schematically in Figure 2.10. Each application runs in its own area of processor memory, so if anything goes wrong in one application, the others are unaffected.

Protected mode therefore improves the reliability of applications running concurrently in a single computer but there is a corresponding sacrifice in performance by restricting processes to particular areas of CPU memory. However, OS/2 compensates to some extent for this through some performance-improving measures. One such is pre-emptive scheduling, which ensures that all applications get their fair share of processing time – no one application can hog the CPU for itself and leave others hanging in suspense. Performance is also improved by support for multiple concurrent threads of execution, which enables the operating system to handle a number of requests from applications simultaneously; this applies equally whether OS/2 is running beneath LAN Manager on a server or supporting applications in single-user mode on a desktop workstation.

Although able to multi-task, OS/2 on its own could only support one user at a time; it could not, for example, handle access to data and applications from other computers or terminals. However, by supporting multi-tasking, the potential is introduced for writing an OS/2 application that supports access by more than one user. That is precisely what LAN Manager was in its first incarnation, an OS/2 application, providing the additional facilities to support multiple users accessing the server across a LAN; OS/2 supplied the underlying file access, management and protection mechanisms, which in the case of NetWare have always been an integral part of the NOS. Novell's approach has the virtue of making it easier to fine tune the operating system for client/server

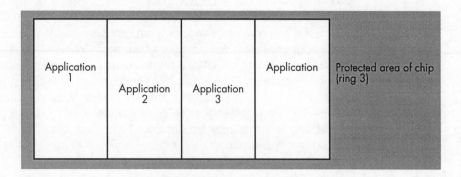

Figure 2.10 Principle of protected mode operation. Applications are confined to their own portion of the CPU, which avoids one overwriting another, but performance is reduced by preventing each application exploiting the whole CPU.

applications on a LAN but Microsoft made it possible to port LAN Manager readily to other operating systems such as UNIX, allowing it to co-exist on the same computer with other applications, such as communications. It also enabled the LAN Manager product to be adapted for incorporation into new Microsoft operating systems, in particular Windows NT, described later in this chapter (Section 2.3.3), and Windows for Workgroups, described in Chapter 3.

The client or shell portions of LAN Manager can take a variety of forms. In the case of Windows for Workgroups and NT, they are part of the same overall operating system as the server components but on earlier versions of LAN Manager the client portion of the NOS was typically one of two graphical user interfaces (GUIs), either Microsoft Windows 3 or OS/2 Presentation Manager. Users interact with the server across the network through pull-down menus, dialogue boxes and point-and-click instructions; they can then browse through the network to control their print jobs, and discover what resources are available.

To link the client and server parts of an application, data transport protocols are needed. Novell, as explained earlier in this chapter, developed its own protocol stack called IPX/SPX, deeming this the best way to maximize performance. Microsoft, on the other hand, plumped for existing industry-standard protocols, starting with the NetBIOS extended user interface (Netbeui). Subsequently, Microsoft added support for other transport protocols, notably TCP/IP.

Network interface cards (NICs) with appropriate drivers can emulate all the popular transport protocols. Therefore client PCs, for example, with such NICs can attach to a LAN Manager LAN irrespective of the transport protocol used, provided it is one for which an NDIS (network device interface specification) driver has been written. Microsoft's support of *de facto* standard transport protocols allowed for more elegant configurations than were usually possible with networks running Novell's IPX/SPX, avoiding the need for protocol conversion gateways in many cases. However, with the introduction of support for ODI (open datalink interface), Novell was able to support other transport protocols.

Transport protocols provide the basic channel of communication between applications but more sophisticated software tools called APIs (application programming interfaces) are available to facilitate higher-level interaction between applications; these make it easier to develop client/server applications in networks. The primary API supported by LAN Manager is Named Pipes, which wraps up lower-level communication processes in higher-level function calls, making distributed applications easier to program. The relationship between APIs and the NOS is described in detail in Chapter 8.

LAN Manager file sharing

File sharing in earlier LAN Manager versions was based on the OS/2 operating system file system for 386 processors, called HPFS386. Microsoft originally built its NOS strategy around OS/2, which was designed to handle multi-tasking on an Intel-based PC efficiently and reliably. This made it suitable as a basis for a server operating system where it is obviously necessary to handle a variety of tasks on behalf of many users simultaneously. HPFS386 was optimized for high performance when multiple files are being accessed simultaneously; like NetWare, features such as caching of directories, files and data are available to minimize the amount of disk access needed to obtain information from large directories of files.

A range of other facilities is provided to maximize the performance, reliability and security of the LAN Manager file system: disk mirroring and duplexing are supported, as is management of uninterruptible power supplies, and data is replicated to protect against server failure. Data can be backed up to other servers on the network or to workstations.

Subsequently, LAN Manager was ported to the UNIX operating system, marketed as LAN Manager for UNIX, then in 1993 Windows NT was introduced, embodying many of the file-handling features of OS/2 and LAN Manager in a completely new network operating system.

LAN Manager printer and peripheral sharing

Although earlier versions of LAN Manager failed to match NetWare for performance, they provided stronger competition in the area of networked printing. The ability to match print queues with different types of printer on a LAN was available from the outset. Figure 1.7 shows a typical set up where one queue of standard draft print jobs is feeding a dot matrix printer, while two laser printers are set up to take two kinds of job – small high-priority and large low-priority jobs. LAN Manager allows more complex queuing arrangements than this; for example, high-priority jobs can be categorized further according to their size. Jobs can also be designated according to the type of paper they need, so that all similar printing jobs can be printed in one batch when the appropriate printer is set up.

Server management

This is another area where LAN Manager's advantages over NetWare have been extinguished, in this case when version 3 of NetWare arrived. LAN Manager has always supported the concept of domains, allowing network administrators to manage a group of servers from a single location; this might include all servers on a network or just a subset, such as those at a particular site. This process enables new users to be added at a stroke, with a single password giving them access to all resources for which they have authorization in their domain. By the same token, all other users in that domain immediately have the ability to send messages to the new user and, if desired, access applications and data on the new user's workstation; this is made possible by keeping information about users within a domain on a common database residing on a central server called the domain controller. Details of all changes to the central database are relayed automatically to all other servers in the domain, so that requests for sessions and data can be handled locally without the performance overhead of involving the central server.

However, a weakness of this approach is that overall network operation is dependent on the single domain controller holding the database. To remedy this, it is possible to have a backup domain controller that is kept completely up-to-date and can take over from the primary controller if necessary.

2.3.2 Other versions of LAN Manager

Novell's approach to NetWare has been to maintain tight control of the core NOS software and encourage third parties to develop additional networked applications on top, such as to provide a specific communications requirement or to back up data. Microsoft have taken a different view, forging strategic partnerships with large IT vendors and allowing them to embody LAN Manager technology in their own NOS software; such partners include AT&T, DEC, Hewlett-Packard and NCR. DEC's Pathworks system, for example, was initially based on LAN Manager. These companies took the basic version of LAN Manager from Microsoft and added features to fit their own systems and the needs of their own customers. Some vendors exploited the communications features of LAN Manager to integrate different components of their systems portfolio; for example, Olivetti used it to tie together its DOS, OS/2 and UNIX systems.

Microsoft itself, as already noted, has also enhanced LAN Manager in various ways. The first notable development was Microsoft's LAN Manager for UNIX version 1.0, which involved shifting, or porting, the LAN Manager software from OS/2 to UNIX. From then on, the original version of LAN Manager became known as LAN Manager for OS/2 to distinguish it from LAN Manager for UNIX. However, both support the same commands and client software, so that users can access LAN manager for UNIX applications without the need for retraining and without having to learn UNIX commands. As shown in Figure 2.11, client workstations were thus able to connect simultaneously to files, printers and applications attached to both UNIX and OS/2 LAN Manager servers.

Some of Microsoft's major hardware partners, for instance Hewlett-Packard and Unisys, used LAN Manager to make their systems function as powerful servers that could be accessed by standard LAN Manager client systems such as OS/2 and Macintosh workstations. LAN Manager for UNIX was also taken by Santa Cruz Organization (SCO) as the basis for its networking software to complement its successful desktop version of UNIX.

Version 2 of LAN Manager for UNIX was developed by Microsoft in partnership with NCR and announced in October 1991. An important enhancement introduced with this second version was support for mixed-platform domains, so that both UNIX and OS/2 LAN Manager servers could be managed as if they were a single server. In addition, users were able to access all the

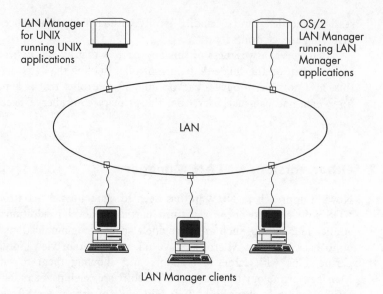

Figure 2.11 Use of LAN Manager to provide simultaneous access to both UNIX and LAN Manager applications.

resources, data and applications to which they were entitled with a single password, whichever server they were on or attached to.

An advantage of LAN Manager for UNIX is that it makes the application and development base of UNIX available to existing LAN Manager users. This has been exploited, among others, by SCO, which has made a twin-pronged attack with its version of LAN Manager for UNIX. At the low end, it has been wooing Windows for Workgroups (WfW) users by offering a dedicated LAN Manager for UNIX server to run new applications and manage the network. SCO argues that Windows for Workgroups, as it is designed mainly to operate in peer-to-peer mode without a dedicated server, runs out of steam as the network grows in size beyond a handful of nodes. Users therefore need a dedicated server to provide centralized data management, which simultaneously opens up the whole spectrum of UNIX applications. The second prong of SCO's attack was to promote a more powerful version of LAN Manager for UNIX as a connectivity tool for turning Windows PCs into clients accessing large-scale UNIX applications.

2.3.3 Windows NT

Windows NT is a product of convergence between the Windows desktop graphical user interface, built originally on the DOS operating system, and LAN Manager, built originally on OS/2. The arrival of NT in a sense heralds

Microsoft's final weaning from the formative influence of IBM, breaking away from both DOS and OS/2.

NT possesses many of the components of a complete network operating system, as defined in the Introduction, and does not rely on any underlying operating system. Although it is designed to communicate with other operating systems such as UNIX, and also with proprietary systems like IBM's MVS, it is nonetheless essentially a competitor to UNIX as a distributed operating system capable of running on a variety of hardware platforms.

The first version of Windows NT came in two types, which are easy to confuse. The core operating system, Windows NT 3.1, is a 32-bit operating system that also runs existing Windows, MS-DOS and character-based OS/2 applications. It runs either on Intel-based systems with at least a 386 processor, or on RISC systems, in particular those based on the MIPS R4000 or DEC Alpha processors, and requires a minimum of 12 Mbytes of memory and ideally at least 90 Mbytes of hard disk storage. Essentially, LAN Manager is also built in, although some of the more sophisticated features are absent from Windows NT 3.1. However, as it contains a superset of the networking features of Windows for Workgroups, it can be used for any network for which WfW is suitable or where it is already deployed.

The second flavour of this first version of NT was called Windows NT Advanced Server 3.1. Originally, Microsoft called this LAN Manager for Windows NT but this title was somewhat misleading because, as already indicated, Windows NT 3.1 already incorporates much of LAN Manager. The difference lies in scale, in that NT Advanced Server (NTAS) provides extra features for security, reliability and performance; it is designed for larger networks running critical applications supporting multiple servers. As far as the server components are concerned, it is comparable with NetWare 3.12 rather than NetWare 4.0, given that the first version did not incorporate a global directory. However, it is likely that the gap between NTAS and NetWare 4.0 will narrow so that the two will become comparable in future, although NTAS also incorporates a graphical user interface for clients. In 1994, therefore, NetWare 3.12 in conjunction with UnixWare was a more direct competitor to NTAS. Future versions of UnixWare will probably incorporate NetWare facilities and compete head on with Windows NT and NTAS in its own right.

In late 1994, Microsoft introduced a major new release of NT called NT 3.5. Now the server part was renamed NT client rather than NTAS. This new release of NT had been code-named 'Daytona'.

The similarity between the first two flavours of Windows NT gave a clear indication of Microsoft's intention to introduce a single distributed operating system by the end of 1994. This project, code-named 'Cairo', aimed at producing a single scaleable Windows NT product for larger networks, with different components to suit systems and networks of varying sizes. On desktop workstations, for example, there would be a client component providing the GUI and support for cooperation with other systems on the network. On central servers, components providing the functions of LAN Manager would be available but, because the different components are all part of a single distributed or network operating system, it should be easier to tune them to optimize performance and management. The evolution of NOSs into distributed operating systems is discussed further in Chapter 10, and in Chapter 9 we look further at cooperation between different computers in a network.

Figure 2.12 clarifies Microsoft's strategy with Windows NT, indicating how the different products interrelate. The figure shows where Microsoft's other strategic project, code-named 'Chicago', fits in, as a progression of its current DOS and Windows systems for single-user PCs. Chicago incorporates emerging object-based operating system methods, which are described in Chapter 10. Chicago was called Windows 95 when released in early 1995.

It is possible to start with DOS 6 on standalone PCs, install a LAN and upgrade to Windows 3.11, so providing peer-to-peer NOS facilities. The next step might be an upgrade to Windows NT as the network grows. However, this migration process has been simplified with the launch of Windows 95 and NT 4.1, following respectively the Chicago and Cairo projects. As these had not been launched when this book was published, they are described in Chapter 10 under the heading of future developments. The descriptions given are based on details of pre-release versions of the software supplied to application developers.

2.3.4 Other related components of LAN Manager: database access and integration with other operating environments

Database access

LAN manager was designed specifically for client/server operation on LANs, which generally involves performing file access and management functions on a server. For any serious application, files are arranged in a database, so to support client/server operation effectively, Microsoft had to provide some means of accessing databases on the server. The obvious method, which Microsoft adopted, was to implement the industry-standard SQL (structured query language), which provides English-like commands for accessing, defining, manipulating and managing data. Microsoft purchased the SQL Server and enhanced it to run not just under LAN Manager but also under other popular NOSs such as Novell NetWare, Banyan Vines and IBM LAN Server. Microsoft also developed software gateways that allow desktop applications on LAN Manager LANs to access and update data on other databases that support the SQL standard, including IBM's DB2, Oracle and Ingres. A product called the Comm Server, developed by Microsoft in partnership with Digital Communications Associates (DCA), enables LAN Manager LANs to cooperate with host systems in IBM SNA networks.

However, the most significant step by Microsoft in the database arena came with the development of open database connectivity (ODBC); this is an API (application programming interface) for developing software that requires

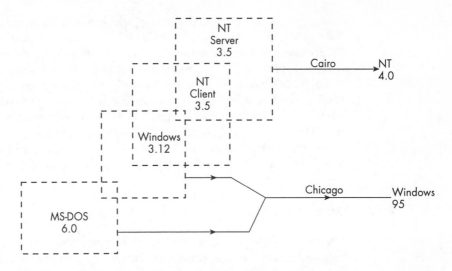

Figure 2.12 Relationship between Microsoft's various operating systems. With Windows 95 and NT 4.0 the distinction between singer-user and network operating systems ends. The single-user version becomes a special case of the overall operating system.

data from a variety of databases. It is discussed further in Chapter 8 but here is a summary of its key features:

(1) locating requested databases, which can be of different types and at any location on the network;

(2) establishing connection with the database using appropriate communications links;

(3) sending requests to the database in a standard format, thus avoiding the need for different instructions for each type of database;

(4) returning data to the application in a consistent format, irrespective of the database management system in use on the database being accessed.

ODBC is a key component of Microsoft's WOSA (Windows open services architecture), described in the next section.

Integration with other computing environments

The overall thrust of Microsoft's strategy is to deliver products that allow applications and systems to cooperate effectively across a wide area network. Other vendors have the same strategy but the difference is that Microsoft is working outwards from its huge base of installed Windows applications. The rails of Microsoft's strategy therefore radiate outwards from Windows.

Microsoft's core product for achieving interoperability between so-called heterogeneous computing environments, which essentially means systems from different vendors, is the WOSA (windows open services architecture) interface. WOSA has something for both users and programmers: it presents users with a single familiar GUI (graphical user interface) for accessing applications, wherever they are located on the network; for programmers, it provides a consistent set of APIs for communicating with back-end services such as databases and electronic mail systems. ODBC, as already described, is the API for communicating with databases. Another key component is called object linking and embedding (OLE), which helps programmers develop Windows applications that interact effectively with applications on different systems.

2.3.5 Other vendors' versions of LAN Manager

A number of other vendors have produced versions of LAN Manager under their own banner, adding various features to the core product; these include large system companies, notably DEC and NCR, whose versions of LAN Manager are aimed primarily at those companies' existing customer bases. We shall focus here on LAN Manager for SCO Systems, from Santa Cruz Organization (SCO), which is in some ways complementary to Microsoft's own products and does not depend on a particular vendor's hardware.

SCO made its name through a version of UNIX for Intel-based PCs, the well-known SCO Xenix. This gave 386 or 486 PCs access to the growing body of UNIX applications, enabling them to function either as multi-user systems accessed by low-cost dumb terminals or desktop workstations running powerful graphics applications. The company built on this base with SCO Open Desk Top, which is a GUI environment for systems running SCO UNIX.

To enable its UNIX systems to communicate across a LAN and access servers based on a NOS, the company developed LAN Manager for SCO systems. As with its UNIX developments, the advantage of this was that SCO did not have to provide the great investment needed for building a new operating system from scratch. Instead, it adapted LAN Manager to work with its existing desktop products. SCO's version supports access from desktop systems, not just to other versions of LAN Manager but also to NetWare servers. The company envisages that a major market for its LAN Manager servers will be sites that have installed Microsoft's Windows 3.11 and find they really need a central dedicated server for administration and management. WfW, described in Chapter 3, is designed for peer-to-peer operation in small workgroups without access to a dedicated server.

□ 2.4   IBM LAN Server

In the past, this would have been included in the LAN Manager family, to which it is still closely related. It was IBM's version of LAN Manager for OS/2 but diverged in 1992, since when IBM has integrated it with various large-scale operating environments and management systems. Initially the parting with Microsoft was painful for IBM, with LAN Server lagging far behind both LAN Manager and NetWare in performance benchmarks. However, the situation changed dramatically in 1992 following the release of LAN Server 3.0. In November 1992, benchmark tests performed by LANQuest Labs in the USA found that LAN Server 3.0 had overtaken Microsoft LAN Manager as the fastest of the three leading NOSs, with NetWare 3.1 in third place. Since then, new versions of LAN Manager and NetWare have come along but these results indicate that IBM has overcome its teething troubles and is now a serious contender in the NOS field. The improvement in performance was explained partly by the fact that this was the first version of LAN Manager to be based on OS/2 version 2.

In fact, LAN Server is positioned slightly differently from LAN Manager and NetWare. IBM also markets NetWare, so LAN Server only competes head on with LAN Manager, and promotes its own label of NetWare to sites that are either already Novell customers or want to follow that well-trodden route. The company promotes LAN Server to customers that require strong integration with existing large IBM systems, and indeed argues that its ability to integrate well with large computer systems sets LAN Server apart from NetWare and LAN Manager.

The integration and communication functions of LAN Server are provided by a related product called Extended Services for OS/2. This consists of three parts: a communications manager, database manager and distributed database connection services/2 (DDCS/2). The communications manager provides a variety of facilities needed to access other computer systems at the network level, in other words the basic underlying transport mechanism. The database manager and DDCS/2 give the higher-level support needed for interaction with remote databases; the database manager supports access to client/server databases using the SQL standard; and DDCS/2 is designed to provide tight integration with versions of IBM's own DB2 relational database.

In terms of its basic server controlling functions, LAN Server is still quite similar to LAN Manager. It is available in two versions: a low-price entry server, to entice first time NOS buyers and competing with the low-cost peer-to-peer NOSs described in Chapter 3; and Advanced Server, which adds a high-performance file system and enhanced fault tolerance, making it more suitable for larger networks.

Apart from performance, an important feature of LAN Server version 3.0 is improved support for Microsoft Windows. IBM has enhanced its DOS LAN Requester (DLR), which is the shell software for client workstations, to allow network files, printers, applications and other LAN Server services to be accessed through the Windows GUI. The following features are supported under Windows:

- users can log onto and off a LAN server domain (comprising one or more servers);
- ability to view, connect and disconnect LAN server files, and printers;
- ability to view, install and use LAN server applications;
- ability to send messages to other network users.

Otherwise LAN Server provides the kind of facilities normally expected of a major NOS – these include disk mirroring and duplexing, comprehensive security features, such as password encryption, and ability to specify which users can access a given resource, such as a printer or file.

LAN Server – future directions

IBM's overall LAN strategy has been to embrace the distributed computing environment (DCE) and distributed management environment (DME) technologies being developed by the Open Software Foundation (OSF), of which IBM is a founder member. These are all defined in Appendix 10. As far as LAN Server is concerned, this means supporting DCE standards for distributed file systems, directories and printing. DME, on the other hand, failed to gain market acceptance, so that IBM is instead adopting a variety of less comprehensive industry standards for LAN management, such as SNMP (simple network management protocol).

IBM has promised to implement key standards step by step as they are defined and ratified; meanwhile it will also follow Microsoft by migrating LAN Server to platforms other than OS/2. However, unlike Microsoft, IBM will be focusing on its own host computers as well as *de facto* standard platforms such as UNIX, so that for example LAN Server could run over its mainframe MVS operating system, enabling PC LANs to exploit the security, storage management and backup facilities of centralized host systems. Essentially, IBM intends to make LAN Server a key component of the overall operating environment for distributed, or network, computing, which is discussed further in Chapter 9.

Some of these advances, such as easier use through a new graphical user interface, were planned for inclusion in LAN Server 4.0, due for release early 1995.

□ 2.5 UNIX

2.5.1 Introduction

UNIX is not strictly a NOS but in some manifestations has come to resemble one – in its support for communications and role as an operating system for large servers. Its history, Byzantine in its complexity, merits a PhD thesis in its own right. However, to summarize, it emerged from AT&T's Bell Laboratories to dominate the market for multi-user operating systems that are largely independent of the computer hardware they run on.

The initial growth of UNIX during the 1980s was as a replacement for proprietary operating systems on mid-range departmental computers, commonly called minicomputers. Firms such as Data General and Hewlett-Packard began to phase out their own proprietary operating systems, believing that the future lay in portable operating systems that would enable applications to be moved between computers relatively easily without a major rewrite.

On such systems, UNIX ran initially just as a multi-user operating system, accessed from dumb terminals with all application software and data held centrally at the same location as the computer. However, from this base the credentials of UNIX as a portable operating system grew, as it became available on a wide range of host computers, including also large-scale mainframe computers from Unisys and Amdahl, for example, and even on super-computers from Cray Research. The upshot was that an increasingly rich seam of multi-user applications became available to run under UNIX. UNIX also became the standard operating system for a new breed of powerful graphical workstations from Sun Microsystems, Hewlett-Packard and others.

At the same time, the PC revolution was under way, bringing increasingly powerful machines at affordable prices, and this led to the development of PC versions of UNIX, so opening a new market for business and office applications already written for the operating system. This enabled standard PCs to act as multi-user systems accessed by a small group of dumb terminals. Nevertheless, there were limits to the scale of application that could be run on desktop PCs, and a new role for UNIX emerged as a server operating system, supporting applications accessed by PCs on a LAN. UNIX was helped in this role by having associated communication technologies, in particular the TCP/IP network transport protocol and the network file system (NFS). TCP/IP provided a means for transporting data between non-UNIX computers and host UNIX systems, while NFS enabled applications to access and update files held on UNIX systems.

UNIX does not, however, provide all the functions of a NOS: it is not optimized for client/server applications on a LAN, in which the server performs tasks on behalf of applications running in client desktop workstations, and has no shell components running in the client PC to coordinate with the server. Instead, applications running on client PCs use standard protocols such as NFS to field requests to a UNIX server. NFS, developed by Sun Microsystems, is

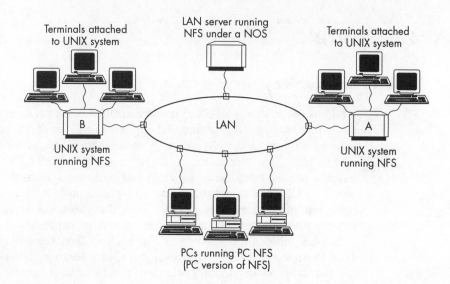

Figure 2.13 The role of network file system (NFS). The PCs can access files on both UNIX systems as well as the LAN server. Users attached to each UNIX system can also access files on the other UNIX system and on the LAN file server.

the most important of a number of systems that allow more than one computer to share files on a UNIX system. This makes UNIX more like a NOS in function, because it enables a number of PCs, for example, to share files managed by the operating system on a central server, via a LAN if desired. The role of NFS is illustrated in Figure 2.13, which shows it working in various guises. You will see that NFS does not just allow computers to access files on local or remote UNIX systems but also UNIX machines to access files on other UNIX systems, or on computers controlled by a different operating system, provided this also supports NFS.

For desktop PCs, a stripped-down version of NFS, called PC-NFS, is used to access UNIX systems. The advantage of PC-NFS is that it is smaller and consumes less processing power and memory on a PC. The disadvantage is that it only allows a PC to access data on UNIX systems, and not the other way round. So if you want UNIX systems to access a non-UNIX PC, some other method is needed.

UNIX, as we have noted, does not have all the features that a NOS possesses for managing and controlling a server-based LAN. However, it provides an ideal base for a NOS and has the advantage of being a more mature application development environment, increasingly able to compete with traditional mainframe operating systems. Microsoft came into the field with LAN Manager for UNIX, allowing its customers to access files and applications on UNIX systems without having to get to grips with a new operating system or GUI, but Novell's was the more dramatic development, introducing UnixWare for Intel-based PCs and servers, as described in Section 2.2. This incorporated NetWare's various protocols, including IPX/SPX, and really completed the apprenticeship of UNIX as a server operating system.

2.5.2 Structure of UNIX

There has always been something of a contradiction about UNIX. Partly to give it widespread appeal, its developers over the years have made it very flexible and relatively easy to mould into different versions. This factor has helped make UNIX popular with hardware makers and software developers but it has also damaged its cause as a universal portable operating system.

Many different versions of UNIX evolved, and an application that runs on one implementation will not automatically run on another, so there has been a conflict between two aspects of the operating system's universal appeal – flexibility and portability. It was not until 1993, when Microsoft's Windows NT operating system threatened to take customers away from UNIX vendors, that there began a really concerted effort to move towards a single version of the operating system: vendors such as IBM, Hewlett-Packard, Novell and Santa Cruz Organization (SCO) formed a new group called the Common Open Software Environment (COSE), partly to harmonize efforts in finally unifying UNIX.

The flexibility of UNIX springs from having a reasonably small and simple core, or kernel, around which there are a variety of software utilities or tools, which enable the operating system to be tailored in different ways. The kernel and the utilities are in fact two of the three components of UNIX: the third, called the shell, comprises software to interpret commands from applications and to execute them using a combination of the kernel and utilities. The relationship between these three components of UNIX is shown in Figure 2.14. When switched on, the computer first goes through a routine sequence of operations in the process called booting up. The kernel is then loaded into the computer's main memory and remains there throughout the time that UNIX is controlling its operation. The kernel is the essence of UNIX, providing the key operating system functions, described in Chapter 1, of dealing with the CPU and memory, and with all attached peripheral hardware devices, and it also controls input/output operations. Although small compared with some traditional large-scale operating systems, such as IBM's MVS, the UNIX kernel is nonetheless a large set of programs, which is why UNIX is not ideally suited for less powerful desktop PCs. As a computer can do little without access to data held in files, all actions on a UNIX system involve the kernel.

Like the rest of UNIX, the kernel is written in the popular C programming language, which, being well known, makes UNIX relatively easy to understand and program in – another factor contributing to the operating system's success. However, the functions of the kernel are relatively low level and hardware specific so that, even though written in an accessible programming language, a detailed understanding of file structures and hardware design is required if they are to be exploited effectively. Therefore to protect programmers and users from having to deal directly with the underlying

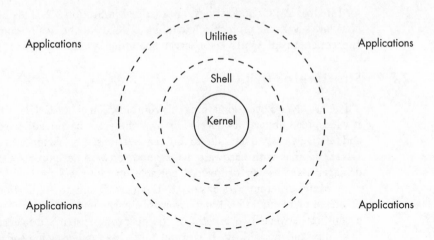

Figure 2.14 Basic structure of UNIX.

hardware, UNIX provides a layer of software known as the shell, depicted in Figure 2.14, wrapped around the kernel. The role of the shell is to interpret commands from users and applications, so helping them manipulate the computer's resources as easily and effectively as possible. Unlike the kernel, the shell is not hardware specific and in an ideal world would be the same on all versions of UNIX so that applications could be ported without change between any computers on which the operating system was installed. However, in practice there are many UNIX shells, providing not just different options but also varying implementations of the same option. UNIX is therefore rather a pot-pourri of different versions, although there are signs now that at last the industry is converging on a common set of shell functions.

The shell incorporates some executable software of its own but mainly it just interprets commands from applications or users, and submits calls to other programs called UNIX utilities. In Figure 2.14, utilities are depicted in a ring round the shell; they provide most of the actual executable programs, written in C, required by the UNIX kernel. Users' applications are depicted in the outer ring surrounding the utilities. Strictly speaking, utilities and applications belong to the same group because UNIX, like most operating systems, does not distinguish between them, both being programs written in C. It is convenient, however, to distinguish between them, in that utilities are generally facilities that help the operating system do its job or help programmers develop software. Applications, in contrast, are programs that meet the final business need, such as processing accounting information. It is the richness and variety of the utilities usually available that has helped UNIX become the *de facto* hardware-independent operating environment, making it easier to develop a wide range of applications. This was one factor in Novell's decision to give UNIX a parallel role to NetWare 4.x, in its strategy to be a major player in the distributed network computing systems of the future.

☐ 2.6 OS/2

OS/2 was originally developed jointly by Microsoft and IBM as a successor to DOS, providing better support for more powerful PCs and more sophisticated applications. In particular, OS/2 avoided the 640 Kbyte main memory limitation of DOS and supported multi-tasking, so that more than one application could run simultaneously. As well as having more memory and the potential to run multi-tasking applications, a new role for PCs was emerging as file and print servers in LANs. OS/2 was designed with this in mind, as a base for LAN Manager, also designed jointly by IBM and Microsoft. However, these two companies underestimated the momentum behind DOS and the task of persuading users to ditch their investment in DOS applications – a major mistake was in not enabling OS/2 to support DOS applications so that users could migrate gradually in their own time. It emerged that it was possible to circumvent, to some extent, the limitations of DOS; indeed, new versions of DOS are still being developed by Microsoft, which has progressively turned it into an operating system capable of supporting multi-tasking applications and sophisticated graphical user interfaces (GUIs).

Nevertheless, IBM has persisted with OS/2 since its split with Microsoft in 1990, and in April 1992 came out with a major new version, OS/2 version 2. On this occasion, the ability to run DOS applications (and also Windows applications) was provided.

2.6.1 OS/2 version 2 key features

OS/2 version 2 is IBM's competitor to Windows NT with built-in support for networking and distributed computing. It can operate as a standalone operating system for powerful PCs, preferably with at least a 386 processor, 8 Mbytes of memory and 90 Mbytes of hard disk storage; alternatively, in conjunction with IBM's LAN Server NOS software, it can form the basis of a distributed LAN operating system.

The key features of the operating system are support for multi-tasking, a high-performance file system, an icon-based graphical user interface (GUI) and in-built support for networking. It can also install other operating systems as guests and run programs written for DOS and Microsoft Windows 3.1.

The GUI is called the OS/2 Workplace Shell – this relates to users through objects presented on the screen as icons, with instructions entered by pointing-and-clicking with a mouse. There are four types of objects: data, which may contain text files, letters, spreadsheets or sound recordings; program, containing OS/2 executable programs, such as word processing software; device, representing physical peripherals that can be accessed from the computer, such as printers and modems; and folder, which is an object containing other objects. Objects contained in the folder may themselves be subfolders, so this allows a hierarchy of facilities to be provided. On a LAN, one such folder would be the network folder, which provides the facilities needed to access LAN resources.

OS/2 version 2 is 'network aware', which means in effect that it incorporates the client shell features that enable applications to access LAN servers, printers and other resources without any additional software.

In October 1994, IBM delivered version 3 of OS/2, called OS/2 Warp. This reversed previous trends in operating systems by requiring less memory than its preceding version, running in 4 Mbytes. It came with a range of new networking facilities, including software to help access and browse through the global Internet network.

☐ 2.7   Banyan Vines

Introduction

Vines has a unique position in the NOS world, having been designed more as a platform for electronic mail and directory services on large networks than as a high-performance file system for workgroup LANs. It began at the opposite end of the spectrum from Novell but the two have converged recently to some extent. It was only in NetWare 4.x, for example, that Novell introduced the support for distributed directory services that had been available with Vines since the product was introduced in the mid 1980s. On the other hand, Banyan has followed Novell and others in producing versions of Vines suitable for small networks, starting with five users. Recently, it also introduced a new file system that moves closer to the performance of the leading NOSs.

Vines has been most successful in the USA, where it is installed at just over 10 per cent of all sites with LANs, according to several surveys, compared with 70 per cent for market leader NetWare. In the UK, Vines has been considerably less successful, owing more to lack-lustre marketing than to any deficiencies in the product. Its main focus tends still to be for large networks and as an integration platform providing comprehensive gateway and communication facilities. In reality, the core Vines NOS itself is only part of the overall product set; the most significant of the related products is the StreetTalk global directory service, which can be used separately from Vines itself. StreetTalk itself forms the basis of a newer family of Banyan products under the banner of ENS (enterprise network services), which enhance other NOSs by providing global directory, messaging and security services. The most important of these is ENS for NetWare, although at first sight this would seem to have been overtaken by NetWare 4.x, which provides similar services. However Banyan's claim is that in practice most large NetWare customers will not upgrade all their servers to NetWare 4.x at a stroke, and that some will be reluctant to do so at all if equivalent services can be obtained more easily and cheaply elsewhere. ENS for NetWare is designed to integrate servers running under different versions of NetWare, including NetWare 2.2 as well as 3.1, into a coherent enterprise-wide network operating within a single distributed directory.

Banyan also focuses on linking different types of client workstation into a single LAN, enabling DOS, OS/2, Windows and Macintosh workstations to share data and applications, and to send messages to each other.

Banyan's overall strategy is thus to provide the glue linking server and client workstations based on different operating systems into an enterprise-wide network. Now, with smaller versions of Vines available, 'enterprise' can mean anything from a small business with five users to a global enterprise with over 1000 servers. Banyan also argues that Vines is the easiest to use and administer of the leading NOSs, and can cite some market research to back this claim; for example, a survey by the US Business Research Group found that Vines was 'across the board' the easiest and least time-consuming NOS to administer.

The various versions of Vines

The core Vines product provides typical NOS facilities as described in Chapter 1, including a file system, support for remote network printing and the ability to be accessed from the leading client PC operating systems – DOS, Macintosh, Microsoft Windows and OS/2.

Vines was initially built on the UNIX operating system, which at the time rendered it unsuitable for PC LANs of the sort served by early versions of NetWare. However, UNIX has now been available on PCs for some time and Banyan has developed versions of Vines suitable for PC platforms; the smallest version, Vines 5, is for just five users. The latter can be upgraded first to Vines 10, then to Vines 20, supporting respectively 10 and 20 users, and these all come with support for file sharing, distributed directories and security as standard. Furthermore, additional options, such as host connectivity, network management and electronic mail, can be added at any stage. After Vines 20, Vines Unlimited is available, which allows any number of users. There is also a version of Vines for SCO UNIX now available.

We shall conclude by summarizing the principal Vines features and associated products, particularly for the benefit of UK readers who may be less familiar with what is a significant NOS player in the USA.

Strengths

- support for large distributed networks with global directory, messaging, management and security services;
- ability to embrace different types of NOS and a wide range of systems within a large network;
- ease of use and administration;
- support for integration with IBM host systems and networks;
- version now available for small networks providing full range of communications and management options.

Weaknesses

- file system performance does not match the big three: LAN Manager, NetWare and IBM LAN Server;

- although a well-established and successful product, lacks the momentum behind the big three. Inevitably, Banyan cannot match the investment of Microsoft, Novell and IBM, and will have to focus on key areas; in others, such as support for document image processing, it may lag behind. By the same token, Banyan does not attract as much support from third-party developers to enrich the overall Vines environment;
- probably not cost-effective for very small LANs.

Associated products

1. *StreetTalk*
Apart from Vines, this is Banyan's most famous product, for some years having the field of distributed directory services virtually to itself. It allows a whole distributed directory of names and network addresses to be updated from a single workstation and is still the market leader in its ability to unite disparate systems and software into a single global directory structure.

2. *Communication Services*
These include a variety of features for accessing remote LANs and host computers from PC LANs based on Vines servers. Facilities include software for bridging with other LANs, accessing TCP/IP networks and connecting to IBM host mainframes. There is also the ability to connect with remote Vines servers via the popular WAN protocols such as X.25, SNA and, again, TCP/IP.

3. *Intelligent Messaging (IM)*
StreetTalk and Vines Communication Services are utilized to provide enterprise-wide electronic mail. This can be accessed from a variety of front-end user interfaces, including those available with DOS, Macintosh and OS/2.

4. *Vines Security Service*
This comes bundled with every version of Vines software, providing security facilities comparable with NetWare. Access to every network device, service and communications link can be controlled individually by having unique identifiers for each. Lists of these names can be associated with each user, so that navigation of the network can be strictly controlled. Each individual directory and file on the network can also be controlled.

□ SUMMARY

Having described and contrasted the major large-scale NOSs, the next chapter continues the process for products that are either less well known or aimed at smaller LANs.

3

Are low-cost NOSs available for small LANs?

CHAPTER OBJECTIVES

- To describe leading NOSs suitable for small networks and the differences between them
- To explain peer-to-peer networking, the basis of low-cost LANs
- To detail the limitations of low-cost NOSs
- To explain how low-cost NOSs can be expanded as your network grows, and when they need to be replaced
- To describe how low-cost NOSs differ
- To detail the role of low-cost NOSs in workgroup computing and so-called groupware products

□ 3.1 Introduction

Low-cost NOSs evolved as a means of sharing data and printers between a small workgroup without the need to buy dedicated hardware such as a central server or printer. The idea was for several users, each with a PC, to permit the others to access their machines in order to obtain data and possibly to use a printer. By this means, the advantages of a LAN, in terms of distributing data and allowing resources to be shared cost-effectively, could be obtained without the usual initial investment for a dedicated central server. The main issues to be considered when choosing a low-cost NOS are highlighted in Chapter 4.

□ 3.2 Basic functions of peer-to-peer NOSs

As well as costing less to buy, low-cost NOSs save money on small networks because the software is less sophisticated and therefore easier to maintain than mainstream products (although this is not the case on larger networks). The original major NOSs, such as NetWare, required a dedicated central server, which held all the shared data and also provided access to one or more printers, perhaps via separate print servers. Low-cost NOSs, in contrast, designated desktop PCs to hold data or applications needed to be accessed by users on the LAN.

The distinction is illustrated in Figure 1.4, which shows a traditional LAN built round a central server and printer alongside a low-cost alternative without a dedicated server. Such low-cost LANs are commonly described as 'peer-to-peer' because all PCs participate as equals, rather than having one machine dedicated to the service of the others. Note, however, that not all computers on a peer-to-peer LAN have to be designated as servers – some might operate purely as clients serving one person, while others might perform a dual role as both client and server. Typically, the more powerful PCs, with at least an Intel 386 chip and preferably a 486 or higher chip, are designated as servers; older and less powerful PCs operate purely as clients. Yet there is no hard and fast rule that servers must be more powerful than clients: if, on a peer-to-peer LAN, a PC exists that is rarely used as a client, this can usefully function as a server, even if it is not particularly powerful. This indicates that the distinction between peer-to-peer networking and client/server operation is far from being well defined.

Apart from resource sharing, peer-to-peer NOSs increasingly provide facilities to support and enhance workgroup computing, such as the ability to schedule tasks and meetings, and to work on common documents and files. These and other facilities are provided by separate groupware packages, such as Lotus Notes 3.0 and WordPerfect Office 4.0. Microsoft's Windows 3.11, however, combines a peer-to-peer NOS and extensive groupware facilities in a single software package, and most peer-to-peer NOSs provide at least rudimentary groupware facilities such as electronic mail. The boundary between low-cost NOSs and groupware packages is becoming blurred, and this trend has been accelerated by Novell's acquisition of WordPerfect in March 1994. Although in this chapter we describe Lotus Notes 3.0 and WordPerfect Office 4.0, these being two of the most popular groupware packages, note that they are not really intended for low-cost LANs, even if increasingly some of the functions they provide are available on small networks.

□ 3.3   Introducing the contenders

The market for peer-to-peer NOSs was shaped from around 1989 by Artisoft, along with a few smaller NOS developers such as Performance Technology and Sage. The field later intensified into a major battleground that drew in the major players, Microsoft and Novell. From the user's viewpoint, the peer-to-peer NOS has become increasingly indistinguishable from the emerging field of groupware software, which provides facilities for cooperation within specific workgroups or departments. It is true that groupware applications require an underlying NOS to run but developments such as Novell's acquisition of WordPerfect indicate that there will be increasing integration of the NOS with groupware applications.

The chief factor distinguishing low-cost NOSs from their more powerful siblings is the support for peer-to-peer operation. This is important because it avoids the need for a dedicated server machine and so reduces by one the total number of computers needed for a given group of users. For small workgroups, peer-to-peer networking is an efficient means of utilizing hardware resources, as PCs often have spare capacity that can readily be used to provide common print services and data access, although as a network grows, such operation generally becomes less attractive because of the mounting problem of managing a proliferating population of non-dedicated servers. This can be a nightmare on a network of 100 PCs, where each can in principle provide services to any of the others. The number of potential interactions becomes enormous, so careful management is needed to make peer-to-peer operation a success on larger networks.

Nevertheless, where network growth is anticipated, peer-to-peer NOSs that provide the option of supporting dedicated servers should be considered. Then, as the network grows beyond about eight users, a dedicated server can be installed to provide centralized administration and management. Note, however, that even if a NOS does support dedicated servers, it may still be suitable for larger networks – it may not have a sufficiently fast file system or it may not support the fault-tolerant features that become important when many users depend on the network to do their jobs.

Some low-cost NOSs, such as Performance Technology's Powerlan, do have the option of running dedicated servers, while others, such as Novell's Personal NetWare, do not. In the latter case, the NOS has to be replaced with a more sophisticated product when network growth calls for centralization of data and/or network management. With Microsoft's Windows 3.11 a third possibility prevails – to install a Windows NT server to cope with network growth.

In the rest of this chapter we look at six of the leading low-cost NOSs: Powerlan from Performance Technology; LANtastic from Artisoft; 10 Net from Tiara; Personal NetWare from Novell; Mainlan from Sage; and Windows 3.11 from Microsoft. Note that the versions of Banyan Vines suitable for small networks are described in Chapter 2.

In addition to the six NOSs just mentioned, we shall look at Apple Computer's AppleTalk in this chapter; this differs from the others in that it is intended exclusively for Apple computers and is typically used for relatively small workgroups. However, AppleTalk is stronger than most other peer-to-peer NOSs in its support for interoperability with other computer systems, partly because it has generated a sufficiently big market to encourage the development of relevant communication products from third parties.

□ 3.4 Powerlan from Performance Technology

This product, distributed in the UK by CMS Software, has consistently out-performed rival low-cost LANs in performance tests both in the UK and the US, being beaten only by more expensive products, such as NetWare 3.11, designed for larger networks. Powerlan is also good at interoperating with other types of networking environment and, by supporting dedicated server operation, can handle considerable network growth. As its performance does begin to flag on large networks in excess of 100 users, it is therefore pitched primarily at small-to-medium sized workgroups. In this arena the product's virtues have been acknowledged by one of its competitors, Artisoft, which was on the verge of acquiring Performance Technology early in 1992, although the takeover fell through.

In fact, the one area where Powerlan is inferior to Artisoft's LANtastic is in ease of management. Powerlan is straightforward for end users to operate but the huge range of options makes it hard to install and manage. However, Powerlan scores well in the key area of print management – while it allows printers to be attached to any workstation on the LAN, the task of running the print spooler is handled by just one machine. Furthermore, print jobs are routed not to a specific printer but to a print profile and this can be useful on larger networks, enabling multiple printers to be deployed in parallel for a given type of job, such as address labels or reports. Nevertheless, careful administration is required to ensure that users are aware of the location where their print jobs are to be carried out.

3.4.1 Powerlan's performance-enhancing features

This product has various options that enhance performance, depending on the configuration required. For non-dedicated servers, disk caching is available to speed up disk read/write operations, which can often prove a bottleneck, particularly on peer-to-peer LANs based on lower-specification PCs. Disk caching involves the use of memory chips, which have much faster data access times than hard disk drives, as temporary storage for data that is most likely to be accessed. Data that has either been recently read, or that the system knows is about to be read, is held in cache.

For dedicated servers, more advanced caching techniques are used, which has enabled Powerlan to score highly on benchmarks despite being based on the DOS operating system. Up to 32 Mbytes of expanded memory can be used for caching and there is a prioritizing method which increases the cache-hit rate. The latter means that there is a greater chance of the data you require already being in cache. Many disk input/output operations then take place effectively in the background, with less impact on file seek and access times.

3.4.2 Other Powerlan features and options

1. *Security and administration*
These two are not synonymous: administration of some form is compulsory on a LAN in order to make it work, while security is optional. On Powerlan, however, both are delivered via the logon server application running on one designated PC on the network, which can either be a dedicated or non-dedicated server. This provides a central point of control over access to all resources on the network. Users therefore have to go through the logon server whenever they want to access data or an application that does not reside in their own PC. If no security is required, logon is automatic but the logon server still plays an important administrative role in adding or removing users from the network. When security is needed, users can be given passwords and all shared files can be protected from being read, modified or deleted, or a combination of these three. The logon server should be duplicated on another PC so that users can gain access through this secondary logon server should the primary server go down.

Users can also be assigned different privileges; for example, some may be allowed to alter print queues while others may be given full network administrator status. User groups can then be set up, with members of each group having the same privileges and facilities.

2. *Printing*

Powerlan goes further than some low-cost NOSs in supporting fully distributed printing – it allows printers to be dispersed through the network while maintaining the advantages of a single centralized print spooler. Figure 3.1 shows the technique. Printers can be attached to servers, both dedicated and non-dedicated, and also to non-serving workstations. A single server is dedicated as the spool server and all machines to which printers are attached are configured as unspoolers. Each printer is driven by the so-called unspooler software, residing in the machine to which it is attached. The unspooler knows where the central spool server is located, enabling it continuously to issue commands to the spooler server to check if files exist that it should be printing. If this is the case, the files are transmitted across the network to the unspooler, which controls the actual printing of the job. The process is efficient because each unspooler only has to look at one central spool server. Furthermore, the unspooler software takes up only 3.5 Kbytes of memory in the PC in which it resides, so there is plenty of room left for users' applications.

3. *Data backup*

A package called Powersave is available to back up data automatically on both servers and client workstations. It can be used with a variety of tape drives, including DAT (digital audio tape) drives with SCSI (small computer system

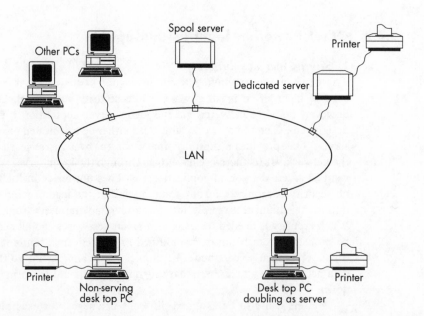

Figure 3.1 How Powerlan NOS supports printing. PCs on the LAN can access all printers, whether on non-serving PC or both dedicated and non-dedicated servers.

interface) controllers, providing unattended backup for up to 36 different disk drives. It is optional with Powerlan and can also be used with other leading NOSs, including Novell NetWare, Banyan Vines and Artisoft's LANtastic.

There is also a package called Powermirror available for more critical applications. This provides more complete protection against disk drive failure by writing data simultaneously to two or more drives, via more than one controller if required.

4. *Network expansion and access to other systems*
A software package called Powerbridge allows Powerlan networks to be interconnected locally or remotely, either with each other or with other networks based on NetBIOS protocols (see Section 1.4). Also, Powerfusion is available to allow PCs running on NetBIOS LANs to access UNIX file and print services. A related package called Powerfusion for Novell permits PCs to access UNIX and NetWare services simultaneously, providing some of the facilities available with Novell's UnixWare (see Section 2.2). In addition to these, there are options available which enable Powerlan users to connect to most other leading NOSs, including LAN Manager, IBM LAN Server, NetWare and Vines.

□ 3.5   LANtastic from Artisoft

Although other vendors came into the peer-to-peer market at roughly the same time, Artisoft became the leader through a combination of astute marketing, having an easy-to-use product and offering value for money. According to International Data Corporation (IDC), LANtastic had 35 per cent of the worldwide market for peer-to-peer NOSs in 1992, with 225 000 networks installed and a total of 1.2 million users.

Performance was only average, at least until version 5.0 came along early in 1993, but this has been less relevant at the lower end of the market. Furthermore, the product scores highly on the key areas of administration and printing; it is well endowed with features to ease administration of the network in general and to manage print queues, and security, although an optional extra, is sufficient to allow larger networks to be built than are feasible with most peer-to-peer LANs.

3.5.1   Main features of LANtastic version 5.0

Unlike some rivals such as Performance Technology, Artisoft has decided not to cover both potential markets by trying to sell its NOS as a platform for client/server computing as well as peer-to-peer networking. With version 5.0, Artisoft remains unabashed in its enthusiasm for peer-to-peer networking and makes no attempt to compete with high-end server-based NOS products like NetWare 4.x. This is not to say that LANtastic is not used in some quite large networks but it is always as a peer-to-peer system and, when used in larger networks, it typically, although not always, co-exists with other server-based NOSs. So although Artisoft has not itself promoted dedicated servers, it recognizes that many organizations, including some of its own customers, are not prepared to build large networks exclusively with peer-to-peer networking.

Not surprisingly, therefore, a major thrust with version 5.0 was to improve and simplify co-existence with other leading NOSs, especially Net-Ware. Version 4.0 allowed PCs on a LANtastic LAN to access NetWare servers on an individual basis but this quickly became an untidy solution if a number of users wanted to do so. Therefore version 5.0 has the ability for LANtastic PCs, or peers as they are called, to access a NetWare network through a single LANtastic non-dedicated server, acting as a bridge. This provides a common shared gateway into NetWare for all members of the LANtastic network. The principle, which also extends to some other networks, such as those based on UNIX, is shown in Figure 3.2.

Most of the other improvements in version 5.0 relate to administration and management, and go some way to answer criticisms that peer-to-peer operation becomes hard to manage on large networks; for example, users now need only to log onto one server to use resources throughout the network, and all user accounts can be set up on a single server. This means that, as far as both users and administrators are concerned, a LANtastic LAN functions more like a client/server LAN, while retaining the advantages of peer-to-peer operation, such as the ability to make effective use of all the network's processing resources. Version 5.0 is also able to manage servers remotely, and introduces file level security, so that individual files can be protected from

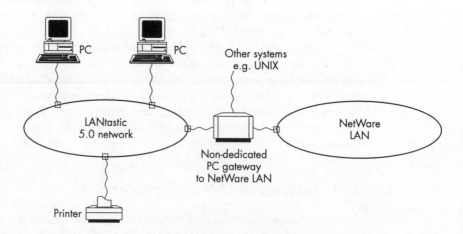

Figure 3.2 How LANtastic 5.0 users can access NetWare LANs and also other external systems such as UNIX hosts.

access by specified users. These are the type of facilities required for larger networks.

Some of the new facilities should have been made available earlier, and their introduction now suggests that, despite protestations to the contrary, Artisoft has only just decided to target the market for larger networks. Other such overdue features include support for uninterruptible power supplies and diskless workstations. The former has become an essential component for any network running critical applications, while diskless workstations have become popular on larger networks because they help control LAN usage and also enhance security by making it difficult to introduce viruses into the network. However, Artisoft does have a nice touch of its own with a feature called LAN Radio. This is available with the Windows version of the product in combination with LANtastic's Sounding Board, providing a voice intercom system across the network.

A more serious factor distinguishing Artisoft from most of its competitors is that the company makes its own Ethernet adapters called Node Runners. These enable it to supply complete networking solutions optimized for LANtastic, including adapters as well as the software. Artisoft is planning to go further by working with PC makers to have single-chip versions of the Ethernet adaptors implemented on the PC's motherboard; then, perhaps in partnership with PC vendors, Artisoft will supply total computing solutions including PCs as well as the NOS, and possibly the applications software running on top of this platform. LANtastic can be purchased in starter kits for two PCs, comprising Artisoft's own adapter boards as well as the requisite software.

□ 3.6   10 Net

10 Net, developed by the US company Tiara Computer Systems, is a mature NOS with a loyal and medium-sized user base about half as big as Artisoft's, having 700 000 nodes installed worldwide. However, some customers became unsettled when Sitka, the Sun Microsystems subsidiary, ended its cooperative licensing agreement for the product with Tiara. Sitka was initially planning to combine 10 Net with other products of its own design in a new all-embracing range of networking facilities called OpenTops, but then decided to omit 10 Net from this strategy, deciding that it overlapped too much with its own products, such as DOS Tops.

In the UK, this left the product in the hands of less well-known distributors like Interquad. Inevitably, the withdrawal of one of the industry's big players raised doubts about the product's future, even though Tiara and its distributors remain committed to it. It is a fact of life that big customers home in on the comfort factor provided by a big company like Novell, Microsoft or even Artisoft.

However, as a solution for small networks, 10 Net retains considerable merit – it is rich on features, and performance, while variable, holds up well on moderately loaded networks. There is evidence from some benchtests that the product is unstable under heavy network loading; unlike LANtastic and Powerlan, it only really thrives in quite small networks. It is available in starter packs for just two or three workstations, depending on the distributor, comprising the software and documentation for installing modules running under DOS and Microsoft Windows. The Windows version requires the basic DOS version to be already installed, along with Windows 3.0 or higher (meaning a later version such as Windows 3.1). It also requires at least 256 Kbytes extended memory in addition to 640 Kbytes conventional memory, although with falling prices of memory chips this is a decreasing deterrent. Like most other low-cost NOSs, 10 Net can be upgraded one node at a time and in addition there is a so-called value pack for ten-node networks.

Support for electronic mail is increasingly important for peer-to-peer NOSs with a trend towards more dispersed workgroups. 10 Net scores well as the product comes bundled with the popular and comprehensive Da Vinci eMail package.

□ 3.7 Windows 3.11, from Microsoft

Any new product launch from Microsoft sends shock waves rippling through the rest of the industry. So it was when WfW Windows for Workgroups (now part of Windows 3.11) arrived in late 1992, although other vendors of low-end NOSs also derived a spin-off benefit. Microsoft's arrival in the market for peer-to-peer workgroup LAN solutions signalled that the field was sufficiently big and mature to merit the attentions of the world's premier software company. Novell would argue that its earlier launch of NetWare Lite had already legitimized the peer-to-peer market but be that as it may, the launch of WfW hit Novell itself because it was priced aggressively by Microsoft. The product also represented a bid by Microsoft to exile Novell from the desktop by providing all the shell functionality required for accessing NetWare servers within WfW. The appeal of this was that, as Microsoft's Windows operating system was already installed on so many desktop PCs, it made sense to use WfW to provide peer-to-peer links between them and at the same time to support any other communications links needed, including access to NetWare LANs.

Microsoft hoped this would enable it first to penetrate the networks of Novell customers, and ultimately to prise them away from NetWare by offering a complete set of networking software, embracing both clients and servers, based on Windows NT. This led to a legal dispute between the two companies, with Novell claiming that an agreement between the two companies allowing Microsoft to implement NetWare shell software did not extend to WfW. The dispute was settled late in 1993 with Microsoft agreeing to let Novell supply the elements that were subject to copyright dispute. So now half the software drivers on Windows 3.11 providing the NetWare shell come from Microsoft, while the rest are provided freely by Novell, either from bulletin boards or via other distribution channels.

3.7.1 Features of Windows 3.11

Windows 3.11 combines Microsoft's original Windows 3.1 desktop operating system with a subset of the LAN Manager NOS organized to support just peer-to-peer networking. Features supported include the ability to share files and printers located anywhere on the network between all users of the LAN, and support for workgroup applications such as email and scheduling tasks or meetings. These functions are shared by some groupware packages with which Windows 3.11 competes alongside other low-cost NOS products. Features present in full-blown Windows NT Server but lacking in Windows 3.11 are those needed to support larger networks based on dedicated servers; these include support for fault tolerance, servers based on multiple processors and more advanced features for administering large networks comprising more than one server.

Whereas NT Server is intended for systems with over 12 Mbytes of memory and preferably at least a high-end Intel 486 or RISC processor, Windows 3.11 is aimed at systems with less than 4 Mbytes of main memory, typically low-end 486 PCs or older 386 PCs.

However, the starting point, and therefore basis for comparison, in most cases is Windows 3.1; Windows 3.11 inherits all its characteristics. In essence, Windows 3.1 is an enhancement of MS-DOS, overcoming some of its limitations and making it easier to use (for the majority who prefer graphical user interfaces based on mice and icons to traditional DOS commands). Microsoft was motivated to develop Windows by the realization that the huge base of DOS applications was not going to be rewritten at a stroke to take advantage of new, more advanced operating systems such as OS/2. Windows 3.1 provides some of the benefits of OS/2 while running existing legacy DOS applications. The great mistake Microsoft and IBM made (although only IBM has suffered permanent damage from this) in developing OS/2 was in not supporting DOS applications. OS/2 version 2 now does support DOS as well as Windows 3.1 applications, but the move came too late to halt the inexorable onward march of Microsoft's Windows family. DOS was designed purely as a single-user operating system and originally provided no mechanism for sharing files between more than one user or application. At this stage it would have been impossible to build any sort of NOS on top of DOS without rewriting part of the underlying operating system. For this reason, early NOSs such as NetWare were built from the bottom up, because DOS did not provide the fundamental ability, necessary for a LAN or any shared resource system, of allowing a file to be shared between more than one user. To support sharing of data, the operating system needs the ability to lock files so that only one user at a time can access them. Otherwise there is the risk of a file being updated simultaneously by two users, leading to inconsistencies and corruptions of files. Microsoft finally introduced support for file locking in MS-DOS when the Share command was added to version 3.1 of the operating system. This opened the door to the use of MS-DOS as a base for low-cost peer-to-peer LANs, and Microsoft itself exploited this with WfW. Therefore WfW can also be distinguished from full-blown LAN Manager by being built on MS-DOS rather than UNIX, OS/2 or Windows NT.

All network operations are executed through the Windows GUI. To do this, the Windows GUI was enhanced to include a tool bar with icons for commonly used network commands such as sharing resources and connecting to other machines. The specific NOS features provided by Windows 3.11, in addition to the basic Windows 3.1 features for single users, can now be summarized:

(1) *File sharing.* Files and directories on hard disks of all PCs attached to the network can be shared, subject to access controls. Different levels of access can be allocated to each user, including read only, read/write, copy and execute (in the case of a program file).

(2) *Printer sharing.* As with other peer-to-peer NOSs, printers attached to any PC can be shared.

(3) *Network DDE and clipbook viewer.* Microsoft's DDE (dynamic data exchange) protocol allows interactive links to be created between data items such as documents on different PCs on the network. Changes initiated on one PC can be automatically propagated to others; for example, a group of users might all be revising a report containing typographical errors – corrections made by each user would propagate automatically to the versions being worked on by the others. However, this feature only works with applications that support DDE, which excludes DOS programs.

Note that in Chapter 10 we describe object linking and embedding (OLE), which is Microsoft's sequel to DDE, providing more sophisticated facilities for cooperation between applications and information sharing between documents.

(4) *Electronic mail.* Microsoft's MS Mail 3.0, which is also available as a separate email package, is integrated into Windows 3.11. This allows users to read, compose, forward and reply to mail messages, supported by features such as a point-and-click address book. However, to access remote email systems outside Window 3.11, which many organizations will want to do, a separate upgrade has to be purchased.

(5) *Scheduling.* A graphical scheduling application called Schedule+ is integrated into Windows 3.11; this provides standard facilities for managing diaries and schedules electronically. For example, to schedule meetings with other members of the Windows group, the same address book used for email needs to be accessed to select the desired people to attend the meeting. Schedule+ then looks up the diaries of each of these people to see if they

are free. When a commonly available time has been determined, email messages requesting the meeting can be sent, although currently this process is not done automatically.

(6) *Security.* Users can protect their shared directories and printers by using passwords, and they can allow different levels of access such as read only.

(7) WinMeter. This is a cunning device allowing users to specify what proportion of their CPU will be available for other members of the workgroup, if their PC is shared. This could become anarchic if not controlled, because users might become frustrated if their PC is being slowed down by network tasks on behalf of other users, and decide to turn off access to the CPU from the network.

(8) *Interoperability with other NOSs.* Windows 3.11 can interoperate with higher-level Microsoft products to the extent that, for example, Windows 3.11 PCs can become clients to an NT server. This means that, should a Windows 3.11 network grow to such a size that a dedicated server becomes desirable, a smooth upgrade can be achieved by simply installing a version of NT Server on one of the PCs, if necessary upgrading the PC so that it has at least 8 Mbytes of main memory.

Windows 3.11 includes NetWare client software, which enables Windows 3.11 users to access NetWare servers over the same adapter card and cable as other Windows 3.11 PCs. This is made possible through the use of Microsoft's dual redirector technology, which allows more than one set of network protocols to operate through a single adapter card.

□ 3.8 Personal NetWare (originally NetWare Lite)

Like most peer-to-peer NOSs, Personal NetWare is an extension of DOS. Just as Windows 3.11 supports NetWare, so Personal NetWare will work with Windows 3.1, which is also based on DOS.

However, unlike Windows 3.11, Personal NetWare is a separate product written specially for peer-to-peer operation. It is not a stripped down version of existing NetWare versions, largely because these provided no facility for peer-to-peer communications, and this meant that the product had some teething troubles, the first version being unreliable and poor on performance. However, Novell pulled out the stops, and the second release, NetWare Lite 1.1, was dramatically improved to the extent that it was given the coveted accolade of top low-cost LAN product by the UK *PC Magazine* in December 1992. The main remaining criticism was that it cost more than most other low-cost NOSs, but there is often a premium to be paid for a big name brand which has better-than-average prospects of future enhancement and support.

Personal NetWare has been designed to look and feel as much like its more powerful siblings as possible; the commands are mostly the same, making it easy to migrate upwards to NetWare 3.1 or NetWare 4.0, for example. However, a disadvantage of being a new product is that the upgrade path is not as seamless as from Windows for Workgroups to LAN Manager. The product does have to be replaced for users who want full-blown NetWare facilities but existing NetWare networks can be left intact and will interoperate excellently with Personal NetWare.

In addition, being a new product, Novell has taken some trouble to ensure that Personal NetWare is easy to install and use, providing a relatively pain-free entry to networking, although areas where the bigger versions of NetWare excel, such as security, are weak. This all points to Personal NetWare being a fine starter product but unsuitable as a vehicle for growth beyond, ideally, 10 users or so, even if the maximum allowed is 25.

3.8.1 Features of Personal NetWare summarized

Personal NetWare provides a set of frequently used commands which allow standard tasks to be performed without going through the menu. However, supervisory tasks, such as giving a network name to an existing directory on a PC so that other users can access it, have to be executed via the menu. Specific features can now be summarized:

(1) *File sharing.* Users can create or modify network directories, and can provide restricted access. However, the default is for users to have complete access, so if you want others to read your files only, this must be specified. Also note that if you only want other users to access a particular subdirectory on your PC, you have to specify just that subdirectory as available to the network, otherwise your whole root directory will be open to other users.

(2) *Printer sharing.* Only supervisors can specify that you can use a particular printer on the network, unless it is directly attached to your own PC. However, if a printer is specified as being for networked operation, all users then have access to it by default, although you can create a list of individuals who are not allowed to use a particular printer. The command Capture is used to specify which printer your jobs are sent to and the Print command is used to specify files for printing, with the option of overriding the printer specified in the Capture command.

(3) *Electronic mail.* There are fairly basic facilities for sending and receiving messages to and from users that are currently connected to the network.

(4) *Server configuration.* A strong point of the product is the ability to tune servers to maximize performance, drawing on Novell's experience with its other NOSs. Users are allowed to modify their own PCs but others can be modified only by supervisors if such PCs are designated as servers.

(5) *Network management.* On a small peer-to-peer network, management extends to lists of network users, directories and printers, configuration of servers, and details of access rights. This information is vital for administering the network properly and so Novell provides the ability to backup and restore network management files. Unlike other versions of NetWare and also some other low-cost NOSs, there are no in-built facilities for backing up other files, such as users' data and programs – this is left to individual users.

□ 3.9   Sage Mainlan version 4.0

For those who prefer a British NOS, this is the prime candidate, provided your networking requirements are relatively humble. Initially, Mainlan was pitched right down at the bottom of the NOS market, for networks with at most six users, particularly those that already ran the Sterling accounting software from the same company. However, several weaknesses in security and performance were tackled in version 4.0 of the product launched in 1993; this replaced two previous products, Mainlan Easy and Mainlan GTI, which both offered comparable performance and features, even though the latter was twice the price of the former. Mainlan v4 is much improved, yet prices are only slightly higher than Mainlan Easy, and the product now represents good value for money on a small network. Nevertheless, although Mainlan v4 can support up to 60 PCs, it is still not a realistic proposition for networks with more than ten nodes.

The product is now compatible with the leading makes of network adapter or NIC (network interface card) from leading manufacturers such as Novell and Western Digital. It can, like Artisoft's LANtastic, be purchased in two node starter kits comprising two adapters, the Mainlan software, and the cabling and components required to connect up the network. The network can be extended in single-user increments.

□ 3.10   AppleTalk

Apple is well known for leading the world into the era of windows and icon-based desktop operating systems with the Macintosh. Less well known is that the company was also quite visionary in its approach to networking with its AppleTalk protocol and services. The key move was building the AppleTalk protocol into all Macs, which have come 'network ready' since their launch in 1984.

Initially, AppleTalk was used mainly for linking Macs to printers but, with the growth of workgroup computing, users soon realized that they had an advantage over those using Intel-based PCs running MS-DOS: they did not need to buy network interface cards (NICs) because this functionality was in-built. This also meant they did not have to install client shell software to access the NOS services, which not only saved the cost of NICs but also made it much easier to establish a low-cost simple peer-to-peer LAN with the ability to exchange messages and to share files and printers.

However, AppleTalk networks also had some limitations compared with those based on other NOSs; these resulted not so much from the Apple's NOS software but from the fact that AppleTalk was based on a slower-speed LAN than Ethernet or token ring. Note that AppleTalk is not just a NOS but also a complete set of network services spanning all seven layers of the OSI model from cabling up to the application level with print and file services. Figure 3.3 shows the structure of AppleTalk which is entirely consistent with the OSI model (see Appendix 3). The bottom two layers are referred to by Apple as Local Talk, which is the equivalent of Ethernet or token ring. The function of the NOS spans the top three layers in the diagram, layers five to seven. This layered protocol structure has enabled AppleTalk to evolve and overcome some of its earlier limitations. Furthermore, the use of windows in the Mac has allowed Apple to provide access to other types of network in an easy-to-use well-structured manner; the result is that AppleTalk networks can now readily provide access to LANs based on other NOSs, as explained further in Chapter 5.

Alternatively, Mac users can access networks controlled by other NOSs directly from a window – one window could be used to access files on an AppleTalk network while a NetWare server is being accessed through another,

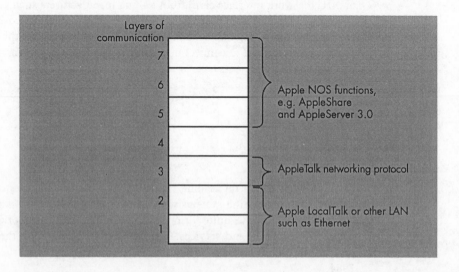

Figure 3.3 Structure of AppleTalk.

although this does necessitate running the appropriate version of NetWare shell software on the Mac.

3.10.1 Key points of the AppleTalk NOS

Apple's approach to networking is rather different from other vendors', which can lead to confusion when comparing NOS functions. As noted in Section 3.10, AppleTalk is the generic name for Apple's whole range of networking services. Apple refers to these as AppleTalk network services, which embraces the NOS functions and contained within these is the seven-layer AppleTalk protocol, as illustrated in Figure 3.3.

As already noted in Section 3.10, basic peer-to-peer file and print-sharing facilities are built into the Mac operating system, the current version being System 7 at the time of writing (1994). However Apple was quick to realize that larger networks would require more sophisticated centralized file sharing facilities for client/server applications. The software that runs on dedicated Mac servers is called AppleShare, which is functionally similar to NetWare 3.1, for example. An important difference is that the client software already present in the Mac also provides access to dedicated AppleShare servers as well as to peers in an AppleTalk network, so that no additional shell software needs to be installed.

AppleShare Server 3.0 was the current Apple server software in 1994. It supports up to 120 concurrent users and up to five AppleTalk printers, and is still therefore unsuitable for the largest networks. However, Apple does provide a range of options for expansion through use of other vendors' systems: one such is EtherShare 2.0, which allows UNIX servers or workstations from vendors such as IBM, Hewlett-Packard, Sun Microsystems and Digital Equipment to provide NOS file and print services for AppleTalk networks. These AppleTalk networks can also access the leading host environments such as IBM mainframes.

☐ 3.11 Groupware packages: Lotus Notes 3.0 and WordPerfect Office 4.0

Groupware involves integration of messaging with office applications like electronic diary, word processing, calendars and scheduling, to produce a whole system greater than the sum of its component parts. A key aspect of more sophisticated groupware products is workflow automation, in which the system directs tasks that need to be done in the correct order.

Most NOSs come equipped with some groupware fundamentals, incorporating some form of electronic mail package allowing users and applications to exchange messages. Microsoft's Windows 3.11 NOS, as we saw in Section 3.7, goes further by coming bundled with a complete range of groupware functions including scheduling and the ability to link documents across a network via a clipboard facility. Windows 3.11 competes directly with other groupware products, such as the two considered in this section, the difference being that the others are not specific to a particular NOS and will run on a variety of different networking software platforms.

There are advantages and disadvantages in both approaches. Microsoft's provides a single package combining the underlying NOS with the workgroup software; all software problems can then be referred to a single source without having to worry whether the fault lies with the NOS or in higher-level software. Other approaches provide freedom to match the NOS and the groupware software separately to the particular needs of the business. Also, by supporting all the leading NOSs, they allow different LANs to be bound together in a single workgroup with common access to office applications. This is useful for businesses that have more than one LAN and want to create a single workgroup without having to replace existing NOSs.

Increasingly, groupware vendors are cooperating to make their products work together in a single large network. This makes it more feasible for a business to allow each workgroup to choose its own favourite groupware product, knowing that they will be able to exchange messages, with mutual access to a database containing information on diaries and schedules.

3.11.1 What is groupware?

In theory, groupware should be all things to all workgroups, providing all the basic functions they need plus easy-to-use development tools and options to customize the product to specific types of application like selling, marketing and design. Many of the ingredients are also available as independent packages: the trick with groupware is to integrate them effectively so that they work together to support a whole business process rather than just parts of it. The essential ingredients are:

(1) some form of messaging system or electronic mail so that users and applications can communicate;

(2) a database, with an appropriate management and access system, to provide a common store of business information pertaining to clients, diaries, projects and so on;

(3) scheduling and time management, which extends from running diaries of individuals to planning and assigning tasks. This combines elements of existing diary management software with more sophisticated project management systems. This is not to say that all groupware products come anywhere near the sophistication of leading project management systems but they are encroaching on that area;

(4) workflow management, to tie the other ingredients together and make them support the particular flow of tasks and information; for example, workflow software can ordain that documents are transmitted to the right people for comment and annotation. Similarly, documents requiring authorization can be sent to managers who can record their assent or dissent by clicking on an appropriate icon on the screen.

There are other features of growing importance, such as the ability to work with different vendors' groupware applications and support for the leading NOSs. Also important are development tools allowing applications to be built readily, and software to manage the whole process.

3.11.2 Lotus Notes 3.0

Introduced in 1989, this is the trail-blazing groupware product allowing users within a workgroup to cooperate on common documents and applications and to exchange messages as easily as possible. Rather like NetWare in the NOS world, competitors such as WordPerfect have been forced to acknowledge the presence of Notes by enabling their software to interoperate with it.

The thrust of the product is office and workgroup productivity, leading to the increasingly hyped concept known as workflow, which involves automation of the tasks of a workgroup or department, such as the construction, amendment and circulation of documents, reports, minutes of meetings and so on. From the point of view of users, one of the product's strengths is its ability to be customized to suit the working environment without requiring programming skills. The simplest option is to use application templates supplied by Lotus, which merely need some parameters filled in to customize them to your requirements. Alternatively, if none of the specific templates is quite right for your needs, you can use various development tools to build your own application. Although these require no real programming skills, you do need a detailed grasp of how your business works. However, having to sit down and work out what your workflow requirements are can itself help tune the workings of your business before they are automated.

Foundation of Lotus Notes

Technically, the product rests on three foundations: a distributed database that allows information to be replicated so that it is available on servers within local workgroups; email facilities so that applications and users can exchange messages; and graphical facilities that make the product as easy to use as possible. Around this base are the development tools and applications themselves, and there are also optional added-value functions available that not all users need and would add substantially to the cost were they included as standard. Such facilities include: the ability to handle document images as well as standard coded data; multimedia capabilities such as support for voice and video; and workflow management software.

Improvements introduced in version 3.0 of Lotus Notes

These come under five headings:

(1) *Support for different client and server operating systems.* The main point to note here is that Notes, unlike WordPerfect 4.0, is based on the client/server concept. Users' applications running in desktop PCs or workstations are clients utilizing services such as database management and remote communications provided by servers. At the server level, the idea is that Notes dovetails with the NOS, providing additional security and communications services that can straddle several different NOSs within a single network. In earlier versions, Notes ran on clients based on the leading graphical operating systems such as OS/2 and Windows. Release 3.0 adds support for Apple Macintosh for the first time, and also for servers running Microsoft Windows. Most importantly, the product now runs on UNIX and Windows NT clients and servers, and Notes for NetWare is also available, which can run as a NetWare loadable module on NetWare servers.

(2) *Greater ease of use, through simpler document management, improved graphics and better support for remote users.* The latter includes a feature called selective replication, which allows users to define a subset of documents for storage at their local site in a large distributed network.

(3) *Application development tools.* This includes support for development of workflow management, where the system guides the flow of documents and the actions that should be taken, or synchronizes the execution of tasks.

(4) *Back-end services and management.* Back-end encompasses things that do not directly impinge on key day-to-day business tasks; in this case it relates to management of the application. Lotus Notes now provides support for statistics and alarms in much the same way that leading NOSs do (see Chapter 7).

(5) *Working with other applications.* Lotus has now completed the job of integrating Notes with its own popular electronic mail package cc:Mail. Although not an integral part of Notes, which instead has a different watered-down email facility, cc:Mail can now be accessed directly from the Notes menu. There is also improved integration with the even more popular Lotus 1-2-3 spreadsheet package. In 1993, Lotus introduced a feature called Version Manager, which makes it easier for spreadsheets to be shared and worked on simultaneously by different members of a team. Until now, although they have been able to share common data, spreadsheets have not themselves been readily shareable because of problems in maintaining consistency when users update them at the same time. Also, by supporting industry standards such as vendor-independent messaging (VIM), Lotus at least allows the basic exchange of messages with users of different group-

ware products. With WordPerfect Office, closer cooperation is possible, as explained in Section 3.11.3.

Strengths and weaknesses of Lotus Notes

The strengths of the product are its replicated database and application development tools, which make it ideal for building applications focused on the database, such as sales order processing. A notable weakness so far has been the lack of effective scheduling capabilities, which makes it less useful for work-group and project management applications. Also its messaging system is relatively weak – all the more surprising given that Lotus has one of the leading and best-regarded email packages in cc:Mail. However, Lotus now seems to be addressing the problem by integrating cc:Mail with Notes, rather than improving the email software already built into Notes. The reliance on its own database could also be regarded as a weakness, although Lotus does support communication with other databases through industry-standard interfaces.

3.11.3 WordPerfect Office 4.0

Coming into the groupware market four years after Lotus, WordPerfect has at least managed to exploit its strong presence in the word-processing market to strike some effective alliances. Novell was the ideal partner because it did not itself sell groupware applications, but provides the best framework for large-scale workgroup applications with NetWare 4.x. WordPerfect and Novell signed an agreement to jointly promote and market each other's products through their respective distribution channels, highlighting the synergy between the NOS and groupware. Indeed, this synergy became so strong that Novell bought WordPerfect in March 1994, creating a company more closely matching Microsoft's range and size. The impact of Novell's acquisition of WordPerfect is examined in Chapter 9.

A rather less ideal, but necessary, partner for WordPerfect was Lotus. WordPerfect and Lotus already shared many common customers and, given Lotus Notes' established base, WordPerfect had to ensure that Office 4.0 could integrate closely with it. This objective has been achieved, because not only is a gateway based on the VIM standard provided, allowing messages to be exchanged between the two, but also closer coupling of the products at the data-base level. WordPerfect is supporting the Lotus Notes database format, the aim being for Office 4.0 users to use the Notes database as their common repository for information. Not having a well-established database product of its own, WordPerfect's approach is to support a wide variety of other vendors' products, including popular desktop ones such as dBase and FoxPro, as well as more powerful ones based on the SQL standard, such as Oracle, Sybase and IBM's DB2.

An important related product is WordPerfect Informs, which provides

facilities for creating and distributing forms electronically, via both Word-
Perfect Office and other messaging systems.

Features of WordPerfect Office summarized

WordPerfect has taken pains to enter the market with a product covering the
whole range of groupware functions, to make it hard for competitors to knock
it down before it has gained any momentum. Foremost among them are:

(1) *Electronic mail.* Here the company has exploited its word-processing
expertise to provide a comprehensive mail editor incorporating speller and
thesaurus, the ability to attach unlimited numbers of files and also the
facility to launch programs from within a message.

(2) *Time and task management.* Meetings and associated resources such as video
projectors can be booked, and tasks can be scheduled with automatic
forwarding of assignments between people in a distribution list.

(3) *Electronic forms support.* As mentioned above, users can create forms
through the related Informs package and have them distributed and tracked
automatically among designated people in the network.

(4) *Workflow services.* Messages can contain instructions to recipients on tasks
to be performed, and can be routed according to whether particular tasks
or conditions have been completed or fulfilled. To work effectively, this
requires the cooperation and competence of members of a workgroup, but
it can then prove a powerful tool.

(5) *Directory service.* WordPerfect has developed its own proprietary distributed
directory service to support transmission of messages to a variety of different
recipient types (often called objects); these include users themselves and
various different types of computing device like PCs, printers, servers and
fax machines. WordPerfect argues that it had to develop yet another
proprietary directory system because its products commonly straddle a
variety of NOSs that each has its own directory system; by interacting with
these proprietary systems, its directory can act as a universal facility binding
them together. However this is hardly the ultimate solution, because it still
requires more than one directory system to be maintained. WordPerfect
therefore plans to integrate its system fully into leading NOS directory
services, such as Novell's NetWare directory service (NDS) and Banyan's
StreetTalk directory assistance. All addresses can then be found within a
single directory system, without the need to maintain consistency between
multiple directories. Another possibility is that as vendors increasingly
support the international X.500 standard, their products will all fold into
each other to form a universal distributed system composed of different
elements that automatically keep in step.

(6) *Integration with other groupware systems.* As already mentioned, WordPerfect
is working hard with other vendors to allow their products to interoperate
through standard interfaces such as VIM and MAPI. Note, however, that

these are essentially only messaging links, and that the level of cooperation and interaction possible between users of different groupware systems is far less than can be enjoyed by users who all share the same product; for example, scheduling and calendar-based applications of one groupware package cannot be accessed by users of another.

Strengths and weaknesses of WordPerfect Office summarized

The product's strengths lie in its messaging system, the quality of its word processing and in its support for integration with other products. Whereas Lotus Notes is focused on client/server computing in which client applications have direct sessions into servers, WordPerfect Office transmits messages through the network without requiring links with specific server machines. This allows a greater range of network configurations to be supported, because it does not require direct paths between clients and servers, and also permits different types of NOS and database environment to be embraced within the same overall workgroup, since messages can be transmitted between computers using common multivendor standards.

The disadvantage is that this technique is not very suitable for handling applications where fast response is critical, even though WordPerfect has added performance-enhancing features to mitigate this problem. For this reason, WordPerfect Office is inferior to Lotus Notes for a variety of database-based transaction type applications, such as telesales and airline reservations, where fast reliable access to data is required.

☐ SUMMARY

This chapter completes the description of the main NOSs, clearing the way for the discussions in Chapter 4 of the issues involved in selecting a NOS. Chapter 5 then takes up the story from the point of view of an organization needing to integrate more than one NOS in a single unified network. Remaining chapters discuss other networking issues and the role of the NOS in them.

4

How do I choose a suitable NOS for my systems?

CHAPTER OBJECTIVES:

- To help decide which NOS best meets your current requirements
- To point out the importance of a well-formulated business plan
- To emphasize that the commitment and stability of the supplier are often more important than the technical merits of a NOS
- To examine other important factors, including performance, resilience, security, ability to integrate with other networks, availability of information and training, and price

☐ 4.1 Introduction

For many networks, particularly small ones, the most important choice to be made is that of the NOS itself; suppliers and sources of support are also highly important but these to some extent are bound in with the choice of NOS.

Having chosen the NOS, other issues can be considered, including whether to go for Ethernet, token ring or some other topology, and which type of cabling system to opt for. Appendix 5 summarizes topology issues, while Appendix 4 does the same for cabling. These lower-level LAN issues are covered in more detail by other books in this series (such as Hunter, *Local Area Networks: Making the Right Choices*, 1993, Wokingham, Addison-Wesley).

The choice of NOS is driven by present and future business requirements, and the rather separate issue of which suppliers are deemed fit enough to stay the course. Until almost 1990, Novell virtually had the field to itself and the main decision was about who should install and maintain the network. However, there are now perhaps six serious and relatively stable contenders to consider. With the LAN market still growing quickly, few of these companies are likely to go out of business in the near future but there are considerable differences in the resources being committed to support and further development. Also, the bigger-selling NOSs such as NetWare are better equipped with training courses and places to go for information and solutions to problems, such as user groups and bulletin boards. The weight given to all these factors will depend on the size of your network, the in-house expertise you have available, and the prospects for future growth.

Having narrowed down the field by considering the relative merits of different potential suppliers, you are left with price and the various technical factors to consider. The final choice may finally come down to whom you personally prefer to have dealings with. These factors are explored in more detail in the rest of this chapter.

☐ 4.2 Business strategies

The first aspect to consider is why a NOS is needed and what applications it will support. What are the overriding business objectives that it will help fulfil?

In some cases a LAN may be needed for a new workgroup in an organization that already has LANs elsewhere, for instance for a new design team or for a telesales group to handle a new product. In either case, key aspects to consider are the strategic role of the new workgroup, how it is likely to develop and what information its members need to do their job effectively. It may be that this information is already available on computers or LANs elsewhere, in which case communication links will need to be established with the relevant systems.

Such business considerations should be thought out and ordered clearly. They can then be translated into an outline of what the LAN needs to achieve, and in turn into a more detailed specification of the network and of the NOS at its heart. For example, a workgroup might initially be established on a trial basis with just four members but with provisional plans to expand to twenty. Ignoring other factors for the moment, this points to a modular NOS with an economic version for four users, yet having the capability to expand to twenty users without sacrificing performance and without becoming hard to administer.

The nature of the applications to be supported now and in the foreseeable future is determined by business strategy. The applications also influence the choice of NOS; if, for example, some require intensive use of a large central database, such as a system for booking concert tickets over the telephone, then it is important that the NOS provides good support for dedicated servers. This is because a robust database providing fast guaranteed response cannot readily be supported by a non-dedicated server that also functions as a desktop PC.

If, on the other hand, the network is just for applications involving communication and interaction between members of a workgroup, with no requirement for running transactions off a central database, then a NOS able to support peer-to-peer groupware applications should be considered. In this case a suitable groupware application could be chosen first, followed by an appropriate NOS to underpin it.

For a small business such as a firm of solicitors or architects with little likelihood of substantial growth, then a low-cost peer-to-peer LAN may be ideal. It may also be worth considering packages such as Sage's Mainlan that can be bundled with suitable financial application software. The overall strategy then decides:

(1) what applications you will be running on the LAN;

(2) how the LAN is likely to grow;

(3) any external systems or networks it will need to connect to.

These all shape how you should formulate a request for proposals that can be addressed to potential suppliers.

☐ 4.3　Request for proposals (RFP)

Table 4.1 lists the issues that an RFP should address. The RFP need not, indeed should not, be specific about the kind of LAN solution and NOS that you want. It should not even rule out alternatives to conventional NOSs, such

Table 4.1 Issues that should be addressed by a request for proposals for a local network controlled by a NOS.

---

1. Idea of network size and anticipated growth over next few years. Can specify number of PCs and other devices that need to be attached, again with growth forecasts.
2. Description of applications to run on the network, identifying which are most critical.
3. Performance requirements, perhaps specifying maximum acceptable response times.
4. An indication of the amount of data that will be stored on file servers and how heavily the network will be used at peak times.
5. Additional features such as support for electronic mail and remote access via dial-up connections should be specified.
6. Requirements for access to other computer systems such as mainframes.
7. An idea of the kind of network management features that will be needed. These could include the ability to configure devices from a central point, monitoring of traffic to maintain or improve performance and identification of faults (see Chapter 7 for a complete list of possible network management features).
8. Cabling requirements – for example, should the network be based on optical fibre or copper? Also describe the site, specifying where the cable has to go and whether it has to cross any natural barriers such as a river.
9. Specify implementation and payment schedules.
10. Ask to talk to reference sites.
11. Include details of training requirements for your staff, and provision of on-going maintenance and support.

---

as a UNIX system driving terminals based on the X terminal standard. As we saw in Chapter 2, UNIX has advantages over the conventional NOS for some applications. Also products such as Novell's UnixWare allow UNIX to function as a server operating system interacting with PC LANs controlled by NOSs such as NetWare.

The main consideration about the RFP is that it should invite proposals based on a variety of technologies, while ruling out those that do not fulfil the business requirements. The differing proposals themselves may then help to clarify further what kind of system you really want, or suggest alternatives you might not have considered. The RFP should also make clear how proposed solutions would integrate with existing systems and networks, and should specify any future requirements for connectivity.

4.3.1 Evaluating proposals

The issues involved in choosing a NOS are expanded in the rest of this chapter. However Table 4.2 summarizes the points to look at when evaluating proposals. One point is the possibility of involving consultants to help with the choice,

Table 4.2 Points to consider when evaluating proposals.

1. Pedigree of vendor: the financial health of the vendor should be considered, along with the apparent commitment to the product.
2. Does the proposal adhere well to your original RFP? In other words, has the vendor taken the trouble to put forward a solution that fits your stated requirements as closely as possible?
3. Does the proposal incorporate some additional features that you had not thought of but which seem relevant and increase your confidence in that vendor?
4. Is the cost unacceptably high or suspiciously low?
5. Does the proposal include some unproven or leading-edge technology that you would rather not risk on your network? Or does it include some technology that is too old?
6. Does the proposed solution include proprietary components that may lead to problems interoperating with other existing systems or in expanding your network in future?
7. If you did not specify the NOS, is the one proposed to your liking and does it provide sufficient scope for network growth?

and perhaps with the subsequent installation. At this stage it is worth working back from the proposals to see whether they really do meet your present and future requirements. Price is naturally of importance at this stage but you should bear in mind that the straightforward purchase and installation costs are not the whole story. There will also be differences between the proposals in the costs of administering, managing and expanding the on-going networks that would result. The potential cost of upgrades, or in some cases of having to replace the NOS completely, may be worthy of consideration.

The proposals should not necessarily be taken at face value. Naturally, suppliers want to accentuate the positive, and sometimes may be creative in crystallizing reality out of vapourware. This refers to the tendency many IT vendors have of pretending that products or technologies still at a relatively early stage of development will definitely be available by, or soon after, they have installed your network. In practice, the promised solution is often late or in some cases never quite arrives. Also note that products already on the table may not be of the calibre implied in the proposal, and may not even be widely tried and tested. In the case of the NOS, this may apply to optional extras such as security, network management or groupware software. If your organization lacks the expertise to evaluate the proposals accurately, then outside help should be sought from independent sources. In addition to this, you should insist on seeing reference sites. This will not guarantee that the product will meet your needs but it does provide some indication that it has been run in successfully elsewhere. The greater exposure a product has had before reaching your network, the more stable it is likely to be.

□ 4.4 Supply channels

Table 4.3 highlights the different sources of NOS and other LAN components. Suppliers differ in the level of their expertise and service. In some cases the NOS is just a necessary component of a complete networked application, while in others it is the key element of a networking platform designed to serve a variety of applications now and in the future.

Suppliers also differ in their degree of impartiality. Even dealers claiming to represent several NOS vendors may have favourites, or may have greater financial incentives to promote one above the others. One way round this is to make your choice before seeking a source of supply, if necessary with some independent advice, from a consultancy perhaps. Then you can contact the NOS vendor itself for advice on appropriate sources of supply; for a smaller company this may be a dealer, while for a larger site it could be a bigger systems or software house. At this stage you may wish to seek references if the product is not so well known. Even for big name products such as the NT Server, contacting existing users may elicit information that influences your decision; for example, you may find that the latest release is still unstable in particular circumstances.

For small LANs, everything you need to get a network up and running can be purchased from a dealer in a single shrink-wrapped box, apart from the end devices such as PCs. Figure 4.1 illustrates schematically how these components fit together. Such packages comprise cabling and connectors, adapter cards for the devices, manuals and the NOS itself. At this end of the market we are talking about peer-to-peer LANs, where the NOS code is implemented in every computer on the network. Then machines can be configured either to act purely as clients or to act as servers as well. Some low-cost NOSs can also be equipped with dedicated servers.

An advantage of purchasing in this way is that any problems, whether with the cable, the adapters or the LAN software itself, can be referred to a single dealer or source of supply. Furthermore, technical support may be available, either from a reseller or the NOS developer itself, covering all

Table 4.3 Different sources of NOS and other LAN components.

Dealer
Consultancy
Application software supplier
Systems integrator
Mainstream computer company

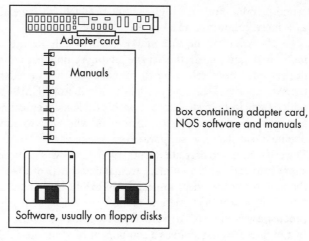

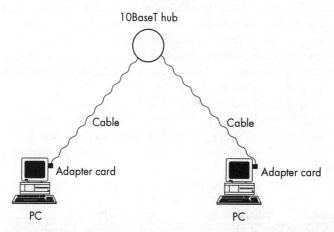

Figure 4.1 How the components contained in a 'shrink-wrapped' peer-to-peer LAN fit together. In this case the PCs are connected using the 10BaseT Ethernet standard through a central wiring hub. Other cabling configurations are possible, such as via a single backbone coaxial cable.

ingredients of the network. Again, all components should be covered by a single warranty or maintenance agreement.

In the case of low-cost peer-to-peer LANs, the balance of responsibility between the dealers, who sell to the end users, and the supplier or distributor for a particular country or region often depends on how many users the product has. The most successful products that sell in large quantities require more central support for customers, as dealers may not be able to cope with the volume of technical queries, and also are more likely to encounter problems they cannot handle. For such high-volume products, the role of dealers may be more as a mere conduit to market.

However, in the case of Powerlan, which despite considerable technical merit had not joined the league of big-selling peer-to-peer NOSs by 1994, dealers have been relied on to provide the bulk of technical support. Nevertheless, in the UK the product's distributor, CMS Software, has always undertaken to help dealers out with problems they cannot handle. CMS will also provide direct help to customers who, for whatever reason, have not obtained satisfactory support from their dealer. In fact, as shipments of Powerlan began to escalate during 1993, CMS was considering providing direct support to end users on a more formal basis. Artisoft, whose LANtastic became the most successful peer-to-peer LAN before Novell and Microsoft entered the fray, also prefers customers to contact the dealer or reseller that sold them the product as a first step. Artisoft is also stepping up its use of value-added resellers that bundle LANtastic in as a component of a complete solution for a particular type of business. Such so-called vertical market resellers addressing specific business needs now account for about 55 per cent of Artisoft's sales. However, with 45 per cent of Artisoft's products sold through commodity dealers that add little value to the product and often lack experience of networking products, the firm has to make a technical support service directly available to customers as well as to its resellers.

Components can be obtained from single sources for larger networks too, although in this case these will more likely be systems integrators, value-added resellers or consultancies rather than small local dealers. Yet the principle is the same – to have a one-stop shop for support, maintenance and possibly training.

A welcome development for both large and small users is the growing cooperation between leading vendors of NOSs and groupware software over marketing and distribution of their products. In Chapter 3 we noted the overlap between NOS and groupware products. Microsoft has integrated both into the same product, Windows 3.11. Novell, on the other hand, did not sell groupware software until its acquisition of WordPerfect early in 1994, although the two companies had been cooperating to forge common distribution channels for their respective products before then. The relationship also extends to technology, the aim being to provide an integrated package that competes more effectively with Microsoft. The idea is to make the combined package appear to come from a single shop as far as customers are concerned. Technically the products overlap smoothly, with NetWare 4.x providing the lower-level NOS facilities including messaging and directory services, and WordPerfect 4.0 the office applications. The aim initially was just to bring the products to market through a common channel, giving the customers a single point of contact for maintenance and technical support. Then as the two companies discovered that they had compatible cultures as well as complementary product strategies, the way was paved for the takeover.

The inexorable rise of Microsoft as a single shop for all things software also motivated Novell to strike deals with leading vendors of other types of software. Most prominent of these was the strategic agreement announced in June 1993 between Novell and relational database vendor Oracle. Initially this went further than the relationship with WordPerfect by folding the two companies' respective products into a single range called OracleWare. This encroached on the groupware field, as Oracle had a product called OracleOffice that provides messaging and scheduling. The three members of the OracleWare range all include this office product, along with the Oracle7 database environment. The difference between the three products is that one comes with NetWare 3.1, one with UnixWare and one with NetWare 4.x.

The Oracle deal provided an even greater number of ways of buying NetWare than existed before, for those who also want Oracle products. In addition to Novell's extensive network of dealers and resellers, OracleWare is sold by Oracle's direct sales and consulting division. This is aimed primarily at large customers, particularly those who also want help with the implementation of key applications on client/server platforms. The role of the NOS in client/server applications is discussed in Chapter 9. Oracle and Novell have also coordinated their approach to training and technical support by establishing a programme to qualify, train and then certify resellers for the OracleWare product range, much as Novell does itself for NetWare. This programme has been developed by Oracle but is administered through Novell Authorized Education Centres.

However, not everyone wants products from both NetWare and Oracle. Users who want to mix and match products still generally have to handle more than one point of contact, but since 1991 the problem of knowing who to contact when problems occur on a multivendor network has been tackled by a loose vendor grouping called the technical support alliance (TSA), which is described in Section 4.8.

Role of systems integrators

Some companies provide complete systems integration services, embracing all aspects of network installation from physical cabling right up to application software. Such services may be worth considering, although companies in this field rarely possess an equal spread of expertise across the whole spectrum. In practice, it may be better in some cases to opt for two or three suppliers, with one perhaps for physical aspects of the network, another for the underlying software platform including the NOS and perhaps relational database, and a third for the applications that run on top. Note, however, that suppliers, where there is more than one involved, have a habit of blaming each other when things go wrong. Therefore if your company lacks sufficient in-house project management expertise, it may be worth hiring consultants to oversee the whole operation and act as a single point of contact (see Section 4.6 for the role of consultants).

Some systems integrators undertake to obtain equipment from a wide range of suppliers to provide maximum choice. Others offer just a limited portfolio of options for the various network components, such as hubs and routers, arguing they are then using their expertise to select the best systems available and weed out weaker ones. By sticking to a limited range of products for which they are in fact distributors, they may offer better prices, greater expertise and a higher degree of integration, at the expense of a wide choice. Examples of such systems integrators in the UK include Datarange and Chernikeef.

□ 4.5   Assessing suppliers

Criteria for assessing suppliers are summarized in Table 4.4. These include obvious ones like price and how closely they adhere to your RFP but also include points that do not relate directly to the product itself, such as how financially stable the supplier is and how much further development is likely to take place. If you want a product to grow with you into the future, you obviously need a supplier that is going to be around for some time but also one who is going to invest the necessary resources in product development and support.

The relative importance of these criteria will naturally vary with the size and the type of the network under consideration. Factors such as financial strength and size of potential suppliers will matter less to a small company buying a peer-to-peer LAN than to a large organization looking to make a strategic purchase of NOSs for 4000 regional offices. Larger companies tend to favour the big NOS vendors such as Novell, IBM and Microsoft, although some vendors of low-cost peer-to-peer LANs, notably Artisoft, have made inroads into the corporate market. At this level more subtle factors come into play; for example, what is one to make of Novell's growing appetite during 1992 and 1993 for collaborating ventures with major players in other key software areas? At first sight this is a totally positive development, as it gives users a single source for support and training.

However, there are some potentially less desirable side effects. Novell argues that by creating a family of alliances with leading vendors in all of the

Table 4.4. Criteria for assessing suppliers.

1. Size of company and its financial strength.
2. Apparent commitment to the products concerned and their future development.
3. References from other users.
4. Quality of support and training provided.
5. Adherence to relevant standards.
6. Adherence to your RFP, and ability of the company to understand your requirements.
7. Grasp of key issues relevant for your network, such as security, network management and integration with various computer systems.

major fields, such as relational databases and groupware, it can provide customers with single shops for whatever combination of product they need,
without limiting their freedom of choice. After all, Novell would say, if a
customer wants a database from, say, Sybase rather than Oracle, they can have
that and still enjoy the full range of support from Novell if they also want
NetWare.

Yet there are two points to consider. Firstly, when a vendor, even one
as large as Novell, strikes up numerous alliances, there must always be some
doubt as to how committed it is to each one. The history of networking is
littered with the corpses of failed alliances, and only a minority become
enduring if there is no formal merging of the companies. Secondly, by linking
with other vendors, Novell is to some extent encroaching on territory previously
occupied by its resellers. Some of these resellers had added value to NetWare
by integrating it with other software products to deliver complete solutions.

Neither of these cautionary notes means you should shy away from
products like OracleWare but they pose some questions that should be
considered, such as where best to obtain the product and what role the dealer
or reseller should play. If the objective is to provide 'oven ready' products,
perhaps including the hardware, the role of intermediate dealers may be
marginalized. The question then for smaller customers especially is: will Novell
and Oracle themselves provide sufficient support and training at the right price?

A vendor might be big, but will it continue supporting your product?

Even if you have established that a vendor is financially sound, it does not
automatically follow that a particular product in its portfolio will continue to
be enhanced in line with emerging technologies. Sometimes software products
wither on the vine, continuing to be supported while there are still users, but
no longer being upgraded. Novell's NetWare 2.2 is such a product. Therefore
before committing to a particular NOS, especially if you intend it to play a
starring role in your network for years to come, it is worth investigating as far
as possible how committed the vendor is to that product.

Microsoft, for example, is by far the largest and financially strongest
company in the software business. Yet some industry observers originally
questioned the sincerity of its commitment to Windows for Workgroups. There
is no question of Microsoft leaving its customers in the lurch, and the rumours
may turn out to be false anyway. The risk here, if there is one, is not that the
product will stop being supported but that its users may be coerced into moving
up to Microsoft's strategic product, Windows NT. They may then end up with
a more expensive and complex networking software environment than they had
originally wanted.

☐ 4.6 Role of consultants in helping choose NOSs

Consultants can provide invaluable help in selecting both the NOS itself and an appropriate reseller or systems integrator to assist with the installation. In some cases the consultancy itself, if it is a large one, will provide systems integration services but then it obviously cannot be relied on to provide impartial advice regarding potential suppliers! It may be that you want a consultancy to take charge of installation, and provide impartial advice only to the extent of selecting the NOS and other networking components. Consultants may then advise the use of several suppliers for different elements of the installation.

As consultants can prove to be expensive sources of cheap information, they should be chosen carefully. Given the high price they charge, it is important to ensure that their role is clearly defined and focused. Some consultants are only too happy being busy doing nothing useful while gobbling up fees. The following checklist should be applied:

(1) Define clearly what you want the consultants to achieve and the scope of their work. This can range from merely helping select other suppliers to managing the whole acquisition and installation process on your behalf. At this stage, timescales for the project should also be clarified.

(2) Having established a framework for the project, the little matter of cost needs to be discussed. The way in which costs are determined is particularly important for consultancy, because some methods of payment can lead to unexpectedly high bills. Payment can be a fixed fee for the project; or costs plus, in which case there is a set fee with bonuses for work that was not described in the initial contract; or it can be on a time basis with additional payment for materials and expenses. All have their merits and minuses. Fixed fee has the advantage that costs are largely predetermined but can mean paying more than the project merits, although this can be mitigated by seeking quotes from several different consultancies. Time and materials contracts are open-ended of course, and need to be tightly linked to carefully worded contracts that relate fees to targets. Contracts should be carefully scrutinized by a solicitor or lawyer with expertise in the general field of consultancy contracts.

(3) Ensure that there is a proper reporting structure. The consultant or consultants should have someone in your company to report to, rather than being vaguely answerable to more than one director or manager. Even when the consultants are taking full charge of an installation, there should be close liaison with someone in your company to ensure that timescales and milestones are met.

(4) It is important that consultants adhere to well-defined procedures and

technical standards, and that the project is well documented so that you are not left stranded if for some reason they pull out of the project. Specify key components such as the NOS, LAN type, communication protocols and database. Consultants may give useful advice about these – indeed this may be partly what you hire them for – but the ultimate decision is yours and this needs to be spelt out clearly in contracts.

(5) Many businesses have failed in the past to ensure first that there is a clear definition of what constitutes a completed project, and then that consultants provide an adequate guarantee. The answer is to be specific both about what constitutes a completed project and about acceptable levels of faults or problems with the resulting network. At this stage it is well worth specifying any maintenance and on-going support agreements, and their costs.

In certain cases, consultants will be called in just to help evaluate proposals and perhaps oversee other suppliers. Some or all of the above principles will apply to each party concerned; for example, on-going support and maintenance may be provided by the installer of the network but it is still important to define clearly what consultants are expected to achieve for the price they have quoted.

□ 4.7   Importance of reliable NOS performance

Performance at the file-system level is no longer a major differentiator between the big name NOSs, in particular NetWare, LAN Manager and IBM's LAN Server. However, the NOSs do vary in their ability to support high-performance networking over wide area networks of interconnected LANs. Novell realized from the outset that a high-performance file system was the crux of a good NOS, and must continually score well in bench tests. Subsequently, IBM and Microsoft largely or entirely made up the lost ground and as a result vendors increasingly attempt to differentiate themselves on other factors such as ability to work well with other leading software products, which is explored further in Chapters 8 and 9, and support for large-scale networking, which is considered more fully in Chapter 6.

In Chapter 2, performance factors were considered in comparing different NOSs. Here it is worth emphasizing that although relative file-system performance is no longer a major differentiator between the major NOSs, it can be significant for the lower-cost peer-to-peer LANs. This is discussed further in Chapter 3.

More generally, the issue of performance comes into the whole field of large-scale networking, in which LANs are connected to each other and to large computer systems. This is discussed in Chapter 6. The main point to note is that over larger networks in which LANs are interconnected by telecommunications links that have to be paid for, it is more important to use communication protocols that make efficient use of bandwidth. Most NOSs operate over a variety of universal communication protocols such as TCP/IP, as described in Chapter 6. However, NetWare, while it also supports other protocols in various ways, was originally built around the IPX protocol, as explained in Chapter 2. As a result, IPX is still widely used in NetWare networks.

NetWare session emulation can impair performance on large networks

When used on networks of multiple remotely connected LANs, NetWare requires connections between all elements of the network to be maintained at all times. This allows status information to be exchanged even when no application is actually transmitting data. So, for example, if there are two servers interconnected by a leased line, they continuously send information about the state of the network to each other.

An adverse factor to be considered is that this process could impair performance on a large network because the amount of status information can then become significant. This is a particular problem when dial-up links are used between LANs over a public ISDN network since a connection needs to be made every time status information is sent between a remote pair of servers, yet in many cases this status information serves no useful purpose.

Happily some vendors have developed solutions that avoid sending unnecessary status information across telecommunications links. They do this by emulating the status details at each end of the link, so that servers are provided with the information they are expecting. Some status information still needs to be transmitted across the link, for example when a new user is added to the network, but this can be kept to a minimum and where possible status updates can be packaged with user data, to minimize the number of dial-up calls that need to be made. Among vendors providing such solutions for NetWare networks is the UK dial-up connectivity specialist Sonix.

□ 4.8   Catering for future expansion

The ability to move forward with your network, supporting new applications with increased size and reach, is an obvious requisite for a NOS, especially in larger sites. In a small business that is unlikely to grow much in size, cost and performance may be more important, but even then it is desirable to choose a product that is going to be upgraded to take advantage of emerging technologies.

Table 4.5 lists features or issues that should be considered in this context,

Table 4.5 Issues to be considered for NOS expansion.

How strong is the NOS supplier (the ultimate owner, not the dealer or distributor) and how committed is it to the product?

Can the product be upgraded to support the numbers of users you anticipate may be connected to your network in future?

Will performance still be adequate or does it tail off as the number of users and amount of network traffic increase?

Will the product operate as effectively over a large-scale network of interconnected LANs?

Does the NOS support necessary links with existing computer systems in your organization, for example an IBM mainframe or SNA network?

Does the NOS support the leading desktop software environments?

Does it provide sufficient server management and administration facilities?

although only some will be relevant for individual networks. These will be considered in turn.

1. *Is the supplier strong and committed enough?*

The issue of supplier and strength has already been considered. Larger user sites in particular tend to gravitate towards the big players, such as Novell and Microsoft, partly because only they can afford the necessary investment to keep the NOS at the leading edge in key areas like performance, reliability, security and integration with other software components. Smaller NOS vendors, even if they continue to prosper in their market, have to concentrate their development resources on selected subsets of the overall field. The suitability of their products for your network therefore depends on whether these subsets are the relevant ones in your particular case.

Consider, for example, the Powerlan NOS from Performance Technology, which primarily addresses the market for low-cost peer-to-peer LANs. For high performance, and above all the ability to sustain that performance for quite reasonably sized networks, it is hard to beat. Yet if ease of use is top of the wants list, then Personal NetWare, while it scores much less well on performance and expandability, would be the wiser choice.

2. *Technical issues relating to expansion*

The remaining issues of this section can be considered together as they all relate to growth and the technical ability of the NOS to sustain this. These issues are addressed more comprehensively in Chapters 5 and 6. Essentially, they are the ability of the NOS to cope with the growth in numbers of users, physical reach and level of traffic that is likely over the foreseeable future, which typically means over the next five years. Is the NOS robust enough to handle such growth, and will current performance levels be sustained? Does it offer adequate management and security for the size of network anticipated in five years' time? Also, if servers are going to be interconnected at some future time, the NOS should either support global directory services directly or there should be a third-party directory product that works with that NOS.

The market leaders score here not just by virtue of their own efforts but through numerous independent software vendors drawn to the largest honey pots. For this reason NetWare in particular is well served with products that provide specific requirements for connecting or interacting with other systems. For example, large sites may want to interconnect LANs with existing applications running on host systems from one of the leading computer vendors such as Digital, IBM or Unisys. This enables users attached to the LAN to exploit file management and printing services already available on the host system, which could avoid having to upgrade servers or install new local printers. By the same token, users attached to the host system can access print or file services on the LAN. Such two-way interaction opens up an organization's data and applications to a greater number of users, and makes more efficient use of the total resources available. For NetWare there are various independent products that provide links with the leading host environments. In some cases these overlap with facilities available from Novell itself, perhaps providing greater functionality and performance. In other cases they fill a niche not covered by Novell.

Another argument in favour of the big vendors is the greater level of integration between their NOSs and other leading software products, as explained in Section 4.4, and just as important is the growing level of cooperation between leading software vendors over technical support. The goal is to avoid the long-standing problem on large multivendor networks of vendors passing the buck to each other when problems occur. Ideally, you should be able to contact any vendor with which you have a support agreement, and that vendor must endeavour to solve the problem even if another vendor's software is implicated.

This is exactly the target of Novell's Technical Support Alliance (TSA), which was set up in 1991 and whose members now include almost all the leading names in networking and computing, even including Novell's arch rival Microsoft. So while members of TSA may be strong competitors, they are cooperating increasingly with each other over technical support. TSA members undertake to resolve problems even when they are caused by other members' products. However, the advantages of this are compromised if your network also contains ingredients from vendors that are not members of the TSA alliance.

Smaller NOS vendors are not members of TSA and are unlikely to join because they lack the resources to support products other than their own or to liaise with other vendors. This may not matter much for a small business but should be considered on a network that embraces products from several vendors. If, for example, you have a NetWare LAN at one site linked to a LAN Manager network at another, both running Oracle's relational database, then you should be able to resolve calls by phoning any one of these three vendors, without being bounced between them.

It does not matter how well a NOS is supported if it cannot handle your future requirements. Sometimes a NOS may appear on paper to meet your future needs but turn out in practice to buckle under the strain. The chance of installing a NOS that runs out of steam can be reduced by assessing clearly what your requirements will be and then seeking reference sites that have already reached that stage. If the NOS has already proved itself elsewhere in circumstances similar to those envisaged at your site, then you can install it with greater impunity.

□ 4.9 Support for industry standards and ability to integrate with other networks

This section overlaps considerably with Section 4.7, as maintenance of standards and ability to integrate with other networks are essential to support expansion in many cases. Only by maintaining key *de jure* and *de facto* standards can a NOS integrate with other LANs, other parts of a wide area network or even the networks of other organizations. The latter is becoming more relevant with the growing use of applications such as EDI (electronic data interchange) which require interaction between the networks of different organizations.

However, standards are also important for other aspects of expansion, in particular the ability to run future applications. Of course support for standards is not the sole preserve of the NOS but as the NOS is the nerve centre of LANs, which are the elements of larger enterprise-wide networks, it is vital that it does support the relevant interoperability standards.

Key standards are described in other chapters under relevant headings: for example, network management standards are covered in Chapter 7 which deals with that subject. Here it is worth summarizing the types of standard that you may well want your NOS to support:

(1) relevant desktop operating systems or software environments, such as DOS, Microsoft Windows and PC versions of UNIX;

(2) key network data transport and access protocols, such as TCP/IP and NFS;

(3) leading application programming interfaces (APIs) and software development environments, described in Chapter 8;

(4) major network management standards or systems, such as SNMP and IBM's Netview.

Note that, as with other lists of desirable NOS features, these are not all relevant in all situations. For example, support for Netview is almost certainly totally irrelevant for a small firm of architects seeking a simple plug-and-play peer-to-peer NOS.

□ 4.10 Training

NOS vendors vary considerably in their commitment to training, depending partly on the complexity of the product and the sophistication of the networking environments in which their products operate. Novell and Microsoft therefore invest heavily in training, although they do not in general provide courses for end users. Rather they rely on distributors or resellers, and also specialist training companies, which provide courses both on the NOS itself and on other aspects of networking and information technology.

Companies providing NetWare courses must all be Novell Authorized Education Centres (NAECs), of which there are 25 in the UK and over 900 worldwide. These deliver courses, developed by Novell, to end users, leading in some cases to certificates of competence in the given field. Novell, for example, has its Certified Network Engineer (CNE) qualification, which can be taken by NetWare users requiring basic all-round competence in installing and managing a NetWare LAN. There is also a more advanced qualification called Certified NetWare Administrator (CNA), typically taken by someone responsible for managing a larger NetWare network and providing help to other users. To give such courses, you must be a Certified NetWare Instructor (CNI), trained directly by Novell at one of its main education centres.

Microsoft also endorses training centres that provide courses in the basic products together with numerous related topics in networking and other fields. Again, like Novell, Microsoft has a certified professional programme leading to exams for individuals to qualify as experts in one or more of the company's products. Microsoft also has a programme to back up its authorized training centres, including free licences for software, marketing materials, referrals and other forms of promotion such as publicity in published case studies.

Vendors of peer-to-peer NOSs for smaller networks argue that as their products are easy to use, training is largely unnecessary. Artisoft, for example, has not been highly committed to training but has relied on its resellers to handle end-user training, merely providing the backup materials. However, as the company is hoping to sell LANtastic into larger networks, it is now having to provide more extensive backup for resellers. Also, hoping to tap into the huge NetWare customer base, Artisoft launched LANtastic for NetWare, which allows NetWare users to add a peer-to-peer LAN segment to an existing NetWare network, although support is a slightly grey area here. Given that users are not always sure in such cases which of the two vendors' products caused the problem, they may not know at first whether they should contact Artisoft or Novell. Artisoft confirms it would always consider the problem carefully but admits that it does not have great expertise in NetWare. Therefore should such a problem turns out to be NetWare specific, Artisoft would refer the customer to Novell. Similarly, Novell would refer LANtastic-related problems to Artisoft. However, what if both vendors blame each other? As

Artisoft is not a member of Novell's TSA support alliance, there is no formal mechanism for resolving such conflicts.

□ 4.11 Sources of information about the NOS: user groups and bulletin boards

Apart from suppliers, training companies and books, there are two main sources of information about the NOS: user groups and bulletin boards.

User groups are a valuable source of solutions to practical problems, and of tips that you may not obtain from a formal training course. Also, as new revisions of the NOS are released, fresh problems and issues arise. Within a user group there will often be someone who has already experienced and solved a problem that has just struck you.

User groups evolve around particular vendors of hardware or software, or around a specific well-established product like Microsoft Windows. There may be several relevant user groups available, possibly one for your NOS, one for your PC and others for applications such as word processing and spreadsheets. It may not be necessary to join all of them: the NOS one will cover most aspects of LAN operation, for example. Vendors or dealers should be able to put you in touch with relevant groups.

Electronic bulletin boards that can be dialled up from a PC are another useful source of information, particularly about widely used NOSs such as NetWare. Like user groups, they can provide information about fixes to bugs in a new release of software, and tips that may help you exploit some of the less well-known features of a product.

Bulletin boards also provide a wide variety of other information, including details of courses, products for sale and relevant news items in a particular field. They are available on well-known public electronic mail or information networks such as Compuserve, CIX and BT Dialcom's services. These include bulletin boards that deal specifically with popular LAN and PC products; for example, on both CIX and Compuserve there is a NetWare bulletin board, on which Novell itself displays information about new products or solutions to particular problems. Subscribers can also display information freely, the only cost being the on-line charge of the particular service.

Novell also offers a dedicated information service called NetWare Express, which has various bulletin board features. This is available worldwide on GE Information Services' BusinessTalk System 2000 electronic mail and bulletin board service. It provides access to sales and marketing data pertaining to NetWare, complementing existing bulletin board services that offer mainly technical information. It can be used to order some lower-cost NetWare products and utilities.

A possible criticism of bulletin boards is that they appeal most to enthusiasts, the material often being haphazard and poorly laid out. However, for people familiar with using them, they provide a congenial way of keeping abreast in general with the given specialist field.

☐ SUMMARY

This chapter has brought together the main issues involved in NOS selection, building on the first three chapters which focused on product issues. A key point is that while the NOS typically represents at most 10 per cent of the cost of a LAN, getting it wrong is much more expensive than that. Making the wrong choice of NOS will jeopardize your ability to utilize the other 90 per cent of the LAN, including the applications, cabling and NICs.

5

Can I have more than one NOS running on my network?

CHAPTER OBJECTIVES:

- To show how different NOSs can cooperate in a network by allowing data and applications to be shared between users of each, and to demonstrate how this is more relevant at larger sites, as small businesses are less likely to have more than one NOS

- To define when different NOSs need to interoperate

- To determine what users want to achieve

- To show how different NOS vendors have made it possible for their products to interoperate

- To explain the protocols that enable different NOSs to interoperate

□ 5.1 Introduction

In Chapter 4, issues involved in selecting NOSs were discussed. You may have concluded that within a large organization a single NOS might not be suitable for all applications. A small workgroup of four people dealing just with accounts, for example, might be best served by a low-cost simple peer-to-peer LAN, while a large department handling a variety of different applications might want a more powerful NOS better suited to client/server-based operation.

In any case for a variety of reasons, both good and bad, many organizations now find themselves with two or more NOSs in different parts of the operation. Also there is increasing demand from users to interlink different local networks within the organization to provide wider access to data and applications, which means either the organization has to standardize on a single NOS, or enable different NOSs to interoperate. The former would mean wasting substantial existing investment in NOSs, and incur additional costs in new software licences and retraining users and administrators of the LANs where the NOS was to be changed. In practice, therefore, larger organizations and even some smaller sites need at least some degree of interoperability between NOSs. This chapter looks at the issues involved in making this happen.

Note that the discussion often assumes that just two NOSs are involved, in order to explain the issues as clearly as possible. However, the arguments can readily be extrapolated to networks containing more than two NOSs. It is also worth noting that two interoperating NOSs are not always on different computers, they can also interoperate on a single server, an example of which is shown later this chapter (see Figure 5.5). Also note that, by enterprise network, we mean the whole network of a medium-sized or large organization, typically though not necessarily spanning more than one site.

□ 5.2 Situations where different NOSs interoperate, or where this is desirable

Although NetWare in its various versions is the dominant NOS for medium-sized and large LANs, it has been less successful for very small sites. Novell pitches Personal NetWare for small LANs but its share of the peer-to-peer market is much less spectacular than that held by NetWare 3.1 and 4.x in the larger-scale network arena. Furthermore, Personal NetWare was not released until other peer-to-peer products such as LANtastic were already well established. The upshot is that a number of organizations already had a combination of NetWare LANs for larger networks and peer-to-peer LANs serving more remote departments. There was thus a growing need for interoperability between the peer-to-peer NOSs and NetWare. Since NetWare was already widely installed when the first peer-to-peer NOSs arrived around 1989, vendors of peer-to-peer NOSs had to ensure that their products would interoperate with it. The pressure was on them rather than Novell, and they tended to support the NetWare IPX/SPX protocol stack, as explained further in Section 5.4.2.

Instances of sites with more than one NOS are not necessarily those where this is desirable. Sometimes, for historical reasons, an organization inherits workgroups with a different NOS from the one generally used, for example when one company acquires another. Alternatively, local departments may have been allowed to choose their own NOS, and although the choice may have been correct in each individual case, for the corporate whole it might have been better to standardize on one particular NOS.

5.2.1 Situations where different NOSs have been installed

(1) When one company acquired another that standardized on a different NOS.

(2) When departments or workgroups within an organization have the autonomy to choose their own NOS or, on a larger scale, different subsidiaries have each gone their own way.

(3) Where several computer system types have evolved in different parts of an organization; for example, Digital Equipment workstations might be used in the computer-aided design department of an automobile manufacturer but with IBM mainframes for central accounting and financial applications, and PC LANs in the sales department. DEC's Pathworks NOS might have been chosen for the DEC systems, IBM's LAN Server for LANs accessing the mainframe, and NetWare for the PC LANs in the sales department.

(4) When an organization decides to change to another NOS but cannot afford to do all this at a stroke; retraining all users at once, for example, could be impractical and prohibitively expensive.

5.2.2 Situations where it is desirable to have more than one NOS

(1) When two NOSs complement each other within a large-scale network; this could happen, for example, where one NOS better serves the needs of individual workgroups while another provides better communications services. A well-known case of this is the combination of NetWare and Banyan's Enterprise Network Services (ENS), which is a derivative of the Banyan's Vines NOS described in Chapter 2. Until the launch of NetWare 4.0 in March 1993, Novell did not provide global directory services, which presented an opportunity for other networking software companies, such

as Banyan, to come in with products that enabled users of older NetWare versions to interlink their LANs effectively in a large-scale enterprise-wide network. Figure 5.1 shows how this could operate on a typical network. It may also be desirable to mix a NOS such as NetWare with UNIX on a given network. Indeed moves such as Novell's UnixWare initiative, explained in Chapter 2, have hastened the integration of UNIX with leading NOSs. The advantage of this is that UNIX provides a more mature software development environment and access to a large range of existing applications, while NOSs, especially NetWare, are more efficient for managing the server and communications across the network.

(2) When money can be saved by having more than one NOS; for example, before Novell launched NetWare Lite (which later became Personal NetWare) and Microsoft launched Windows for Workgroups, neither company had a low-cost peer-to-peer NOS. As a result some organizations installed low-cost NOSs for small workgroups having already opted for NetWare or perhaps LAN Manager in larger departments. This may in hindsight seem a bad move now that Novell and Microsoft have low-cost peer-to-peer LANs available. However, as is shown in Chapter 3, other peer-to-peer NOSs may still be preferred in some instances.

(3) Where there is a variety of different applications and workgroups on a given network, making it desirable to have several NOSs each tailored to the different requirements. This was also cited earlier in the section, as a number of organizations have perhaps been coerced into purchasing different NOSs by their computer suppliers. The point here is that growing interoperability between NOS vendors makes it increasingly feasible to mix and match NOSs in certain situations. Novell, for example, has cooperated closely with both IBM and DEC, which has led to improved interaction between NetWare and both IBM's LAN Server and DEC's Pathworks.

□ 5.3 What needs to be done to integrate two NOSs

The stock phrase that comes to mind here is 'transparency to the user'. Certainly the process of crossing boundaries between parts of the network controlled by different NOSs should be as simple as possible. Ideally, users should not be aware where the data or application they are using normally resides: it should appear to be an extension of their PC accessed through whatever type of commands or graphical user interfaces (GUI) they are used to. In practice, however, the degree of integration depends on the particular combination of NOSs involved. Some vendors have gone far to integrate their different NOS environments, such as DEC and Novell in allowing NetWare and DEC's

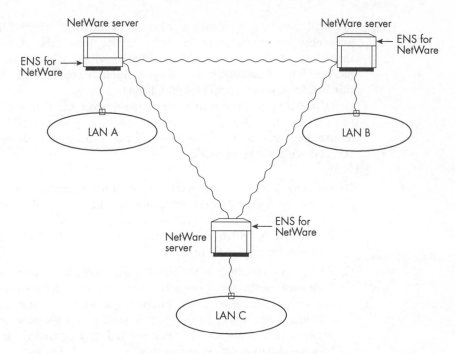

Figure 5.1 How Banyan's enterprise network services (ENS) can interconnect local NetWare LANs in a wide area network. By running ENS for NetWare, NetWare servers running different versions of NetWare can interoperate in a wide area network, utilizing Banyan's global directory services.

Pathworks to co-exist on DEC VAX computers. In this way NetWare client applications running in desktop PCs can access DEC file and print services directly as if they were available via the NetWare server, and vice versa.

Nevertheless, there are no significant products that allow NetWare and Microsoft's NOSs to be integrated at the server level. For sites that have both NT Server and NetWare LANs and want to give users access to both, the usual option is to run both sets of shell software in the PC. In this case, therefore, it is necessary to implement both the NT Server and the NetWare client software in PCs that need to access both NOSs. This uses up a good deal of the PC's memory and processing resources if the user wants to have access to both servers at the same time. This would be the case, for example, when moving data from the NetWare server to the NT Server. DEC's Pathworks, on the other hand, is integrated with NetWare at the server level, which means that PCs need only run one set of shell software, either Pathworks or NetWare. Furthermore, data can be moved between the two NOS environments within the DEC VAX, without having to bring it out onto the network and through the client PC. It is worth detailing what is typically required from a large network to make data, applications and services as widely available as possible.

We shall then be in a position to examine the extent to which different NOSs may need to ·interoperate in order to facilitate this. Note that NOS interoperability is only a small part of the story; also required are higher-level facilities for interaction between different applications. How the NOS fits into this bigger picture is discussed in Chapters 6 to 9.

The Utopian ideal is to make all the services and data available directly to each user through a chosen desktop operating system or GUI. For this to be possible, some or all of the following needs to be done, depending on the size and scale of the network:

(1) Different local LAN segments must be interconnected by suitable devices such as bridges or routers, to ensure that there is a path from each work-station to all resources on the overall network. Such devices are described in Chapter 6, which also examines the role of the NOS in controlling communications across them.

(2) The NOS controlling each LAN segment must be able to route requests from each user to the appropriate remote server or other computer hosting the service that is required. Alternatively, each PC must have software enabling it to connect directly to the services it needs, although on a large network this is usually impractical, and this is where interoperability between different NOSs comes in.

(3) Different application processes must be able to interact across the network using the basic communication paths provided by the NOS(s) and the underlying LAN interconnection devices. This requires application pro-gramming interfaces (APIs), which are described in Chapter 8, and also coordination between different databases to maintain consistency and ensure that the right data is forwarded to the application or user that requested it, wherever they are on the network. The role of the NOS in distributed database operation is discussed in Chapter 9.

(4) The whole network needs to be managed effectively. Chapter 7 looks at how the NOS fits into the overall network management picture.

Thus interoperability between NOSs addresses the second of these four points. To achieve this, some or all of the following four facilities need to be provided, depending on the configuration and scale of the overall network:

(1) access for users of one NOS to printers controlled by the other;

(2) access for users of one NOS to file servers controlled by the other;

(3) a direct link between file servers on the LANs controlled by each NOS;

(4) some integration of each NOS's respective security and administration domains. This may be needed to enable each NOS to identify users of the other, and to allow details of configuration changes to be transmitted between the two networks. The general issue of access control and security is discussed in more detail in Chapter 7.

In general, the last two of these four facilities are necessary to achieve the first two. Although it is possible for the PC to run shells for more than one NOS, this is an inefficient process and it is better to have PCs attached to a LAN controlled by a single NOS which provides access to LANs controlled by other NOSs as appropriate. Integration of the respective NOSs' access control systems then becomes necessary as it is only by this means that consistent procedures can be used to control access to data and network resources, irrespective of the location of the user.

The NOS next needs to provide access to the file and print services of other NOSs. To allow files to be shared with servers controlled by other NOSs or operating systems, the NOSs must be integrated in the following respects:

- Users must be able to access all services through their familiar operating system or GUIs. This can be done either by each NOS supporting all client operating environments that may need to access it, or by having all servers on one NOS acting as clients to other NOSs.

- There must be some integration between the access control regimes of the two NOSs, as already mentioned.

- Each NOS must be able to relay the file and record locking messages to users of the other. Data is locked at the level of files or individual records to prevent two users from updating it simultaneously. It is important that locking is applied equally to all users, and that each user receives messages to this effect.

- Each NOS has to understand a common data transport protocol, even if this is not the one normally used within its own environment; for example, IPX/SPX is Novell's protocol suite but TCP/IP is often used for communication between NetWare LANs and servers controlled by other NOSs. Figure 5.2 depicts a common arrangement where a NetWare LAN is linked with a UNIX server via TCP/IP.

To allow printers to be shared between users, each NOS must be able to redirect output to printers attached to the other. However, it should go further by also allowing users to select the printer they want, submit jobs directly to it and then query it for status and queuing information.

It is worth noting that the functions needed for a NOS to access services provided by other NOSs are really only an extension of those they already provide to support access from client workstations anyway; for example, NetWare has to understand DOS file access and print commands to support DOS clients. The difference is that this is done through shell software running in the client, whereas to provide access to other NOSs the communications software has to run in the server.

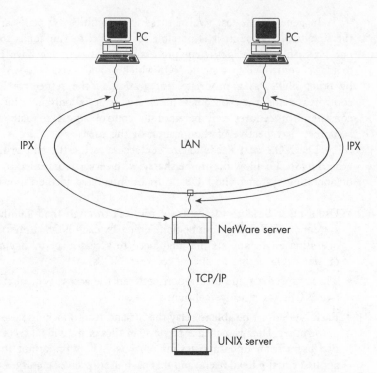

Figure 5.2 NetWare LAN linked to UNIX server via TCP/IP. Novell's IPX protocol is often used, as shown here, to communicate between PCs and the NetWare server. TCP/IP is then used to communicate on from the NetWare server to a UNIX server.

□ 5.4   How different NOSs actually interoperate

5.4.1   Other NOSs accessing NetWare

As NetWare dominates the field, lesser NOS vendors have to ensure that their products interoperate with it. They need to win sales from sites where NetWare is already installed to achieve any lasting success. Essentially, this means that a file server on the peer-to-peer LAN must become a NetWare client, as illustrated in Figure 5.3. The file server must run the relevant NetWare shell software and there must be an application that enables the peer-to-peer NOS to recognize requests destined for the NetWare file server rather than its own file servers. An example of this could be where a user on the peer-to-peer LAN wants to send output to a printer on the NetWare LAN. The peer-to-peer NOS recognizes the name of the NetWare printer and routes the output to it. The

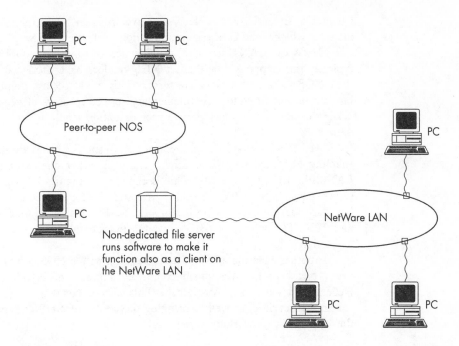

Figure 5.3 How users on a peer-to-peer NOS can access services on a separate NetWare LAN.

job is then handled by the NetWare LAN as normal, with status information being accessed when required by the peer-to-peer NOS.

This is a simple example of a 'server hierarchy', with a server on one network being a client on another. More examples of this are given in Chapter 6, where we shall describe how LANs can access remote host systems. Note in this case the role of Novell's IPX transport protocol to provide a path for the transmission of data packets between the server on the peer-to-peer LAN and the NetWare server.

5.4.2 NetWare accessing systems controlled by other NOSs

A NetWare LAN may also provide access to a remote server controlled by another NOS or operating system. The most common arrangement of this kind, apart from accessing IBM systems, which is described in Chapter 6, is a link between a NetWare server and a UNIX system. Figure 5.2 shows a typical arrangement where a NetWare server provides access to a remote UNIX system – in this case, the NetWare server has to convert between its own IPX transport protocol and the TCP/IP protocol used by UNIX systems. The technical details of this type of link up between LANs and UNIX systems are elaborated on in

Chapter 6. Essentially, the NetWare server runs an NLM (NetWare loadable module) which handles the communication with the UNIX system.

NetWare LANs can also provide access to other NOS servers, and typically this happens where other NOS vendors have produced a version of their NOS to run on a NetWare server. This might seem a pointless exercise but can in fact provide a complementary service to users of versions of Net-Ware that do not support peer-to-peer operation (such as NetWare 3.1 and 4.0).

Artisoft, for example, announced LANtastic for NetWare in May 1993, enabling NetWare servers to function also as either clients or servers on a LANtastic peer-to-peer LAN. This is depicted in Figure 5.4, where the main server hosts both NetWare and LANtastic. LANtastic communicates with NetWare via NetBIOS. Novell supports NetBIOS as an option alongside its own IPX. The role of NetBIOS in NOS interoperability is discussed further in Section 5.5.

Another example of NetWare co-existing with a NOS comes from Novell itself. NetWare for Macintosh comprises a group of NLMs which allow NetWare to run on a Macintosh. This allows NetWare clients to access Macintosh services, as well as bringing the wealth of NetWare applications to the AppleTalk networking scene.

5.4.3 Links between other NOSs

Other peer-to-peer NOSs as well as LANtastic can provide access to NetWare networks to obtain data and route print jobs. Some can also interoperate with other leading NOSs such as Banyan's Vines; Powerlan from Performance Technology, for example, supports access to NetWare, Banyan and UNIX servers. Furthermore, by supporting both SMB (server message block) and NetBIOS, it can access other NOSs including the various derivatives of LAN Manager.

The Microsoft product with which vendors of peer-to-peer NOSs most need to interoperate is Windows 3.11, which incorporates the NOS software formerly called Windows for Workgroups (WfW). This is because WfW was itself a peer-to-peer NOS and has made significant inroads into the market for small workgroup LANs. As a result, the other peer-to-peer NOS vendors need to interoperate with WfW, just as NOS vendors in general must interoperate with NetWare.

Indeed the various derivatives of the original LAN Manager software, including Microsoft's own products, do interoperate with NetWare. However, Microsoft initially took a rather different approach to integration with other vendors' NOSs than did Novell, reflecting the two companies' disparate positions in the market. Microsoft dominates the desktop operating environment, while Novell dominates the LAN server software world. Novell's approach to integration is via the server, where the NOS is in full control.

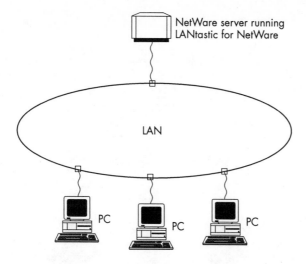

Figure 5.4 Use of Artisoft's LANtastic for NetWare. Users of the client PCs can access the NetWare services and at the same time exploit the peer-to-peer facilities of LANtastic.

Microsoft, on the other hand, has tended to provide integration at the client level, although this has changed somewhat with the growing thrust behind NT Server. Nevertheless, the Microsoft approach has traditionally been for the client NOS software to decide whether to access a LAN Manager file server or one controlled by another NOS. For integration with NetWare, for example, Microsoft originally supported simultaneous access from clients to both NetWare and LAN Manager servers, rather than a direct connection between the two servers. This distinction is illustrated in Figure 5.5, in which both approaches are sketched. On Windows 3.11 this is still the approach taken, the NetWare shell software being supplied partly by Microsoft and partly by Novell under the terms of their settlement, as explained in Chapter 3.

However, it became clear to Microsoft that this would prove an inefficient and unwieldy solution on larger Windows NT networks. The company therefore developed a redirector product allowing NT clients to access NetWare services through an NT server. In other words, Microsoft belatedly accepted that the NOS server is the best place to provide access to other NOS services on larger networks. In fact the NT redirectors can also be obtained from Novell, offering slightly different facilities. The better choice depends on whether the overall network is biased towards Windows NT or NetWare. An organization with a large established NetWare network, which is perhaps trying out NT in a small way, should probably use Novell's NT redirector, because this is more likely to exploit some of the finer points of NetWare. However, if the

(a)

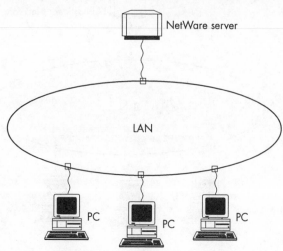

PCs running Microsoft's Windows for
Workgroups peer-to-peer software

b)

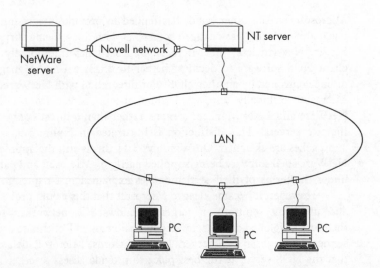

Figure 5.5 (a) Traditional Microsoft approach of accessing NetWare server from PCs directly; (b) the more recently developed Microsoft approach of connecting to a NetWare network via an NT server – recommended for larger networks.

commitment to NT becomes serious, then Microsoft's redirector would be the wiser choice, because it integrates better with the NT services.

With either of the redirectors, you can browse through the NT services as normal and also look at servers available in the NetWare network from the same window. Although the two redirectors fulfil the same function, the two companies naturally have different motives for promoting them. Microsoft sees it as a vehicle for encouraging existing NetWare users to migrate to Windows NT Server, while Novell sees it as just another integration feature to enrich its environment.

Integration between LAN Manager and UNIX servers is driven from the desktop but accomplished elegantly and efficiently. In Chapter 2, the way LAN Manager is built on top of established computer operating systems was discussed: at first it was based on OS/2 but subsequently Microsoft developed LAN Manager for UNIX. The same client software is used for both the OS/2 and UNIX versions, which means that a desktop application can simultaneously access an OS/2 LAN Manager server and a UNIX LAN Manager server. This allows users to control UNIX and LAN Manager applications from different windows on a single screen.

□ 5.5 Work done by different NOS vendors to enable their products to interoperate

NOS players can be split into five categories here: Novell; Microsoft and its LAN Manager resellers; Banyan; Apple and other vendors of low-cost peer-to-peer NOSs; and IBM.

Microsoft's approach to NOS integration, as already explained, has been through using LAN Manager to provide common client access to different server or general computer operating systems. More recently, Novell has favoured this direction too – having ported NetWare to operate on top of other operating systems, an example being NetWare for AIX (AIX is a version of UNIX developed by IBM). Novell's strategic direction is to make NetWare into a distributed operating system platform straddling other localized operating systems, while promoting UnixWare as the platform for running large-scale so-called mission-critical applications.

The first of these objectives is being advanced partly through partnerships with other leading players in the NOS field, notably Digital Equipment and IBM, although cooperation with its arch rival Microsoft is restricted to areas of mutual necessity, such as industry-standards work. However, DEC's Pathworks was initially derived from LAN Manager so, through its partnership with DEC, Novell is in a sense involved with LAN Manager through the back door. DEC then proceeded to support NetWare 3.1 and subsequently NetWare 4.x within Pathworks in the fifth version of the product, providing a bridge between the two rival systems. This version of the software incorporates native code supplied directly by Microsoft and Novell, providing for the first time a single platform capable of integrating the two. Nevertheless, there are numerous sites that already have NetWare and LAN Manager or one of its derivatives, and these gain nothing from such developments because they would have to make a major investment in Pathworks.

IBM's approach is interesting because its LAN Server is also a derivative of LAN Manager although it now follows a separate line of development, as explained in Chapter 2. Like DEC, IBM addresses interoperability with NetWare through a reasonably close relationship with Novell. As with DEC, this means IBM can provide closer integration with NetWare than Microsoft has been able to. Access to NetWare is achieved at the server level, through a product called NetWare Services Manager for OS/2, which defines the NetWare services available to the LAN Server users. IBM's relationship with Novell has also led to the introduction of LANRES (LAN Resource Extension and Services), which allows an IBM mainframe to act as a super server controlling a network of NetWare servers.

Banyan's policy is to sell Vines and its derivative products as a glue for integrating other operating system environments, including UNIX hosts, and IBM mainframes as well as other NOSs. This approach follows naturally from Banyan's strengths in large-scale networking and distributed directories, given that the company will never be a really big player in server operating systems. Thus Banyan is in a strong position in the growing market for products that integrate the leading NOS and operating system environments, in particular NetWare, NT Server, UNIX, and IBM systems. At time of writing, Banyan had yet to complete its product armoury in this field but already had ENS for NetWare, integrating different versions of NetWare, along with products for linking LAN Manager, LAN Server and AppleTalk networks with clients and servers in a Vines network.

Apple's approach is in some ways the mirror image of Banyan's – its strengths have always been in workgroup computing, whereas Banyan has majored in the directory and mail services required for large-scale networks. So while Banyan naturally focused on interconnecting other NOSs acting as a backbone, Apple has concentrated on being able to access other NOS environments that provide backbone services for Mac clients and AppleTalk networks. Apple has provided appropriate interconnection facilities through collaboration with relevant vendors, notably IBM, Novell and Digital Equipment. The collaboration with IBM, for example, led to AppleTalk protocols being supported in the OS/2 operating system.

The peer-to-peer NOS vendors need to sell to organizations that already have other NOSs, especially NetWare. They therefore tend to address NetWare integration specifically, while tackling other NOSs through common industry standards, in particular NetBIOS.

□ 5.6 Standard protocols that allow different NOSs to interoperate

There are two essential requirements for interoperability between two NOSs. The first is a common transport protocol which enables commands and data to be transmitted between clients and servers controlled by the two NOSs. This corresponds to the bottom four layers of the seven-layer OSI interconnection model which is described in Appendix 3. Then, at a higher level than the transport protocol, which merely provides a pipe for data to flow through, there has to be a means for applications to direct requests for data and services to the appropriate server, irrespective of the NOS controlling it. This fits just above layer four of the OSI model, providing a basis for direct links to be established between applications. In this case the link is either between a client workstation and a server application, or between a server under control of one NOS and an application on a server controlled by the other.

When a network is all under the control of a single NOS, these two functions can both be handled by a single protocol stack. Indeed, proprietary protocol stacks such as Novell's IPX/SPX and Apple Computer's AppleTalk provide all the functions needed for communication from client-to-server or server-to-server within these companies' own NOS environments. Also Net-BIOS, which is described in Chapter 1, provides the means for basic communication between applications, and is widely supported by all NOS vendors. It is the principal method of communication for peer-to-peer LANs, and provides a rudimentary level of interaction between NOSs at this level. However, NetBIOS is inadequate for providing more sophisticated interaction between NOSs on larger networks. At this level more sophisticated APIs (application programming interfaces) are required. APIs are considered in Chapter 8.

For two different NOSs to interoperate, it is often necessary to mix protocols to facilitate communication; for example, TCP/IP has become a widely established transport protocol for communication between different vendors' systems and operating platforms. At the same time, NetBIOS has long been a major standard for communication between client applications and NOS servers on a LAN. In consequence, NetBIOS commands are often transmitted over a TCP/IP transport service – a process known as encapsulation. NetBIOS data packets are snipped in two so that the higher-level part, which contains the information needed by the systems to process commands, is carried over the TCP/IP link. Similarly, NetWare IPX packets may be encapsulated over a TCP/IP link so that an industry-standard transport network can be used rather than one which is proprietary to Novell. The process of encapsulation is shown in Figure 5.6, which indicates how a TCP/IP network is used to transport a Novell IPX packet. In principle, networks using any one type of protocol can be used to transport packets formatted in any other. TCP/IP networks, for example, are also used to transport NetBIOS and IBM SNA data, among others.

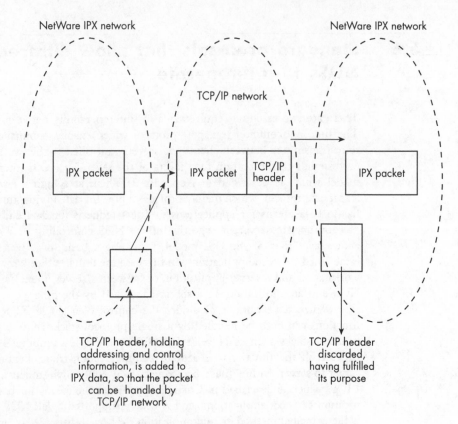

Figure 5.6 Use of TCP/IP network to transport IPX packet.

Other protocols used to provide the network transport include DEC's LAT (local area transport) and OSI transport services.

☐ SUMMARY

To facilitate communication between applications which may reside on systems controlled by different NOSs and other operating systems, a range of APIs is now available, as discussed in Chapter 8. In Chapter 9 we shall build on the work of this chapter and in Chapter 8 in particular we shall examine the rise of the network as a single computing entity providing services to the whole user community, and the role of operating systems in general within this wider scheme of things.

How the NOS provides the LAN with access to other networks and computer systems

CHAPTER OBJECTIVES:

- To describe the methods of accessing systems run by more traditional multi-user operating systems such as DEC's VMS, including UNIX in its guise as an operating system controlling a host computer running corporate or departmental applications
- To describe the products needed to interconnect LANs into a complete network that spans an enterprise

☐ 6.1   Introduction

The three-pronged thrust of the 1990s in IT is towards distributed computing, universal access to data and services, and centralized management. These objectives can only be achieved in an enterprise of any size by enabling all systems to interact at the application level. The role of the seven-layer OSI (open system interconnection) model in defining how computers interoperate is summarized in Appendix 3. This model is universally supported in the industry as the basis for interaction between computers, LANs and applications. Novell's IPX/SPX protocol stack, for example, is based on it.

Distributed computing requires applications to be dispersed to the locations where users need them – on host computers, LAN servers and desktop workstations or PCs. To provide universal access to information, these applications must be able to cooperate at the level of data sharing: this requires physical links at the bottom, network protocols that allow data packets to be routed over these physical links, and higher-layer protocols so that the applications can process commands and requests transmitted between themselves. For the network to be managed centrally, information has to be siphoned back from all parts of the network across the entire protocol spectrum to provide a comprehensive picture. At the physical level, for example, it may be necessary to trace cabling faults while at the application level it could be useful to know if a user has the wrong version of a particular software package.

The NOS plays a key role in all three of the prongs as it controls the LAN which is the local network unit within a larger enterprise. Within each LAN, the NOS needs to address the whole protocol spectrum as it provides the gateway between client workstations and all applications that are not resident on that LAN. This chapter builds up the picture first by examining the role of the NOS in the basic communications infrastructure, which on larger networks typically comprises LANs interconnected by routers in a mesh structure. Next, it moves on to the role of the NOS in providing the higher-level links with operating systems such as IBM's MVS, DEC's VMS and UNIX. Finally, it points the way to subsequent chapters which expand the role of the NOS in distributed computing across an enterprise.

□ 6.2 Defining the problem: what sort of access do users need across the network?

Chapter 5 defined when it is desirable to have links between LANs that are controlled by different NOSs. The same arguments apply to links between LANs and other systems – they are needed to provide users with access to applications, data and resources, irrespective of where they are located. The purpose is to share an organization's resources as efficiently as possible, eliminating unnecessary purchases of systems and reducing the burden of managing the data.

In many organizations, LAN workgroups grew up in isolated fashion, often with only rudimentary links to centralized host computers and with none at all to other LANs. The need grew for stronger links with both central IT resources and with other LANs to enable data, applications and resources such as printers to be shared more effectively. In some cases a drive towards executive information systems (EIS) has provided an additional incentive to link islands of IT together in a coherent network. EIS requires a universal network and appropriate software to funnel information back to workstations on managers' desks so that it can be analysed and presented as required.

Links can now be categorized either by the function required or by the types of system or network to be interconnected. The main functional requirements for links from a local LAN to other systems can be split into the following six groups: (1) access to data; (2) access to applications; (3) access to printers; (4) access to other specialist resources on the remote system; (5) backup – use of the remote system to store data safely; and (6) electronic mail – the ability to send messages to users of other systems.

In the case of links to other NOSs, as examined in Chapter 5, the first three of these are usually most relevant. However, with the growing sophistication of the NetWare environment, for example, there is increasing demand for links between NetWare and peer-to-peer LANs so that the latter can benefit from the more advanced security and backup facilities of the former. Points (4) and (5) apply mostly to a host system controlled either by a proprietary operating system such as Digital Equipment's VMS or by a version of UNIX.

When considering the type of system you may want to access, there are three principal categories: (1) host systems controlled by a proprietary operating system; (2) host systems controlled by UNIX; and (3) LAN servers controlled by a NOS. The third of these was discussed in Chapter 5, while the first two are dealt with in this chapter. However, the distinction between these three categories is slowly fading; for example, UNIX can also function in effect as a server operating system accessed directly by PCs, and host systems such as IBM mainframes are increasingly being used as large file servers in client/server applications, although often they would be backing up a smaller file server controlled by a conventional NOS. Alternatively, the host system may run a version of a NOS such as NetWare on top of its own operating system, enabling it to act directly as a file server on a LAN. In general, host systems are increasingly being attached to LANs and, as a result, wide area networks commonly comprise LANs interconnected by appropriate telecommunications links.

We shall come back to the first two categories above in Section 6.5 but first we shall describe how LANs are interconnected both locally and remotely by bridges, routers and hubs, or a combination of these.

□ 6.3 LAN interconnection

Readers familiar with the methods used to interconnect LANs should skip this section and pick up the story in Section 6.4 where the role of the NOS in the process is described.

The need for devices that enable two or more LANs to be interconnected arose for two reasons: firstly, there was a growing demand for interconnection of LANs at different sites via telecommunications links, so that users at one site could access data and applications residing in the other; secondly, as usage of local LANs at each site increased, bandwidth was occupied. The only method available at that time for maintaining performance was to divide each LAN into multiple segments, restricting the flow of traffic between segments. Note that, as far as the systems and applications on a network are concerned, there is no difference between these two cases.

The word segment in this context is used to describe a single logical LAN connecting all devices attached to it directly without any division of the network by bridges or routers. Figure 6.1 illustrates two LAN segments interconnected by a bridge. The whole network functions as a logical LAN but the bridge only forwards packets if they are addressed to a device on the other side of it, improving performance because overall traffic levels on the network are reduced. Each segment is untouched by data traffic between devices on the other segment.

Bridges and routers evolved to handle both local and remote LAN interconnection, although with configuration differences in each case. For remote interconnection, bridges and routers usually have to funnel high-speed LAN traffic down onto slower long-distance lines, which requires additional processing that is not necessary when LANs are attached directly to each other. Some bridges and routers are therefore dedicated just to local or remote LAN interconnection but cannot handle both; others can interconnect LANs both locally and remotely, although not through the same port. As the processing involved is different in each case, such systems are segmented, with one part of the device handling local and the other remote communication. Figure 6.2 illustrates three LANs interconnected by router 1. LANs A and B are connected locally to each other via two ports of the router, while LAN C is connected to both of them via a telecommunications link which comes into the remote port of router 1. Note that LAN C is attached to the other end of the telecommunications link via router 2. We shall discuss the distinction between bridges and routers in Section 6.3.1.

As well as being connected to each other, LANs may also be linked directly to a host system via devices called gateways; these perform the protocol conversion necessary for devices on the LAN to communicate with the host system. However, with host computers increasingly being connected to wide area networks via LANs, the distinction between gateways and LAN interconnection devices is fading. LANs have become the standard local building block of enterprise-wide networks, therefore bridges and routers, being the

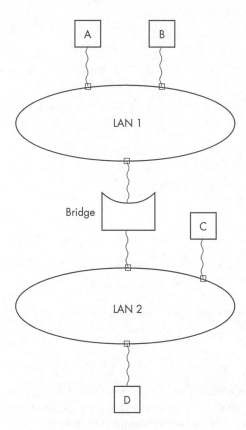

Figure 6.1 Two LANs interconnected by a bridge. Traffic between devices A and B is not allowed to cross the bridge, so it does not occupy bandwidth. The same is true of traffic between C and D. However, the bridge will forward data packets from, for example, A to D.

devices that interconnect LANs, have become essential components of large networks. Also the NOS, as the software controlling the LAN at each site, has assumed responsibility for supporting interaction between LAN applications and remote host-based systems, in effect providing the gateway function. This will become clearer in Section 6.5.

6.3.1 Distinction between bridges, routers, gateways and hubs

These have all converged to some extent, although there is still a clear distinction between the four functions. The functions can now all be integrated in single hardware units, which can be mixed and matched as required. A brief résumé of each will clarify the situation.

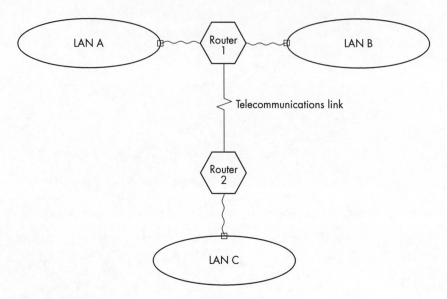

Figure 6.2 Three LANs interconnected by a router.

Bridges

Bridges provide transparent links between pairs of LAN segments, which may be geographically remote or located in the same building, their function being to filter data packets on a LAN according to the layer two MAC (media access control) address (used within LANs) of their destination. Packets addressed to devices on the other side of the bridge will be removed from the segment on which they originated and forwarded to the segment on which the destination device is located. On the other hand, packets addressed to devices on the same segment as the originating devices will be blocked by the bridge so that they do not occupy bandwidth on the other segment. This allows bridges to fulfil two main roles: firstly, they can interconnect two LAN segments that were not previously linked, if necessary via a point-to-point telecommunications link; secondly, their ability to filter packets by not letting them pass allows bridges to divide a LAN into two or more segments, restricting the overall flow of traffic. These two applications of bridges are illustrated in Figure 6.3, one half of which depicts a local LAN split into two segments by a bridge, while the other shows two remote LANs interconnected by a bridge.

Networks comprising multiple LAN segments can be constructed using bridges. However, this can in general be done only by daisy-chaining the segments together, which becomes a severe limitation on large networks. Each bridge can interconnect two segments only. Bridges operate only in the bottom two layers of the protocol stack used by LANs themselves and therefore create, in effect, a single enlarged LAN partitioned into smaller LANs only by traffic flow. As they are impervious to higher-layer protocols, use of bridges does not

(a)

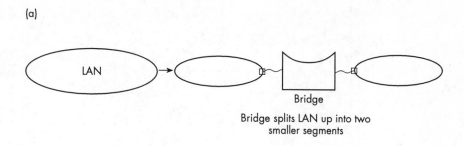

Bridge

Bridge splits LAN up into two
smaller segments

(b)

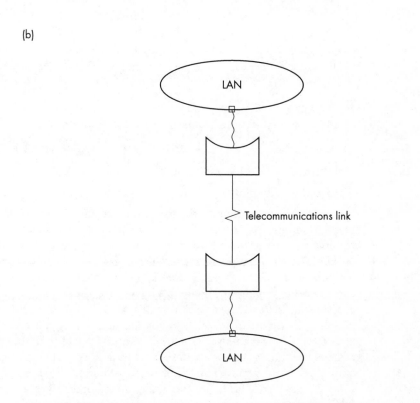

Telecommunications link

Figure 6.3 (a) Use of a bridge to segment a local LAN. Bridge splits LAN into
two smaller segments; (b) bridges at each end of the link allow two (or more)
LANs to be interconnected remotely.

affect the applications that run on the LAN, other than by changing response
times. The role of the bridge is depicted schematically with reference to the
seven-layer OSI model in Figure 6.4. Note that although the bridging function
always takes place in the bottom two protocol layers, there are several variants
on the theme, which are discussed in Appendix 1.

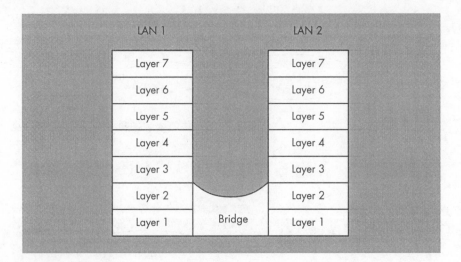

Figure 6.4 Bridges can connect LANs at the datalink level as shown, which embraces the bottom two layers of the seven-layer OSI model.

Routers

Like bridges, routers can interconnect LAN segments either locally or remotely. In addition, also like bridges, they either filter data packets to contain them within a segment or they forward them to another segment. The difference lies in the way forwarding is handled. Whereas bridges can only forward across a point-to-point link to a single LAN segment, routers can connect more than two segments together. To do this they have the ability to make routing decisions to decide which of the paths to take – hence their name. The information needed to make these routing decisions is not contained within layer two of the seven-layer OSI model, which handles only basic addressing of stations or nodes attached to the LAN. Bridges, operating in layer two, know only whether a device to which a packet is addressed is located on one side of it or the other and, based on this information, either filter or forward it.

A router, on the other hand, incorporates tables containing information about the whole network, not just the segments to which it is attached. This enables it to make intelligent routing decisions when there is a choice of paths, taking into account factors such as congestion of the network, availability of specific links and relative transmission costs across the links that are available.

Unlike bridges, routers only examine packets addressed specifically to them, rather than handling all packets on the LAN automatically. A router is itself a device with a layer two address on the LAN to which it is attached, whereas a bridge has no layer two address and simply looks at all packets that reach it, quite transparently to all other devices on the network. So when a packet is addressed to it, a router does not need to examine the layer two field to decide whether the packet needs to be forwarded; it discards the outer envelope of the packet containing the layer two information and looks inside at layer three to decide which route to take. The layer three field of a packet tells the router on which LAN segment the destination node is located. The router may or may not be directly connected to this segment – however, by combining the location of the destination segment with knowledge of the network configuration and prevailing network conditions, it can decide which path to send the packet on. Figure 6.5 illustrates the process in a simple network. A packet is addressed from device 1 on LAN segment A to device 2 on LAN segment C. There are two possible paths, one directly from LAN segment A to C, and the other via LAN segment B. Normally the direct link would be quicker if the lines run at the same speed but in this case we will suppose that the link has failed. The router decides therefore to send the packet via segment B.

Note that in order to take account of prevailing network conditions, routers need some method of deciding on a route. There are various routing protocols that enable this to be done, such as OSPF (open shortest path first) – described briefly in Appendix 1.

The relative merits of bridges and routers are summarized below.

Router advantages

More reliable delivery of data, with greater tolerance of network link failures.

Can link LANs of different types and speeds, such as Ethernet and token ring.

Can take advantage of multiple routes and in general make more efficient use of available bandwidth.

More secure, with greater protection against unauthorized access to resources.

Bridge advantages

Faster transmission on straightforward point-to-point links.

Less expensive.

Simpler to install and configure.

Can more readily handle protocols that do not provide information in layer three, such as Digital Equipment's LAT.

Essentially, routers are preferred for large networks because they provide greater flexibility, better support for network management and superior control over traffic flow. Bridges tend to be preferred in smaller networks because they are usually cheaper, and easier to set up and configure.

Another factor to be considered is that routers need information in layer three of each data packet in order to decide which route to take. Unfortunately, not all protocol stacks provide a layer three – two such are DEC's LAT (local

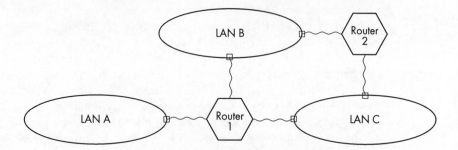

Figure 6.5 If the link between router 1 and LAN C fails, traffic between LAN A and LAN C can be diverted via LAN B and router 2.

area transport) protocol and IBM's SNA/SDLC, although both of these are gradually being phased out in favour of protocols that are fully routable. Nevertheless, there are large numbers of networks where the requirement to transport data formatted using these protocols between LANs still applies.

On the latter networks there may also be a need to use routers to carry some of the protocols, as listed in Table 6.1, that can be routed. This is done by the brouter, a hybrid device capable of routing packets wrapped in protocols that can be routed while bridging those that cannot. A brouter recognizes data packets that cannot be routed, and examines their layer two addresses, just like a bridge, to determine whether to forward or filter them. Most leading systems that perform routing also support some bridging, so that technically they are brouters.

A further point to note is that while each local bridge, since it operates in layer two, is usually specific to the LAN that it serves so that it can only interconnect two LANs of the same type, this is not true of routers. As routers operate in layer three, they are independent of the underlying LAN type, so that they can interconnect, for example, a token ring and Ethernet LAN. However, being dependent on the layer three protocol, two routers at each end of a telecommunications link can be attached to different LANs but they need to support the same protocol in layer three. The most common layer three protocol is the IP (internet protocol) of TCP/IP but Novell's IPX is also widely used for interconnecting NetWare servers and AppleTalk is still common on networks of Apple Macintoshes. While bridges can only support one LAN type, most routers support several layer three protocols, being referred to as multiprotocol routers; this is important because many large networks are not confined to just one protocol. By supporting all the common protocols, routers can be used to build networks of interconnected LANs that will carry all the traffic generated, irrespective of which network layer protocol is used to address data packets. The relationship between the NOS and layer three protocols is expanded in Section 6.4.

Table 6.1 Protocols that can be routed.

Novell IPX
TCP/IP
DECnet phase 4 and phase 5
OSI
SNA APPN
AppleTalk
XNS
Banyan Vines

Introducing the hub

The basic operation of the two most popular LAN types, Ethernet and token ring, and how they have evolved as star-shaped structures connected to central wiring hubs is summarized in Appendix 5. At the simplest level, hubs or concentrators are devices that enable the cabling of LANs to be centralized, providing no additional management or communication capabilities. In the case of Ethernet LANs, the 10BaseT standard has become very popular as it enables networks to be laid out in a flexible star formation using unshielded twisted pair cabling as shown in Figure 6.6. Such devices are in widespread use on both small and large networks; however, more sophisticated hubs have evolved from these humble beginnings, providing focal points for the management and control of the network. This was a logical step as hubs provide central points through which all traffic on a LAN flows, enabling faults to be detected at the hub and management information to be extracted from it.

Hubs also expanded their role by physically interconnecting multiple LAN segments, rather than just being located at the centre of each LAN segment. In this guise, the function of hubs began to converge with routers at the top end of each of the two product ranges; recall that routers can be used locally to join different LAN segments together. As hubs expanded to provide the physical interconnection between multiple LAN segments, it became logical to introduce support for routing as well; without this, the hub would need to be coupled with an external router in order to segment traffic on the network to maintain performance. While this can be and is done, it is not the most elegant solution and requires the presence of two devices, which may increase cost and complexity.

So the backbone hub, sometimes called the powerhub, or hub of hubs, emerged as a device that would interconnect LAN segments locally within a large local site and provide the ability to route, or bridge, between them; manufacturers of such hubs include 3 Com and Alantec. Figure 6.7 illustrates a typical set up in an office building. On each floor are 10BaseT LANs, each with their 10BaseT hub, while in the basement is a backbone hub of hubs to

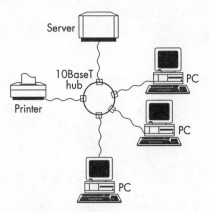

Figure 6.6 Layout of Ethernet LAN using 10BaseT standard. Devices are attached to the hub in star-shaped topology rather than the traditional tree-and-branch-shaped Ethernet bus.

which all of the 10BaseT LANs are connected. Backbone routers provide similar functions, two leading vendors being Cisco Systems and Wellfleet Communications. However, backbone routers provide greater performance than hubs and also provide connection to wide area services, so the two products are not completely interchangeable.

Hubs have also embraced bridging functions, to support filtering for improved performance between attached LAN segments. This development reached its zenith with the deployment of the technique called Ethernet switching in hubs. The principle is that the LAN retains the Ethernet access protocol CSMA/CD (see Appendix 1) but data packets, instead of being transmitted to all devices, are routed only to the destination device which is also attached to the hub. The function is an extension of bridging in that it operates in OSI layer two, and involves filtering according to the destination address specified in that layer.

Functionally, Ethernet switching is more like a local router interconnecting a star cluster of LAN segments, where each segment has just one device or at most a few devices on it, but with the difference that it operates in layer two, involving just a scan of the destination address. This makes it much faster than routing, and Ethernet switches out-perform local bridges and routers by an order of magnitude, while also providing users with the potential to have in effect a whole Ethernet to themselves, as there are no other devices contending for access to their segment. The full bandwidth of Ethernet is available for each session between devices, provided the switch has enough capacity to handle the traffic as it passes through. Ethernet switching is now an option available with the more sophisticated LAN hubs, enabling LANs to provide faster response to users and support applications, in multimedia for example, which require greater bandwidth to each desktop workstation.

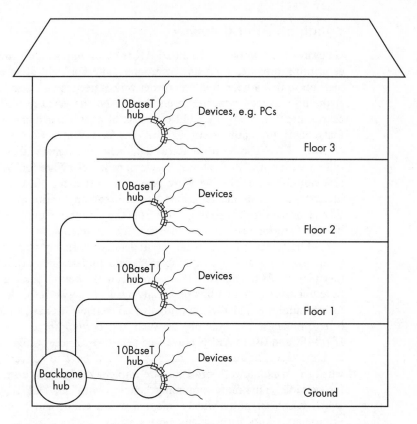

Figure 6.7 Role of the backbone hub in a network spanning a building.

Ethernet switching is described more fully in Appendix 1.

Ethernet switching is, however, likely to be only an interim technology. Ultimately, hub vendors are looking towards ATM (asynchronous transfer mode) as a way of providing high performance and also of uniting LANs and WANs into a coherent end-to-end high-speed network. The growing role of the NOS in ATM and high-speed services is discussed in Chapter 10.

The other key development in hub technology of particular relevance to NOSs is the card-based hub for insertion into LAN servers. This arrangement has the virtue of elegance because the LAN server, already the logical heart of the LAN, now becomes the physical hub as well, although it is only suitable for smaller LANs and cannot compete with dedicated hubs in expandability and sophistication. The principal use of combined server/hubs is, therefore, in branch offices of large organizations where there is little prospect of significant network growth in each branch. The role of the NOS in managing such card-based hubs is discussed in Section 7.4.1.

Bringing in the gateway

Gateways allow workstations on a LAN to access applications and services such as printing provided by a host computer. The host will often be at a remote location so that a wide area link or network is needed to access it from a LAN. If the host is itself attached to another LAN, the gateway may also function as a router but it has the additional task of converting higher-layer protocols that enable the applications to interact. As a simple example, a user on a NetWare LAN may want to access data held on a remote IBM mainframe. In this case Novell's IBM gateway services, called NetWare for SAA (see Section 6.5) would convert the NetWare protocols so that the IBM mainframe could understand the commands issued by the user's application program; it would then reformat the data coming back from the mainframe into the form expected by NetWare for presentation to the user's application.

The gateway function can be understood formally with reference to the seven-layer OSI model. Unlike bridges and routers, gateways can address all seven layers. At the network level, embracing the bottom three layers, gateways have to ensure that a path is physically available between the devices that want to communicate and this may involve conversion between different network layer protocols, for example between the bottom three layers of Novell's IPX/SPX and IBM's APPN (advanced peer-to-peer networking) protocol suites. In some cases, however, the gateway may not have to convert at this level – when the same network protocols are implemented on the host and the LAN, for example. This most commonly happens with the TCP/IP protocol suite, which has been quite widely adopted as an end-to-end protocol, replacing proprietary protocols on many host systems.

Nevertheless, a gateway definitely does have to convert in the higher layers (otherwise it would be redundant), in order to enable the host application to communicate with applications on the LAN via the NOS. We shall discuss this further in Section 6.5 in describing how a NOS supports access to host systems. The point to stress here is that the gateway function, like routing and bridging, can be implemented in a variety of different devices on the network. It can run on the file server itself as a NOS communications application, although this is only really advisable on small LANs, or more commonly on a separate communications server, or, increasingly, gateways functions are available as options on LAN hubs.

The hub, from its humble origins as a wiring concentrator, has expanded to become the visible focal point of the local communications scene, so it is now possible to run all the communications applications in single units. Hubs have therefore become the physical building blocks of enterprise-wide networks, as some of the NOS vendors have been quick to appreciate, emphasizing that the hub is a device that the NOS needs to manage and communicate with if it is to do a proper job of controlling the LANs on a particular site. Novell, for example, has working relationships with most of the leading hub makers, and a particularly close one with SynOptics Communications. The two companies are working together under one of Novell's strategic development alliances to ensure that forthcoming releases of NetWare work efficiently on LANs based on SynOptics hubs, particularly with regard to the emerging switching and high-speed technologies such as ATM. More details on cooperation between NOSs and hubs are given in Chapter 7.

□ 6.4 How the NOS supports interconnection of LANs

A favourite buzz phrase in the IT industry is 'transparency to the user'. What this means is that users on a desktop workstation should not have to worry where the data is located or whether part of the task they are doing involves cooperation with an application running on a mainframe computer 2000 miles away. The ideal is that the network should appear as an extension of the workstation attached directly to it, so that users need to make no effort navigating their way around it. Indeed the whole thrust of network computing, which is discussed in Chapter 9, is to allow organizations to link their systems together and deploy them cooperatively in a cost-effective way, while delivering the results simply and elegantly through windows on their users' screens. Other issues exist, such as support for mobile users and new ways of interacting with computers via light pens and speech recognition, for example, but the crux is this matter of transparency.

The NOS is a key player here; indeed it has the starring role. Fundamental to this is the ability to make a network of interconnected LANs, often called an internet, behave just like one LAN as far as users are concerned. To do this, it must be able to handle different types of printer and support distributed directory services to enable data to be located on a network of multiple servers. However, at a lower level it must be able to handle the LAN interconnection methods, in particular bridging and routing.

6.4.1 The NOS and bridging

Superficially, bridging is easy – indeed the NOS does not even need to know that a bridge is in place, because the function is transparent to the higher layers of communication. Nevertheless, the NOS does need to be aware of the identity and LAN address of any file servers, printers or other services it is responsible for, so that it can transmit requests accordingly. It does not matter in principle whether a bridge has to be crossed at any stage, because the whole network behaves as a single logical LAN.

Thus the bridging function is independent of the NOS, although as an option some NOSs provide the software that enables a server to function as a bridge. While performed most effectively in dedicated hardware as an independent unit, bridging is essentially a software function that can be implemented as a NOS application on a file server or associated communications server. As the preferred solution for small networks, bridging options are offered on some of the low-cost peer-to-peer NOSs described in Chapter 3; for example, Performance Technology offers bridging software called Powerbridge, which can be used independently of its Powerlan NOS, to interconnect LANs controlled by other NOSs, provided they support the NetBIOS protocol, as do the leading ones.

Although the NOS does not have to deal with bridges specifically, it has to be capable of supporting the enlarged networks that result; for example, it must handle the requisite numbers of devices and support multiple file servers. Peer-to-peer NOSs do the latter anyway, and now the larger client/server NOSs, such as NetWare 4.0, are designed specifically for networks of multiple servers.

6.4.2 The NOS and routing

On larger networks, routing tends to be preferred to bridging so it must be catered for by the higher-end NOSs. Unlike bridging, routing is a function that needs to be specifically requested, either by the desktop application or by the NOS. Therefore, to shield users' applications from the need to know where data or services reside, the NOS must either support routing directly as an application or request the services of a separate router; for example, if users or their applications request a particular file that is not contained on a local file server attached to the same LAN, the NOS must be able to transfer the request via a router to a distant LAN, where hopefully the request can be satisfied. In some cases the request may have to pass through several hops before the file is located, after which it is returned, sometimes via a different route, to the LAN that initiated the request.

Figure 6.8 illustrates the process in a case where the request passes first from LAN A to LAN B via a remote telecommunications link. In this case the request is transmitted simultaneously to all three of the other segments, B, C and D, although it will not arrive at each at precisely the same time. As the file is held on LAN D, it is returned via LAN B to the device on LAN A that requested it. Note that the process becomes inefficient on a large network comprising many interconnected LAN segments, because the request is transmitted to every segment on the LAN.

The solution is to have a global directory which enables each LAN segment to look up the location of any file that is requested. The request can then be routed directly to the LAN segment that holds the file, rather than going to every segment. In the case of the network shown in Figure 6.8, the difference is that the request would not have to be processed by LAN B or LAN C, because it is known that the file is held on LAN D.

Where a global directory service exists, the NOS can insert the correct network address into the data packets carrying the instructions to obtain the desired file. The router determines the best path to the segment holding the

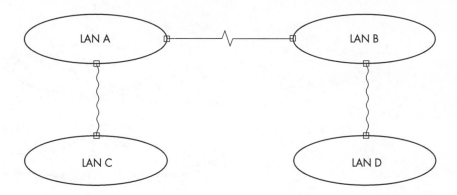

Figure 6.8 How requests for a file have to be relayed exhaustively to all servers on a network in the absence of a directory service. Device on LAN A requests a file held on a server on LAN D. Request has to pass to servers on LANs C and D, even though they do not hold the file.

file, according to what links are available and the prevailing network conditions. The NOSs running in other LAN segments do not have to look up their local directories to see if the file is located on their file server.

Comprehensive support for routing is only provided by the leading NOS vendors, in particular Novell, Microsoft, IBM and, in this context, Banyan Systems as its Vines NOS is designed specifically for large-scale networks. There are three main possibilities, shown in the three parts of Figure 6.9. The first is where the NOS turns the file server into a local router to serve LAN segments directly connected to it. In this case the server is attached to several segments, each segment coming into its own network interface card in the server, the latter routing between these segments. Network performance is the motive for routing in this way: by partitioning the network into different segments, each containing traffic local to it, the overall flow of traffic is reduced.

The second option is for the NOS to provide routing software running on a separate dedicated communications server – this is similar to the print serving function, which can either be run in the file server or in a dedicated print server. The routing server contains standard hardware, is controlled by the NOS and could provide local routing, remote routing, or a combination of both.

The third option is to liaise with a dedicated router, as shown in the third part of Figure 6.9. This differs from the second option in that the hardware is designed specifically for routing and runs software tuned to it – usually the preferred option for large networks with substantial amounts of data traffic between LAN segments. In such situations, only hardware dedicated to the task can handle the heavy processing load required to perform the routing. Although the second option involves a server dedicated to communications, typically it still has to be an industry-standard PC-type server in order to run the NOS

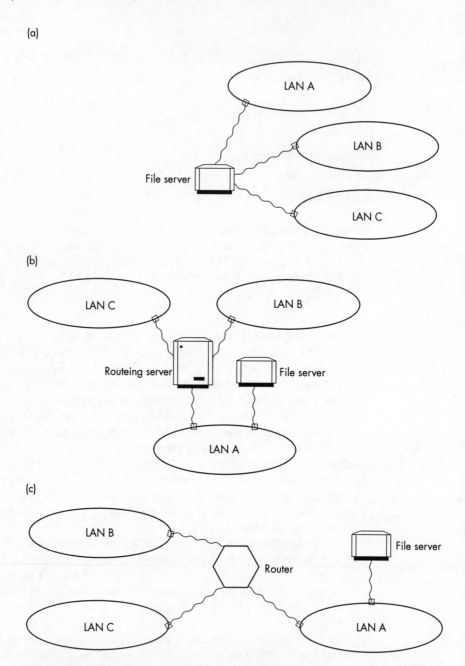

Figure 6.9 How routing is supporting by the NOS: (a) file server becomes local router; (b) NOS controls a dedicated routing server, which is based on standard hardware; (c) NOS liaises with dedicated router.

software. Dedicated routers, on the other hand, contain hardware optimized for the task of routing and designed to cope with a high data throughput. The second option is most suitable for intermediate traffic loads, while the first is only recommended for relatively lightly loaded networks.

Novell covers all three options; for example, NetWare 3.11 can work with dedicated routers but also incorporates external routing software which turns a standard PC into a router. It also supports internal routing within the file server between multiple LAN segments, which would be done to break a proliferating LAN into more manageable parts. As explained in Section 6.3, routers read the layer three addresses of data packets to decide which path to take. The layer three address informs the router of the destination, which will typically be another router attached to a remote LAN segment. In order to achieve this, the software needs to be aware of the router's existence and capable of inserting the desired addresses; in other words, the software running on each LAN segment has to be 'aware of the network'. This software can either be part of the applications running in each client desktop PC or it can reside in the file server. In the latter case, it will usually be a function performed by the main server component of the NOS, generally as a dedicated NOS application, for example a NetWare NLM.

In the early days of LAN interconnection during the late 1980s, it was nearly always the responsibility of the client to decide where to route requests for data or a network service. The client might route a request for a file to the local LAN server in a Microsoft LAN Manager network, or it might go to a distant UNIX computer. At first sight this seemed logical because it is, after all, the client application that has to decide what information and services it needs. However, it runs counter to the notion that the network should appear transparent to the user's application. Particularly on networks containing a variety of different systems, this imposes a heavy burden on the client PCs, each of which has to be able to handle the protocols required to access the systems it needs.

Suppose, for example, you want to give client PCs the ability to access a NetWare server, a UNIX system and an IBM mainframe. Originally the client would have needed to run an IPX protocol stack to reach the NetWare server, a TCP/IP stack to access the UNIX system and the IBM 3270 protocol stack to access the IBM mainframe. These protocol stacks span the upper layers of the OSI model and their role in accessing remote applications is discussed further in Section 6.5.

The point to be stressed here is that the processing of these protocols to perform the underlying routing function needed to send data packets to the desired place takes up considerable memory and processing power, which for clients reduces the capacity to run applications efficiently. In practice, such functions can readily be performed as a service on behalf of a number of clients.

6.4.3 Novell and routing

To coincide with the launch of NetWare 4.x, Novell introduced a new protocol called NLSP (NetWare link services protocol) for routing traffic between networks of NetWare servers. This is a key part of Novell's global networking strategy because it provides the underlying communication layer for large-scale distributed networks of multiple NetWare servers. NLSP overcomes the limitations of Novell's implementation of RIP (routing information protocol) and SAP (service advertising protocol), which only work efficiently for relatively small networks.

Novell has also moved towards support of routing via different protocols as a service provided by the NOS. In Chapter 2 we indicated how the NetWare shell has evolved to enable Novell to support other transport protocols such as TCP/IP and AppleTalk. The aim of this move was to allow a variety of clients to join NetWare networks in addition to their previous links, without necessarily having to support another protocol, or at any rate without having to run more than two stacks. So, for example, an Apple Mac that already used AppleTalk to participate in a workgroup could now access a NetWare server with the same protocol. All it would need would be Novell's AppleTalk version of the NetWare shell.

However, there may also be performance considerations here; for example, IPX is more efficient as a LAN data transport protocol than is TCP/IP, so some clients have two network interface cards – a high-performance one driven by the IPX protocol and a slower one running TCP/IP to access UNIX servers and hosts. This imposes a burden on the client, although happily there is an obvious solution: to revert to using IPX for all communications on the LAN, and then have a dedicated communications service provided by the NOS to translate to other protocols as appropriate. All routing hence becomes the responsibility of the NOS on the server. Suppose, for example, a client wants to access some data that happens to reside not on the NetWare file server but on a remote UNIX host. In this case the client application need not even know of the existence of the remote UNIX system; instead the UNIX services are presented as options available with NetWare. There is no need to have dual protocol stacks running in each workstation; now the user's application selects the service or system it needs to access and NetWare connects to it. Access to the UNIX system becomes a service provided by NetWare as an NLM (NetWare loadable module). This arrangement also brings great benefits in security, control and network management, as is discussed further in Section 6.5. In the present context, it is enough to note that the NOS, in this case NetWare, now becomes entirely responsible for instructing the router on which system to send each data packet to. Requests from users of the IPX protocol are interpreted and converted into the TCP/IP format with the correct network layer three address inserted according to the particular UNIX system the client application requested.

Rather than develop its own product to convert IPX into TCP/IP, Novell utilized a third-party product called Novix from the UK company Firefox.

Further details about this are given in Section 6.5. However, despite the meteoric rise of TCP/IP, the continuing dominance of NetWare in the NOS arena is ensuring that there is also growing demand for IPX to route data across the wide area between LAN segments. We shall now take a look at Novell's recent moves to make IPX an efficient protocol over the WAN as well as within the LAN.

How Novell has made IPX operate faster on LAN internets

The IPX protocol is highly efficient within workgroups for local LAN applications but it was not designed for operation over wide area links via routers between LANs. However, given the huge increase in LAN interconnection, Novell took various steps during the early 1990s to improve the performance of IPX across LAN internets connected by routers. One such measure was to reduce the amount of data transmitted across the network to advertise the availability of services such as file servers and printers. Novell originally developed the SAP (service advertising protocol) to do this – it is widely used on networks based on NetWare 3.11 or earlier versions to advertise the availability of services. However, as this used up network bandwidth that could be used for application data, Novell reduced the need for it in NetWare 4.x by introducing the NetWare Directory Services (NDS) server. The principle is that, instead of servers periodically broadcasting their entire range of services across the network, workstations consult their nearest NDS server to find out where a particular service is located. The NDS servers are updated by servers only when there is a change in the service offered. Information between NDS services is transmitted by NLSP rather than SAP.

Nevertheless, SAP is still used in NetWare 4.x networks by workstations in locating the nearest NDS server when they start up, and most networks continue to use older devices that advertise themselves via SAP. Therefore, to reduce SAP traffic further, Novell introduced SAP filtering, which is analogous to the filtering done by a LAN bridge to restrict traffic to the segments that need it. In this process, SAP broadcasts advertising a service are restricted to workgroups or parts of the network that need that service.

In late 1992 came the introduction of IPXWAN, which enables routers from different vendors to interoperate effectively across an IPX LAN internet. IPXWAN specifies information that routers need to exchange across the WAN links for them to perform efficiently when handling IPX data. This includes details of which links are congested and how urgent the traffic is, enabling the routers to make better and faster decisions about which route to take. Finally, Novell introduced its NetWare Link Services Protocol (NLSP) designed to optimize the flow of IPX traffic in large networks and make it easier to manage; this coincided with the release of NetWare 4.x, also targeted at large-scale networks.

These steps alone would not, however, be sufficient to ensure that IPX was handled efficiently across large-scale networks – the techniques also need to be implemented properly by router makers. Although Novell supplies routers based on standard PC-type LAN servers for smaller networks, it does not have high-end products suitable for the kind of global networks needed by multinational corporations. Significant here therefore was Novell's strategic partnership with Cisco Systems, the world's biggest router maker, struck in August 1993. The companies pledged to cooperate in ensuring that NLSP and IPXWAN would be supported in Cisco routers.

6.4.4 Microsoft and routing

Like Novell, Microsoft has also struck a partnership with Cisco Systems, reflecting Microsoft's growing presence in the large-scale network field. Until the launch of Windows NT in 1993, Microsoft tended to focus on the provision of communication services from the client rather than the server end; this was understandable given the dominance of the company's Windows 3 on the desktop. The approach was to integrate the required communication services into the desktop client workstations as Windows applications. So, for example, if users wanted to access files on both a UNIX server and a LAN Manager server at the same time, they would open two windows, one accessing each server; then, using Windows' familiar drag and drop file utilities, they could move data from one system to the other, provided the applications were properly integrated.

On larger networks it makes more sense to provide communications services on servers rather than clients, because they are then easier to manage and do not divert resources from users' applications. So like Novell, Microsoft too has shifted the axis of its communications strategy from the client to the server, if to a rather lesser extent.

Microsoft also differs from Novell in how routing is supported; whereas Novell implements routing support as NLMs which become part of the operating system, Microsoft decided to have routing and indeed all optional facilities as separate applications running alongside the NOS software on top of an underlying operating platform. Microsoft therefore implements routing as a separate application, working in cooperation with leading players in the field.

☐ 6.5 How the NOS enables PCs and LANs to access remote host systems

We have already established in Section 6.4 what role the NOS plays in enabling LANs to be interconnected over the wide area. Closely related to that is the ability to access applications on remote LANs, which is a higher-level function that assumes the existence of appropriate network services beneath it. Therefore it does not really matter whether the remote system is attached to a LAN or not; in fact a remote host system can participate in a LAN internet without itself being attached to a LAN, provided it runs appropriate communications software to enable it to function like a router. Indeed, IBM's front-end communication processors attached to mainframes can now function as routers, enabling them to deliver services to remote LANs.

As previously indicated, there is a need for higher-layer software operating above the basic network infrastructure, to allow applications on dissimilar systems to understand each other. With reference to the OSI model, this involves layers four to seven inclusive: layer four handles end-to end communication across a network while layers five to seven deal with interaction between applications.

The general requirement is for interaction between client applications on desktop workstations and a remote host application – there may or may not be various intermediate stages. Commonly a LAN server, controlled by a NOS, will be involved, perhaps to determine how to satisfy the request from a user's application. Let us now review the possible ways of accessing remote applications on systems other than a conventional LAN server. The basic requirement is for conversion between the commands and file structures supported by the user's application or desktop graphical interface, and those required by the host system. Traditionally, host systems have been accessed via dumb terminals with strictly defined screen and command formats; therefore, to access these applications, desktop PCs needed to emulate these screen and command formats. Most hosts systems now support other more sophisticated types of command that allow applications to interact on a more equal peer-to-peer basis. Whatever the case, there has to be a layer of software running somewhere to enable the desktop application to access the remote system.

Four possibilities can be identified, which differ according to where the relevant processing and conversion of protocols occur:

(1) The communication software runs in the desktop PCs.

(2) The software runs in dedicated gateways attached to the LANs, providing a shared link with remote systems. Such gateways typically serve client workstations but can also be used by the NOS to provide a service.

(3) The software runs in the host system, having no impact on the LAN and its NOS other than in the data traffic generated by access to the remote application.

(4) The software is integrated into the NOS, so that a separate gateway is not required.

These four options have different advantages and disadvantages. The first one is the oldest, having its origins in the desire to be able to access established mainframe systems to make corporate data available to emerging PC applications. It was relatively simple to implement in this way, and could also co-exist with LAN applications. However, the emergence of LANs meant that desktop workstations were burdened with additional protocol processing. This problem was sometimes referred to as 'RAM Cram' because too much applications software was competing for limited RAM on the user's PC; also, as PC populations proliferated, it became harder to cope with each one having its own communications software. The probability of any one having a problem with this software was correspondingly greater, increasing the burden on those responsible for providing technical support to end users.

The gateway then emerged as an apparent Messiah. The idea was to install on each LAN a system, often a standard PC, running the software needed to allow PC applications like spreadsheets and word-processing packages to access the requisite hosts, such as UNIX systems and IBM mainframes. Gateways spared workstations from having to process additional protocols and gave the host system a single point of contact within each workgroup, although many turned out to be only an interim step because they bypassed the LAN – the designers failed to appreciate the growing power of the NOS and did not integrate the products properly with it. The lack of integration with the NOS meant that many gateways could not participate in the LAN's administration and security systems. Another problem was often the lack of two-way interaction, so that although PCs on the LAN could access the remote host, it was impossible for users attached just to the host to exploit facilities such as printers on the LAN. Therefore they did not fit well with the growing desire to make all of an organization's IT facilities as widely available to its staff as possible. A further practical problem was that many organizations used old PCs as gateways – some still do. Yet this does not make sense when, as is often the case, the function provided by the gateway is as vital to the business as that provided by the file server. Hence the gateway needs to be as reliable as the server, which is not possible if it is an ageing PC.

A better alternative might appear to be to implement the gateway function on the host itself, which will usually provide a much more resilient and reliable environment than a retired PC, but this still fails to address the issue of integration with the LAN. Given that workstations are already attached to LANs, and their users need access to both LAN and host applications, often also with the ability to move data between them, a better alternative emerged. This is listed as the fourth option above: to implement the gateway function in the LAN as a shared service supported fully by the NOS.

There is another alternative which is really a combination of options (3) and (4): to implement the NOS on the host and perform the integration with the other operating environments there – both Microsoft and Novell have been moving towards this.

6.5.1 NetWare and access to remote host applications

Novell has worked with both DEC and IBM to implement NetWare on hosts and integrate it with the respective host operating environments. In the case of DEC, for example, support for NetWare has been built into DEC's Pathworks NOS, which is a derivative of Microsoft's LAN Manager. This means that on a Novell network, a DEC VAX system appears as another NetWare file server to NetWare client systems. Access to DEC file and print services is obtained via the NetWare software implemented within Pathworks. At the same time, unlike the conventional gateway, workstations attached to the VAX system as Pathworks clients can access NetWare print and file services.

In the case of IBM systems there are differences in the way NetWare integration has been accomplished but the upshot for users is similar. The direction of the IBM/Novell collaboration has been to implement versions of NetWare under each of the principal IBM operating systems; for example, NetWare for AIX allows systems running AIX, which is IBM's version of UNIX, to participate as servers in a NetWare network. AIX can run on IBM mainframes but is most often used on the RS/6000 mid-range system. The next development should be NetWare for MVS. There are also products available from independent networking software vendors to integrate NetWare with other host environments; for example, PrimeService, a subsidiary of Prime Computer Inc., offers Connection NetWare for Sparc, a version of NetWare enabling Sun Sparc stations to offer services to NetWare clients.

Full implementation of NetWare on a host system may not be the most practical solution in the case of UNIX hosts; this is because UNIX in its various forms runs on a wide variety of systems, all of which can be accessed via TCP/IP protocols. On a large network this option would then require numerous versions of NetWare, all of which have to be purchased and maintained. It would then be more cost-effective to go for option (3) above, which is to integrate the communications functions into NetWare.

Novell started moving in this direction with its LAN Workgroup product; this centralizes the configuration and control of TCP/IP communication services by bringing them onto the NetWare server. However, it did not go the whole way because it still required each workstation to process the TCP/IP protocols when it needed to access the remote host system, and also meant that both TCP/IP and IPX protocols ran on the LAN. Novell decided to adopt the Novix product from Firefox to complete the job. This brought all the TCP/IP processing onto a server – it is like the gateway option except that it is properly under the control of the NOS. Workstations only need to run the standard IPX protocol; clients see the UNIX services as options controlled by NetWare. As well as saving workstation resources, this makes communications easier to manage and more secure.

Firefox also has a parallel product called Novos, which enables NetWare servers to provide access to remote hosts via OSI protocols. The latter are not as widespread as TCP/IP at the data transport level but they are supported by some large computer system companies: from early 1994, Novos could be used to provide access from NetWare LANs to ICL, DEC and McDonnell Douglas systems, with possibly others to follow.

The approach to accessing IBM host systems and networks has followed similar lines. As already noted, it is possible to implement NetWare on a host IBM system but again this is not practical on a network comprising a number of IBM systems. In any case, support for direct implementation of NetWare under all the IBM operating environments is a fairly recent phenomenon. Furthermore, users within a NetWare workgroup do not want to hunt around a cluster of IBM computers to locate the files and services they require, even when these computers are masquerading as NetWare servers. Novell therefore has a product called NetWare for SAA, which provides access to an IBM SNA network embracing systems operating within IBM's SAA (systems application architecture). A key benefit is the ability for users to locate the services they require on the IBM system without having to find out where they are, and in fact not even being aware that they are not standard NetWare services. NetWare for SAA does this by supporting NetWare Name Service, a feature of NetWare 3.1 and 4.x that allows users to request a service without specifying on which computer or server it is located. NetWare for SAA does not allow IBM users to access NetWare resources, so in this sense it is a one-way tool. For this reason it is likely to be superseded by products that facilitate tighter integration while still retaining the ease of use for NetWare users that want to access IBM services. NetWare for SAA does, however, allow NetWare file and communication services to be monitored from IBM's Netview network management system – more of this in Chapter 7. There are now alternatives to NetWare for SAA from independent suppliers, such as Eicon Technology.

6.5.2 Microsoft and access to remote host systems

With Microsoft the main thrust for integration with remote host systems came from the client end through the ubiquitous Windows 3. At the same time LAN Manager was more readily ported to run over other operating systems than NetWare, LAN Manager for UNIX being the prime example. Other vendors such as DEC and NCR then ported LAN Manager to run over their own operating systems, while IBM's LAN Server product still ran over OS/2. LAN Server shares a common ancestry with LAN Manager, as explained in Chapter 2, and the two can in principle be accessed from the same clients. Furthermore, Microsoft implemented NetWare shell functions in Windows 3.11. This enables a small workgroup to operate within Windows 3.11 for local peer-to-peer functions such as scheduling tasks and accessing diaries, while enjoying access to large-scale NetWare functions, without having to install a separate NetWare shell in each workstation.

Microsoft has now folded its larger-scale efforts into its NT Server product; this is a combination of LAN Manager and Windows NT, as explained in Chapter 2. Microsoft's thrust is to position NT as a competitor to UNIX – as a portable operating system for both servers and clients, providing in turn a range of communication options to other systems.

☐ SUMMARY

This chapter has described the growing role of the NOS in supporting closer interaction between clients attached to a LAN and systems other than the traditional LAN server. Such systems are typically either servers on remote LANs or other systems controlled by different operating systems. Most commonly, such operating systems are either UNIX or an IBM operating system but could also be one of the other remaining proprietary systems like ICL's VME or DEC's VMS. However, the term proprietary is becoming less applicable to operating systems as they come together through common interfaces defined by organizations such as Posix, and through APIs within the X/Open Spec 1170 standard.

The role of the NOS in another key area of IT, centralized network management and administration, follows in the next chapter. In Chapter 10 we then look at the role of the NOS in emerging high-speed wide area networks based on ATM (asynchronous transfer mode).

7

What is the role of the NOS in network management?

CHAPTER OBJECTIVES:

- To define exactly where the NOS fits into the overall process of managing a complete network, including the devices attached to it – a process embracing security and access control as well as management of change and detection of faults

- To explain why a network needs to be managed

- To determine to what extent the NOS provides the requisite management functions

- To explain how the NOS helps manage client PCs and their applications

- To resolve whether the NOS provides all server management functions

- To clarify how the NOS relates to management of LAN hubs

- To show how the NOS relates to existing large-scale network management systems

- To determine whether the NOS helps manage the WAN

- To detail the role of the NOS in network security

□ 7.1 Introduction

It has often been written that the task of managing a network increases exponentially with the number of users on it. The smallest and simplest network possible, with just two users in one room sharing files between identical applications, hardly needs any managing at all beyond the two computers themselves since the only potential source of network problems lies with a single piece of cable that you can see in its entirety.

However, move to the other end of the scale and management becomes vital, some would say impossible. Consider a network comprising 10 000 nodes distributed across the world with multiple protocols and many different types of link including LANs and long-distance circuits. On such a network many things can and will go wrong. The demands on such a network will constantly change: unless traffic patterns are monitored carefully, bottlenecks will form and response times experienced by many of the users will deteriorate. Such a network is likely to carry sensitive data and provide access to applications vital to the business of the organization. So network security will be important to prevent eavesdropping and unauthorized access to systems and data.

On a 10 000 node network, management at present is rather *ad hoc* – there are various management systems each controlling different elements of the network, and not always cooperating well together. Integration between different elements of the management process is nonetheless improving, and the NOS is playing a growing role as it expands beyond single LANs to provide enterprise-wide services, as with NetWare 4.x and Windows NT Server.

Within individual LANs, the NOS is also expanding its role beyond management of the server to integration with other key LAN devices such as hubs and even power supplies. Before examining the role of the NOS in more detail, let us elucidate the scope of network management as a whole. Firstly, in Section 7.2 we shall define the scope of network management with a review of each of the key functions. Next, in Section 7.3 we shall focus on the various elements of the network that need to be managed, and point out in each case which of the functions defined in Section 7.2 are relevant. Finally, in Section 7.4 we shall examine network management from the point of view of the NOS, describing which elements and functions it embraces, and which require other management systems.

□ 7.2 Functions of network management

Table 7.1 lists the ten key tasks of network management. Some of these functions overlap. This is not so surprising as they are all part of the overall process of ensuring that the network does its job of providing all the services

Table 7.1 The ten key tasks of network management.

1. Performance: maintaining satisfactory response times for users.
2. Security: controlling access to applications and preventing data from being eavesdropped.
3. Network monitoring: to collect data that helps identify potential faults or problems before they occur.
4. Troubleshooting: to fix problems as soon as possible and minimize downtime.
5. Configuration control: to respond to changes such as new applications, moves of users within or between offices, and addition of new users and sites.
6. Network mapping: needed to help with the other aspects of management, especially fault monitoring and configuration control.
7. Inventory management: to keep control over network resources.
8. Network planning: to help anticipate the impact on the network of future changes in the business.
9. Cost accounting: to allocate costs to users or departments according to consumption of network resources, and to keep track of network usage.
10. Fault tolerance/data backup: the aims here are to prevent data being lost when network or system failures occur, and to minimize the impact on applications.

that legitimate users need, while minimizing costs and preventing unauthorized access to information and resources. Day-to-day performance management, for example, requires statistics on traffic patterns which will also be used in network planning. The only difference is that network planning involves assumptions about the impact of potential changes that may never be implemented, while performance management focuses on the here and now.

7.2.1 Performance management

LAN performance hinges on the time taken to access the network, and for the server to respond to a particular request. The main factors that cause performance to deteriorate are increases in network traffic and in use of the server. Management of performance therefore entails monitoring the amount of data traffic on a LAN and the usage of such resources as a database server, keeping a historical record so that trends can be detected and acted upon if necessary. The aim is to maintain adequate levels of performance in the face of evolving applications and often growing numbers of users. On a typical LAN there might be sixteen PCs, a database server and two printers, provided for two primary applications – word processing for the production of standard letters, and the handling of sales orders.

The management system should be able to produce statistics of traffic usage over each day to identify overall the peaks and troughs that may occur at various times. It must be possible to break down the traffic figures to look individually at each user and device on the LAN. As far as the network is concerned, the relevant statistics relate to source–destination pairs, because this identifies the combinations of devices that are making most use of the LAN's capacity, and it may also be important to monitor usage of shared resources. In the example above, the database server might be becoming overloaded or queues for one or both of the printers might become excessive. In the case of the printers, the solution would be obvious but with the file server, information about disk utilization would be needed before it could be decided what action should be taken to maintain performance at an acceptable level.

Possible action needed to maintain or improve performance

Action necessary to respond to network performance statistics includes:

- increasing CPU power and storage capacity of the server;
- increasing the number of servers;
- dividing the LAN into segments to restrict overall traffic levels;
- changing the pattern of usage to avoid peak times;
- moving to a faster network, such as from Ethernet to FDDI, or use of LAN switching to give each user the maximum possible bandwidth;
- tuning the NOS to optimize its performance for the network configuration.

7.2.2 Security

The importance of security has increased rapidly as LANs have been utilized for serious applications. Large LANs with powerful servers now process applications that used to require huge water-cooled mainframe computers. Some therefore require levels of security equivalent to that of a mainframe environment in order to protect information from accidental or malicious destruction, and from unauthorized access. Even small businesses are increasingly relying on LANs for critical applications so some security may be needed, although not to the same degree as for large organizations.

The main threats to LAN security are:

- access by legitimate users to data they are not authorized to see;
- electronic eavesdropping, which could be by anyone within close range, even outside the premises;
- hacking into the network from the public telephone network, although this is only possible when dial-up access is allowed;
- tapping directly into the network to intercept or tamper with messages in transmission;
- computer viruses.

Traditionally, computer operating systems have provided the first line of protection against a variety of threats to security or integrity of data. Some aspects of protection, such as control over access to the data and applications residing in the main computer system, have often been aided by additional security products. On LANs this responsibility has been transferred to the network operating system (NOS), as this controls access to servers. Leading NOSs such as NetWare and LAN Manager now provide reasonably sophisticated methods of controlling access to information and resources on the LAN, as will be explained further in Section 7.4. However, there are products offered to enhance the security provided by the NOS, or to meet specialized needs.

7.2.3 Monitoring faults

There are two objectives to this process:

(1) to detect any faults that either have happened or are about to happen;
(2) to restrict the impact of such faults, for example by switching the network to an alternative route to bypass one that has failed. This is partly a matter of designing the network correctly in the first place, in such a way that it avoids single points of failure. Under this category come data backup procedures and uninterruptible power supplies.

These processes apply not just to the network itself but also to the computers attached to it. Users are not generally interested in where a fault lies but they do want it resolved as quickly as possible. Responsibility for the entire fault management application is beyond the scope of network management systems; although they can detect some, it may require more than one management product to cover all potential faults over the network. The same is true for the process of bypassing faults, which enables networks to 'heal' themselves.

Within a LAN there are a variety of faults that can occur in the cable, servers, PCs, other attached devices such as printers, and the network interface cards (NICs) linking devices to the network. LAN management systems should be able to detect a cabling fault but probably will be unable to locate it precisely. In larger networks it may not be immediately obvious where such a fault is located, since much of the cable is concealed under floors or behind walls. In these situations a LAN analyser is required, and these are usually attached to the network for troubleshooting when faults occur – they are too expensive to be permanently attached to every LAN.

Analysers are also used to locate higher-level protocol errors that may be caused by data corruption or by errors in communication software. Network management systems may initially detect the presence of such faults but are usually unable to pinpoint them precisely or resolve them.

7.2.4 Troubleshooting

While the objective of fault monitoring is to maximize the mean time between failure (MTBF), troubleshooting aims to reduce the mean time to repair (MTTR). Troubleshooting has until recently been beyond the realm of ordinary network management systems, requiring dedicated – and expensive – equipment such as protocol analysers. However, growing integration between different network management systems and moves towards more structured cabling layouts are making it easier to implement at least some troubleshooting functions within standard network management systems. The aim is, having identified the broad nature of a problem, to home in on it, pinpointing its precise location and identifying its exact cause so that remedial action can be taken. Such action may involve fixing the fault completely, as would usually have to be done in the case of a software or protocol error, or reconfiguring the network to bypass it. The latter might be done in the case of a cabling break that cannot be repaired readily or sufficiently quickly.

Problems can occur at any level of communication, including cable breaks in layer one and protocol coding errors in any of the higher layers. Tools such as LAN monitors and protocol analysers used for monitoring therefore need to be capable of testing for error conditions right through the protocol stack. At the physical level, for example, analysers based on dedicated hardware (rather than software running on a standard computer) can perform time domain reflectometry (TDR) tests which indicate whether a particular circuit is open or shut. However, to pinpoint the exact location of cabling faults within a particular circuit that links two devices, even more specialized equipment may be needed: typically this would be a specialist TDR tester, in combination with an oscilloscope.

Detailed discussion of such tests is beyond the scope of this book but it should be noted that the network management process has involved a hierarchy of equipment, although much of it is unnecessary for smaller sites. A recent trend has been to rationalize the entire management process by implementing the disparate functions of management, including some troubleshooting, within a single coherent management platform (see Section 7.5).

Note also that the equipment needed to analyse networks for troubleshooting can also be used in a proactive monitoring capacity in permanent operation, gathering information that will help diagnose impending faults before they affect the network. This is a costly option as it involves attaching analysers or probes permanently to each LAN segment, whereas in the troubleshooting capacity perhaps one or two analysers could meet the demands of a complete enterprise spanning many sites. However, as just indicated, troubleshooting facilities are slowly being implemented within the management systems of individual networking components and so will be increasingly widely used.

Given that at present a variety of expensive equipment is still needed to cater for all troubleshooting possibilities, it may be more practical for most smaller organizations and even some large ones to engage a networking specialist to tackle problems, or sign an on-going maintenance contract with such a company. Another alternative, appealing increasingly to medium-sized and large organizations, is to outsource the whole network, the major motive being to avoid the headaches of troubleshooting.

7.2.5 Configuration control

Like some other aspects of network management, the facilities required for configuration control can be viewed in terms of the seven-layer OSI model. The overall need is to be able to reconfigure the network at various levels when changes are made. Such potential changes include the addition or removal of devices from the network, the registration of new users and the enhancement of the network, for example to increase the capacity of particular links.

A general requirement when networks are reconfigured is not just to make any updates to tables and databases that are needed for the network to function properly, but also to revise any management system so that correct information is available to administrators; for example, an existing map of the network needs to be updated. Network maps are described in the next section.

In the physical layer, the requirement is to be able to connect or disconnect devices as easily as possible. This used to be a manual procedure involving patch panels, and still is in many cases. Following the development of manageable hubs, connections can now be effected from a management terminal without manual action.

In network layer three, configuration control must ensure that major structural changes to the network are implemented correctly; typically this might be the addition, removal or relocation of a LAN workgroup. Routers handling the interconnection then need their tables updated accordingly.

In higher OSI layers, tables also need to be updated if users are added to or removed from the network. In some cases the applications themselves, for example security tables or a network mapping database, may need to be updated. Another example is an electronic mail system, to which new user names are to be added; directories of users must also be updated.

7.2.6 Network mapping

This type of mapping serves the other network management functions rather than being an end in itself. Although such a map may look pretty, it serves no useful purpose unless it helps in managing configurations, locating faults and possibly some other functions.

There are two types of map: geographical and topological. The former provides a geographical map of the network and is clearly not needed on single LANs which by their nature are contained within a small area. However, on large national or global networks of interconnected LANs, a geographical map provides a useful overview of network activity; different colours can be used to identify a variety of conditions on the circuits and devices. The use of graphical windowing systems can also simplify an administrator's task of obtaining current or historical statistics relating to components or links shown on the map.

A topological map shows the devices and links of a network in relation to each other, without being precise about their correct geographical positions, and is clearly the most useful sort of map for small networks. However, at the physical cabling level, geographical maps come into their own again, as it is obviously useful to know exactly where each cable is located for maintenance purposes.

For intermediate networks, some combination of the geographical and topological approaches may be needed. This could be similar to maps of metropolitan underground trains, where the primary need is to show how each line and station relates to each other and to the overall network, but where it is also necessary for the map to bear at least a rough resemblance to geographical reality.

On large networks, a hierarchy of maps is usually provided, so administrators can obtain a basic overview map and then home in on increasingly large-scale maps to obtain greater detail of current network performance in particular areas. Typically, the small-scale overview maps of the whole network might be largely geographical, while the large-scale local maps would be more topological.

7.2.7 Inventory management

This is important even for small LANs but becomes particularly significant on larger networks where it is harder to keep track of what items are attached to the network. Inventory management is closely related to configuration management and also network mapping, because on a large network a crude list of contents is fairly useless unless it is related to locations, departments and individual users. The process can help resolve problems, because if a user phones a help desk to report a fault, support personnel can immediately obtain information about the hardware and software that user has. This information may be linked to the network map showing where that user is in relation to other systems.

7.2.8 Network planning

This is the long-range function of the network management process; it is not covered specifically by standard network management systems, although there are software tools to assist with the task of longer-term planning. Whereas conventional network management is concerned with ensuring that the network serves its users well on a day-to-day basis, planning is about making sure it will still do so in the more distant future.

There are various software modelling tools available that allow the effects of changes to the network to be mimicked without those changes actually being made. There are also consultancies available that can help assess the impact of future changes and use such tools on your behalf.

On larger networks spanning many LANs, another option which has been applied successfully by some organizations is to pilot new applications on small portions of the network before extending them to all LANs; for example, a bank might want to introduce a new customer service that requires the implementation of additional application software in each branch. The new application would almost certainly increase overall network traffic as it would probably require access to centrally held data. It could be tried out in just a few branches initially, to gain some idea of its likely impact when extended to the entire network of perhaps 3000 branches. This may help anticipate future problems and decide how the computer network should be extended in preparation for the new application.

7.2.9 Cost accounting

This is a feature that comes into its own only on large networks spanning different departments. In some large organizations, each department is a cost centre that has to submit annual financial results almost like an independent company; for this to happen, costs have to be apportioned to each department on as fair a basis as possible. The network is a resource that costs money, and can be subdivided in a similar way.

The organization first has to calculate how much the network as a whole costs per year, by adding the annual telecommunications bill to money spent on new equipment and software licences, plus the depreciation of existing hardware. The cost of running the network also needs to be added in. Each department can then be metered for use of network resources, and costs allocated on a *pro rata* basis. The exact basis for calculation will vary from company to company but, whatever method is used, there needs to be some form of network management system to measure usage. Network management systems often collect detailed traffic statistics anyway, so cost accounting is a natural extension of this function. Another benefit is that it enables the productivity of individuals and groups of users to be compared with the network costs they incur.

7.2.10 Fault tolerance/data backup

Network resilience and backup are functions of the network management process although not embraced by any single product. There are two closely related aims: the first is to minimize the impact of faults on the overall function of the network, so that users can continue to obtain access to resources and data; then, given that faults inevitably will occur, the second is to minimize critical data being lost or corrupted as a result.

In Section 7.4 we shall see that the NOS has a role to play in both of these objectives. However, fault tolerance also relies on good network design, which ideally should avoid single points of failure and ensure that the impact of faults, when they do occur, is localized and that the overall network can recover as quickly as possible.

Resilience is closely related to security, as both have the aim of preventing unforeseen events destroying data or preventing the network from delivering its usual services. As with security, there are varying levels of resilience according to how much you are prepared to spend. We shall now briefly survey some of the options.

1. *Total redundancy*

This entails duplicating all key components of a network such as routers and file servers, and is a very expensive option, applicable mainly on LANs running applications critical to the business, of the sort previously run on centralized host computers. In the case of a LAN internet, each LAN segment has a duplicate router so that if one fails the other takes over. The file server and all its components are mirrored: one component is designated the master and the other shadows it, duplicating all its operations; if the master fails, the slave is ready to take over almost instantly. Note, however, that the master and slave servers need to be linked by a separate connection running about ten times faster than the LAN they are serving; this is necessary to keep the servers synchronized, so avoiding loss of data during the period of change over from master to slave if a failure does occur.

2. *Duplicating disk drives*

The server's disk drive, being an electro-mechanical device with moving parts, is more likely to fail than the server's central processing unit. Therefore a high degree of resilience can be achieved by having duplicated disk drives, without mirroring the complete server. There are two possibilities: either duplexed drives, in which two drives share a single drive controller; or mirrored drives, in which the controller is duplicated as well as the drives. The second option costs more but protects against failure of the disk drive controller as well as the drives themselves.

A more sophisticated technology called RAID (redundant array of independent disks) is increasingly being used on servers for more critical applications. RAID technology was developed initially to improve performance and reduce costs by using a number of small disks rather than a single large one. This allows less expensive disk drives to be used and can deliver more data to the main processor in a given time by providing simultaneous access to multiple drives. However, RAID has appealed to users more for the protection it provides against failure of single disks than for the greater performance at a given price. By using multiple disks, RAID technology enables high performance to be combined with resilience but there are still some problems with bottlenecks for applications involving large numbers of disk writes.

3. Using lower-cost storage media for backup

Even duplicating disk drives is too costly an option for most LANs, being only really required where the applications are so important for the business that the network has to be fully operational virtually all the time, but it is important on all LANs to ensure that data is protected against faults, even if the recovery process requires the network to be switched off for some time. In such cases it makes sense to use a storage medium that provides sufficient capacity even though speed of access is sacrificed for price. The actual choice depends largely on the capacity required. There are three main options available:

(a) 1/4 inch tape, providing capacities up to around 500 Mbytes. This is a cost-effective option for small to medium-sized networks typically with up to about 25 users, although the actual number depends on the applications. The tapes are typically inserted into a unit that attaches to disk drives via SCSIs (small computer systems interface). The units are often located inside a PC or server.

(b) DAT (digital audio tape). This provides capacities up to around 4 Gbytes per tape cartridge, although this can be increased to 8 Gbytes with the aid of data compression techniques. Given that DAT systems are also fast and relatively inexpensive, with the ability to access a file on the tape in less than a minute, it is emerging as the preferred method for backing up data on larger networks. Aided by appropriate backup software, DAT systems can be used for unattended operation, allowing backups to be made over-night or at other times when the network is not being used.

(c) Video-8 technology. This is based on the 8-track 8 mm tape cartridges used in video camcorders and provides capacities up to around 5 Gbytes of raw data on a single cartridge, although up to 10 Gbytes can be achieved with data compression. Like DAT, it can be used for unattended backup.

DAT devices were about 50 per cent cheaper than Video-8 ones at the time of writing (1994), and also provide faster access to data; therefore they appear to afford the best solution for larger networks. However Video-8 technology might be preferred by existing users who already have libraries of Video-8 cartridges and want to continue with the technology to avoid having to copy files across to new media. The technology also offers significantly higher potential storage capacity on each cartridge because the tapes are bigger. In fact, both Video-8 and DAT use similar techniques for storing data, based on helical scan recording in which data is written across the tape in diagonal stripes, but DAT technology has been better exploited so far.

However, more important than the choice of backup device is the quality of the software used to exploit it. This is where the NOS comes in, to help manage the process of backing up data and ensure that files can readily be found afterwards.

4. Using uninterruptible power supplies (UPS)

Leading NOSs now include support for attachment of UPSs to file servers and increasingly to workstations as well. Where UPSs are installed, support in the NOS helps ensure that networks and the systems attached to them shut down smoothly in the event of power failures and that data is backed up where necessary.

The decision by NOS vendors to support UPSs followed the growing use of such systems on LANs, initially to back up servers and large printers. Centralized host computer systems, such as IBM mainframes, have long been protected against spikes (sudden surges in power), complete blackouts and also brownouts (reductions in power), by uninterruptible power supplies and in some cases by standby generators.

Now that LANs run critical applications for a growing number of businesses, there is a similar need to protect them against power failure as well. Yet many LANs are not protected by a UPS and therefore all processing would cease in the event of a power failure, with the added risk of serious data corruption during more minor brownouts. In many cases it takes a lengthy power cut to make users aware that investment in a UPS, which is relatively modest compared with the overall cost of a LAN, is well worth making. The UPS is often seen as an optional extra but, for any business where main activities cease when the LAN is not available, it should be deemed essential.

Even where a UPS has been installed, protection is often not adequate. A mistake sometimes made is to assume that it is sufficient just to protect the server. However, LANs differ from centralized systems in that a substantial amount of processing takes place on desktop PCs or workstations. Therefore to ensure that the network can be closed down smoothly without any loss of data in the event of a prolonged power cut, it is important that PCs are protected by a UPS as well as the server.

What sort of UPS solutions are available?

It is now possible to purchase small UPSs about the size of a single-volume dictionary to protect individual PCs; these can conveniently sit under each desktop, with the server protected by a larger UPS. Alternatively, all computing devices attached to the LAN, including PCs, servers and printers, can be protected by a single UPS. In this case the UPS obviously needs to be bigger and the electricity cabling needs to be structured either in a ring or so that it fans out from the UPS to each device. Such an arrangement is worth considering when installing new LANs from scratch, particularly if the office is being rewired at the same time; electrical cabling can then be laid in a structured way, as for the data and telephone cabling, making it easy to manage in future. If the UPS has been chosen correctly, the network can be expanded easily without requiring additional investment in power supply equipment. An existing UPS can be more readily expanded, or even replaced, if all mains cabling fans back to a central equipment closet along with the data cabling. However, this arrangement may be too expensive and impractical for small networks, in which case smaller standalone UPSs can be used. It may not be necessary to fit a UPS to every device. For example, PCs might possibly be arranged in pairs, all fed off a single UPS.

Factors to consider when choosing a UPS

The first decision is whether to specify a central UPS feeding all devices or distributed UPSs for every PC, or a combination of the two. The size of the UPS should then be selected. Suppliers can advise you of the precise technical specifications but a basic consideration is how long you want the network to be kept running in the event of a complete power failure. UPS systems rely on rechargeable batteries to provide power but they vary greatly in their capacity – a typical office UPS provides about 1500 VA, and this would be capable of sustaining a network of about 8 PCs, a printer and a server for about 20 minutes. But UPSs are typically rated by power capacity rather than by the number of devices they can handle. Calculations of UPS size therefore need to take account of the power input requirements of the devices on the network as well as the length of time you want to have guaranteed operation of the network in the event of a power failure.

Another important point to consider is support of the UPS for network management facilities. For most networks it is not cost-effective to provide sophisticated standby generators to cope with indefinite power failures, except in parts of the world where long power cuts are a regular occurrence. Instead, the UPS usually provides protection against short power outages or brownouts and facilitates an orderly shutdown of the network in the event of a sustained power cut. Key data can be backed up and applications left in a state from which they can recover smoothly when power is restored. To do this successfully, it is necessary to know immediately that a power failure has occurred. Some UPSs support management facilities provided by NOSs such as NetWare.

UPS systems can also be distinguished according to whether they operate offline or online. Offline UPSs only come into action when there is a power failure; normally they simply channel the raw alternating current (AC) supply through to the computers, sometimes through a filter to smooth out minor fluctuations. Should there be a power failure, they switch to the batteries, which provide a high-quality uniform AC supply, although this can lead to a damaging stutter in supply at the moment of cutover to the batteries. Online UPS systems, on the other hand, provide a continuous AC supply whether or not there is a power cut, so that there is no hitch at the point when a failure occurs. Power is always supplied from the battery, which shields the computer it is serving from fluctuations in the mains supply.

For larger networks, a standby generator may be worth considering, ensuring non-stop operation of the network in the event of power failure. In this case a UPS is still necessary, both to generate a clean supply of electricity from the mains and to ensure a smooth cutover to the generator after a power failure.

Other aspects of fault tolerance

The best NOSs also provide a variety of other techniques that help a network tolerate faults and recover from them. General features are summarized in Section 7.4, while more detail about the resilient features of individual NOSs can be found under the relevant product descriptions in Chapters 2 and 3.

□ 7.3 What elements of a network need to be managed?

Table 7.2 lists the principal components of a network that need managing, and also indicates the OSI layers in which the required management information is transmitted. Note that the whole physical LAN, which embraces NIC (network interface card), cabling and wiring concentrator (if there is one), requires managing only in layers one and two.

The OSI layers from which management information is required, as cited in Table 7.2, are the same as those in which the product operates. This is because networking systems only need managing at the levels at which they operate. A management system can thus be built up in logical layers, each of which relates to some but not all of the network's components. The network management system then has a logical structure that enables it to dovetail neatly with the relevant components of the network.

Such is the theory, although in practice many vendors originally developed their own management systems applicable only to their own products,

Table 7.2 Principal components of a network that need managing.

Component	OSI layers
NIC (network interface card)	1–2
Cabling	1
Wiring concentrator	1
Intelligent hub	1–3
Router	1–3
Bridge	1–2
Workstation/PC	3–7
Printer	3–7
Server	3–7
Modem	1–2
Gateway	1–7
Uninterruptible power supply (UPS)	1

particularly over the wide area. Over the LAN, however, there has been growing consensus behind the SNMP (simple network management protocol) and
this is now supported by virtually all vendors of such LAN components as
bridges, routers and NICs (network interface cards).

SNMP was originally confined to the LAN but with the proliferation of
LAN internets and growing demand for common standards to address end-to-
end network management, it has been extended to wide area devices. It has
become possible therefore to manage WAN devices as well as LANs from a
single management system. Nevertheless there is some way to go before this
can be done with the full range of sophisticated functions required for managing
large networks.

The role of standards, especially SNMP, will be discussed in more detail
in Section 7.5.

□ 7.4   Defining the role of the NOS in the larger network management picture

Originally the managerial role of operating systems was confined to computer
systems rather than networks but that was before a significant number of
networks existed. As soon as operating systems became distributed across two
or more machines, inevitably they had to become involved in the resulting
processes of communication and interaction. With the advent of NOSs, this role
extended to full management of communications within the LAN. Also, with
the growth of LAN internets, NOSs such as NetWare 4.x have been extending
their range into the WAN.

However, there is still some confusion over the demarcation between the
NOS and existing management systems controlling devices on the LAN other
than servers and printers, such as hubs and routers. For this reason some NOS
vendors have struck partnerships with key suppliers of other LAN components
to establish common management frameworks. A good example of such collaboration is the alliance between Novell and one of the main hub vendors, Syn-
Optics, in which a major focus is the common management of the two
companies' respective products. Microsoft is also working with a number of
vendors to enable its management system, called Hermes, to interoperate with
systems controlling other parts of the network. Hermes is designed to control
servers and desktop systems, providing a key part of the overall management
jigsaw; it can either act as an underling to an overall umbrella management
system such as IBM's Netview, or operate as a peer on an equal basis with other
element managers in a distributed arrangement. The latter approach is
becoming more prevalent as organizations lose faith in the idea of ubiquitous
umbrella managers. The NOS thus retains the role of traditional operating
systems in controlling the computers on which it operates – this is primarily

LAN servers but also increasingly includes client workstations. In order to see the NOS's role in network management more clearly, we shall examine its relationship with the functions defined in Section 7.2, and the elements listed in Section 7.3.

7.4.1 Which network management functions come under the NOS's ambit?

Some NOSs provide far more network management functions than others. At the bottom end, some of the low-cost peer-to-peer NOSs, for example, provide only rudimentary facilities for controlling access to data, and no ability to monitor devices other than servers and clients. At the top end of the spectrum, NOSs such as NetWare 4.x designed for enterprise-wide networks now provide many network management facilities themselves, coupled with the ability to feed information to other management systems. In principle, the NOS in its role of controlling the operation of a LAN should be able to manage all aspects of it, and then integrate with any other umbrella systems overseeing the whole enterprise-wide network, if there is one. In practice, though, even the NOSs that offer greatest support for network management, such as NetWare, require the assistance of additional products to satisfy at least some network management requirements – for network management is a broad brush, encompassing a wide range of functions, only some of which will be applicable in most real networks.

Table 7.1 listed the ten key functions of network management. Now we shall indicate to what extent these are supported by NOSs of different types for each of the network elements listed in Table 7.2. Note however that for low-cost peer-to-peer NOSs, not all of these functions are particularly relevant.

1. *Performance*
Top-end NOSs such as NetWare and LAN Manager provide good facilities for monitoring the performance of the server; for example, they give statistics on disk utilization which enables impending bottlenecks here to be overcome before they happen, either by installing larger disks or compressing the data so that it requires less storage. Many NOSs also provide some facilities for monitoring disk, CPU and memory utilization on clients, which can help tune the system and change the proportion of resources allocated to particular applications.

The other important realm of network management for the NOS is the printer. The NOS is responsible for controlling access to printers, managing print queues and responding to status information coming back from the printers. The aim is to ensure that printers, as shared resources, are utilized as efficiently as possible so that users get output printed as quickly as possible. However, NOSs are generally unable to help much with the performance of other devices on the LAN such as hubs and bridges, although leading NOS vendors are trying to rectify this by cooperating with relevant vendors in the field; for example, it is now possible to manage SynOptics hubs from Novell's NetWare Management System (NMS) using the IPX protocol.

Banyan's Vines provides an exception to the rule that the NOS's role in performance is confined to servers and local LAN segments. This is not surprising as Vines has long been positioned as an enterprise-wide NOS providing the messaging and directory services needed to support dispersed workgroups and to give widespread access to data. On the performance front, Vines not only provides the usual statistics to help fine tune the server but also information to help speed up the network as a whole. Facilities are available to view performance across multiple LANs, enabling loads to be balanced to avoid bottlenecks and share processing between servers as efficiently as possible.

Other NOSs such as NetWare 4.x and Windows NT Server are beginning to offer similar facilities as they are also pitched at multiple server networks.

2. *Security*

No NOS can cover all aspects of security, because some are a matter of how the network is configured and others involve controls at the human or physical level. For example, the risk of unauthorized access to critical LAN data can be reduced by keeping main file servers in secure areas. The potential for electronic eavesdropping can be virtually eliminated by using fibre rather than copper cable and opportunities for invasion by viruses can be reduced by using diskless workstations that do not allow software to enter the network via floppy disks. Nevertheless the NOS does have a key role in guarding the server against unauthorized access to data. Even the least sophisticated NOSs provide some help with this through password controls; for example, Mainlan from the Sage Group allows data on all designated servers to be protected by passwords. At the other end of the scale, NetWare 3.11 and NetWare 4.x provide four built-in layers of security to suit different requirements: authentication, authorization, accounting and administration. These are described in more detail in Chapter 2 Section 2.2.4.

NT Server is also well provided with security features, including methods to improve standard password protection; for example, users can be prevented from logging on at times when they are not likely to need to, such as at weekends and at night. Individual accounts can be set to expire at certain times and users can be forced to change their passwords at periodic intervals to minimize the risk of potential hackers getting to know them. Slightly more subtle is the minimum password age, which prevents users from changing their passwords until a specified time has elapsed. This was introduced in an attempt to prevent what became quite a common habit – of switching frequently between two favourite passwords to circumvent the maximum password age restriction, so that users just had two passwords to remember.

Until the release of NetWare 4.x, Microsoft also enjoyed an advantage over Novell in terms of security management through its support of centralized domains; this enables logon, validation of access and tracking of network usage to be controlled centrally for a particular group of servers. Servers within a domain share a common database holding details of user and group accounts, all managed by a central server called the domain controller. An administrator can then determine which users are logged on at any time by submitting a query to this domain controller.

3. *Monitoring faults*

Here again the NOS can only fill part of the picture, chiefly being concerned with faults within the server or applications running on it and those on printers attached to the LAN. Separate products are usually required to monitor faults on other elements such as bridges, cable and also to some extent client work-stations, although Novell's NMS has extended its reach to these elements. However, not all NetWare sites use SMS and typically the NOS may feed information about the server to enterprise-wide management systems that provide a full view of the network, enabling faults to be detected and isolated at a higher level. The NOS's role here is to inform the network supervisor of impending problems so that hopefully they can be remedied with little or no impact on users. It does this by forwarding alerts to a network management station. An alert is the network management jargon for a message informing a management station that some preset threshold has been exceeded; for example, an alert could be triggered if a server disk became more than 95 per cent full of data.

Another network management term is 'agent'. This is software responsible for monitoring a particular device and passing alerts as and when they are generated, as well as other less urgent information, to a central network management station or application. In some cases the NOS provides the agent that monitors the devices and services under control of the NOS. This would always include servers and network printers but could also be extended to other devices, in particular workstations. Examples of typical alerts generated by a NOS as a management agent are:

- printer out of paper;
- no available memory for allocation to a server application or resource;
- disk volume full or nearly full (disk volume is defined in Appendix 9);
- error occurred in writing directory tables to disk.

Note that fault monitoring overlaps considerably with performance management. Alerts could be triggered by events that threaten to reduce the responsiveness of the network rather than bring it down altogether. An example would be the alert 'cache buffers are low', meaning that applications making heavy use of the server's disk would be slowed down because read/write operations have to go straight to the disk drive, rather than via intermediate storage in solid-state memory.

Also note that leading NOSs will relay alerts initiated by other components on the LAN onto network management systems; for example, NetWare 3.1 will pass alerts generated by a token ring LAN onto an IBM NetView management system. Such alerts include faults with the physical cable, which the NOS itself is unable to detect directly.

In the case of NetWare in particular, and also to some extent NT Server, there are various third-party products that either complement or replace facilities provided by the NOS itself, or more often a combination of both. One example worth mentioning, owing to its scope and maturity, is LANAlert from the US firm Network Computing Inc., available in the UK from Peapod Distribution Ltd. For NetWare LANs, this provides facilities, beyond those available from Novell, for anticipating faults before they occur. It also allows the process of monitoring a large network to be delegated to local departments or workgroups, including a paging facility that permits alerts to be transmitted to administrators when they are offsite. Yet perhaps the strongest feature is that it brings workstations fully into the picture through an option called LAN Exam; this allows alerts to be generated by workstations as well as servers and then transmitted to a central management station located either centrally, or within the local LAN to which the workstations are attached.

Note, however, that in NetWare 4.x, Novell has negated some of the advantages of products like LANAlert by completely rewriting its network monitoring facilities. Among new functions available is the ability to delegate monitoring of an enterprise network to local areas or departments. However, firms such as Network Computing will continue to play an important role in adding value to Novell's increasingly solid network management portfolio and meeting specialized requirements that cannot be economically addressed by a large company.

The monitoring facilities of low-cost NOSs are restricted to basic printer and server conditions, such as a printer being out of paper or a disk being nearly full.

4. *Troubleshooting*

NOSs are beginning to provide some troubleshooting facilities; they also provide information that can be garnered by other dedicated LAN monitors and analysers. Also, the leading NOSs are increasingly capable of detecting and locating faults that previously might have required active troubleshooting.

5. *Configuration control*

The role of the NOS here is to allow users to be added and removed from LANs as easily as possible, providing a base for other aspects of network management, particularly security, cost accounting and inventory management. The NOS needs to know when users are added and removed from the servers it is responsible for, so that it can control access to the LAN's resources and in some cases enable usage to be measured.

A key recent development is the ability to register users just once and specify which servers they are allowed to access. Previously, users had to be registered on all servers they were allowed to use, which was time consuming on a large network because it meant that new users' names, passwords and other related information, such as which workgroups they belonged to, had to be keyed into each server. Now such information needs to be entered just once, and the NOS then ensures that it is propagated to all other servers to which that user is allowed access. LANtastic 5.0, for example, allows user accounts on one server to be shared with others; all accounts can thus be stored on one server, making them easier to maintain.

NOSs do not in general support configuration of other LAN devices that need to be updated when new users are added or removed, such as routers, hubs and bridges. Normally these devices need to be configured separately, though there are a few exceptions. One is when the NOS itself provides the bridging or routing functions, as described in Chapter 6; another is when the hub is implemented in card form in the server. In the latter case, the hub is configured automatically whenever changes are made to the NOS's configuration tables; for NetWare LANs, for example, Novell's hub management interface (HMI) is available, which allows hub cards to be managed and configured from NetWare and provides a standard for hub makers to build hub cards for NetWare servers.

Banyan's Vines is worth consideration here, in its capacity as a 'network glue' linking different NOS environments together, which is described more fully in Chapter 5. In September 1992 Banyan launched a new product series called Enterprise Network Services (ENS), and the first member of that family, ENS for NetWare. This is described in Chapter 2. Of note here is that it enables a large network of multiple NetWare servers to be configured from a single point, even if some are on different releases of NetWare from others. From a single station, users can be added or removed from any server, security privileges can be changed, and rights to access file and print services for both individual users and whole workgroups can be amended. These can also all be done within NetWare 4.x but only if all servers on the network run NetWare 4.x.

6. *Network mapping*

This is a function of high-level network management systems rather than the NOS, because it requires information from all elements of the network. The NOS may, however, have a role as a management agent feeding status information about servers, printers and perhaps workstations to a central management system. For example if a printer fails, the NOS would detect this and forward an alert to the management system, so enabling the management system to change the colour of the printer on a map to red to indicate that it was not working. Then, by clicking on the red printer symbol on the map, network administrators might be able to find out what was wrong with the printer, again using information conveyed by the NOS. The printer could just be out of paper or have developed a more serious problem requiring a maintenance visit.

Although NOSs do not yet support detailed mapping directly, there are some NOS applications that do; for example, Network Computing Inc.'s LAN Exam provides a graphical representation of NetWare LANs.

7. *Inventory management*

This is also a function of dedicated management systems, with the NOS in a supporting role; it requires an overall view of the network embracing both hardware components and the software running in each workstation. It has to be said that total inventory management is rarely if ever achieved at present, because network management systems are in general unable to obtain detailed information about applications running in PCs, for example. Management products are available that facilitate centralized distribution and administration of applications software; these can tell a help desk, for instance, which version of a product a particular user has, making it easier to sort out problems.

Such products are rarely integrated into overall management systems, so although the information is available it is hard to bring it all together into coherent inventory reports. One aspect of inventory management that is well catered for, particularly in the NetWare world, is administration of disks and files across both servers and clients. The product for NetWare networks that stands out here is XTreeNet from the US XTree Company, a subsidiary of Executive Information Systems. This is a self-contained system providing powerful facilities for monitoring and controlling use of disk drives, not just on servers but also clients across a NetWare network, although in the version available in late 1993 it was restricted to 26 network drives. An administrator can obtain reports on the arrangement of disk volumes and directories on any of the 26 disk drives, whether local or remote, and then list files and their contents. It is also possible to move files between systems, and delete them, although indiscriminate use of this facility could soon lead to problems.

8. *Network planning*

This is really an extension of the network management process, involving anticipation of future demands rather than day-to-day fire fighting. Some network management systems provide tools to help assess the impact of changes to the network, such as the addition of new users, complete workgroups or even whole sites, and also the implementation of new applications.

The role of the NOS is really restricted to short-term planning, in that it can alert supervisors when disks are nearly full or queues for a particular printer are excessively long. However, there is nothing to stop NOS applications, such as NetWare NLMs, being developed that provide planning functions: these could simulate the impact on a LAN and its resources of an increase in traffic, or new usage patterns.

9. *Cost accounting*

Some network management systems provide facilities that allow subsidiary companies, departments, workgroups or even, if required, individual users, to be charged for use of the network. The role of the NOS depends on the level of chargeback and on how it is defined; for example, if each local workgroup is to be charged for use of the WAN, then the NOS is unlikely to be involved, although this is changing as NOSs such as NetWare 4.x offer more sophisticated wide area services.

Within each LAN, however, the NOS has the potential to provide all necessary accounting information, in particular the use of printing facilities and file services. Furthermore, where the NOS is in control of communications, it can also charge for use of those, although it may be unable to allocate costs accurately unless it knows which routes will be taken to access remote services. If some simple formula is adopted for accessing remote services, the NOS can then provide a complete charging service for users on the workgroup.

Leading NOSs provide quite sophisticated accounting methods based on various aspects of server usage. A typical NOS might support some or all of the following charging mechanisms:

- by length of time connected to server
- by number of data blocks written and/or read to disk
- by amount of disk storage used
- by utilization of the server's CPU
- by number of requests received for network services.

Information gained from these parameters can be used in several ways. Users can be charged individually but more often they would be given limits on their consumption of network resources. The information also allows an audit to be kept of overall system activity, which can help with other aspects of network management such as forward network planning and security.

10. *Fault tolerance/data backup*

As explained in Section 7.2, fault tolerance and data backup are bracketed together because they both aim to protect critical data and applications from being lost or corrupted in the event of hardware, software or cabling failures. However, technically they are two different areas in both of which the NOS plays a prominent part.

(a) *Fault tolerance.* The NOS can provide facilities to ensure that server hardware failures do not cause data to be lost and to minimize the impact on the network's ability to deliver services to users. There are various options, ranging from disk drive duplexing to complete mirroring of the server, the latter being the most expensive and only cost-justifiable for critical applications, and not supported by most NOSs in any case. Novell introduced support for mirrored servers in its NetWare SFT (system fault tolerant) version 3.11. The various hardware options for protection against faults are described in Section 7.2, while the facilities provided by individual NOSs are indicated within the various NOS product descriptions in Chapters 2 and 3.

Note that some aspects of fault tolerance cannot be covered by the NOS. Protection against faults on the cable, or to components outside the NOS's realm, such as bridges or routers, can only be achieved by suitable network configuration. Some LAN types, such as token ring and FDDI, have some in-built protection against cable breaks (see Appendix 5 for a description of these LANs).

If complete protection is required against all network components so that there is no single point of failure, the only sure option is to duplicate all hardware, not just the server; for example, if it is desired to ensure that a LAN segment can immediately access remote services even if the router used to attach it to the relevant wide area links fails, it is necessary to have a second router on standby.

Protection against software failures is quite another matter and here there are no Utopian answers. The NOS can help to some extent by making it difficult for network applications to cause the core operating system to crash but it can do nothing to stop the applications themselves failing if they have bugs in them. Relevant in this context is Novell's move in NetWare 4.x to allow NLMs to run in the protected mode of the Intel processor. This is discussed in Chapter 2, Section 2.2.4, the main point being that it is now possible to prevent the core NetWare operating system from failing and perhaps corrupting data as a result of badly designed NLMs. A third area of resilience involves protection against power failures or fluctuations. The role of the NOS here is to monitor UPSs (uninterruptible power supplies) to ensure that networks are shut down smoothly when there is a power failure. The use of UPSs is described in Section 7.2.

(b) *Data backup.*   Some of the systems available for backing up data on LANs have already been described in Section 7.2. The role of the NOS is to support the backup process and in some cases to automate it. It is important to choose backup systems, typically one of the tape units described in Section 7.2, that are compatible with the NOS; in the case of NetWare, most systems are compatible.

□ 7.5   What standards are there for network management and how does the NOS support them?

SNMP (simple network management protocol) and its close cousin RMON (remote monitoring of networks) have emerged as the most important standards for ensuring that different vendors' systems can be managed, to some extent at least, by a single network management system. Another important contender for multivendor open networks is the OSI CMIP (common management information protocol).

Both SNMP and CMIP are standard protocols defining what management information network elements should provide and how to transmit it. CMIP was originally intended to be the ultimate solution, embracing all layers of the management process from physical media to applications. Yet although it was intended to provide all the information needed for end-to-end management of a complete network, its complexity meant that progress in developing the CMIP protocols was painfully slow. In an attempt to provide a quicker solution, the SNMP protocols were developed and released in 1988 by a US-based standards group, the Internet Engineering Task Force, the original objective being merely to facilitate exchange of basic management information within LANs pending the arrival of the real thing, CMIP. Indeed, it was initially implemented only in Ethernet LANs, primarily to monitor internet-working devices such as bridges. However, as CMIP repeatedly failed to arrive, so SNMP was extended to token ring LANs and to other devices such as printers, plotters, modems and UPS systems. Furthermore SNMP became less simple, with the release in March 1993 of version 2, although it still did not extend to the management of server and workstation applications. For this reason there have been efforts to develop more sophisticated systems for managing complete LANs including desktop and server machines. One such standard was the 802.1D, an extension of the 802.1 series of LAN management standards to embrace desktop systems as well as other LAN devices. These standards are of obvious interest to NOS vendors for two reasons: firstly, they could provide additional information about the status of client workstations; and secondly, the standard enables the NOS to feed relevant information back to other management systems.

However, while awaiting the arrival of more sophisticated LAN manage-ment systems capable of seeing beyond the NIC, the NOS itself, or more specifically the NOS shell, remains the main potential source of information about the workstation. The NOS shell is capable of providing basic information, such as whether the workstation is working or not, although some vendors of network management systems, including the UK company Network Managers, have developed links from their management system to the Novell NetWare shell for this purpose. Yet even this does not allow the management system to elicit information about the status of client applications, because such infor-mation is not available to the NOS or its shell.

RMON is a standard that builds on SNMP to allow devices to be monitored comprehensively from a central management station, providing statistics on performance, alarms and traffic levels. Devices within an RMON network run software called RMON agents or probes to collect the required data locally and then transmit it using the SNMP protocol to a central station. The other principal standards relevant for NOSs are the large-scale so-called enterprise management platforms, which act as the central repository for storage of management information and for building the specific applications needed for different networks. They provide a coherent framework for integration of different components and aspects of the overall management picture.

There are four principal network management platforms – the three best known in 1994 were Hewlett-Packard's Openview, Sun Microsystems' Sun-Net Manager and IBM's Netview/6000. The latter provides close integration between UNIX systems and IBM's existing Netview management system for proprietary host systems. Most NOSs support the host version of Netview to some extent; for example, Banyan's Vines has an option that allows alerts to be sent to Netview and allows devices under Vines control to be managed and monitored from Netview. Similar facilities are provided by Novell and Microsoft.

The fourth key management platform, which emerged during 1994 to challenge the other three, although with a rather different focus, is Novell's NMS (NetWare management system). This is geared towards management of NetWare LANs, particularly in a NetWare 4 network comprising multiple distributed servers. NMS can work with the other platforms, either in a subordinate role or as the principal management platform, and is likely to feature prominently in large Novell sites, where it may preside over other management platforms used to control IBM mainframes or UNIX workstations for example. Some organizations that have not until recently had any significant network management may even have NMS as their sole platform, managing other systems directly rather than via another management platform. In yet other cases, for example where the Novell network is not so significant, NetWare servers may themselves be managed directly from another management platform such as HP Openview.

☐ SUMMARY

In this chapter, network management has been considered in its widest context rather than within the limited orbit of individual management systems. We have explained where the NOS stands in the overall network management scene and how leading NOSs are expanding beyond their traditional pasture in the LAN. Network management has become a battleground in which many IT vendors are fighting to ensure that they have some control over the strategies of their customers. If the NOS is to have a key role in large-scale enterprise networks, it must provide management facilities commensurate with its expanded orbit.

8

What are application programming interfaces and how are they supported in the NOS?

CHAPTER OBJECTIVES:

- To establish what APIs are and how they differ
- To define APIs in the wider context of components needed for distributed network computing, setting the scene for Chapter 9
- To identify which APIs are provided with or supported by the NOS
- To sort out the confusion between different names for various types of API component, such as middleware, and remote procedure call

□ 8.1   Introduction

The term application programming interface (API) is misleading, because an application is commonly understood to be the end product that serves users, such as a word-processing package, but API in its broadest sense is something that provides a link either between two software components, whatever their purpose, or between a software component and an underlying network or hardware platform.

The main purpose of APIs is to break the structure of computer systems, networks and the software that runs on them into standard components. This enables application developers to assemble their products from standard components without having to expend effort on ground already broken by others. A major objective of APIs in general is that applications, once written, should be able to run on a variety of computers and operating systems without additional programming work. They should also be capable of communicating with other applications across a network without requiring new code to be written to facilitate such interaction.

The term network computing is sometimes applied to the cooperation between different applications and software components across a network. The role of the NOS in network computing and some of the key issues to consider for organizations planning a distributed network are discussed in Chapter 9. In this chapter we shall complete the framework for network computing by describing the APIs that enable applications to interoperate on a network, coordinated by operating systems and NOSs.

The definition of API has expanded greatly since it was first used in the mid 1980s to describe the link between an application and the underlying protocol used to transport data about the network. It now embraces any link between the various software components of a network. Like many acronyms in the IT business, the definition of API has shifted to the point where the words represented by the letters, application programming interface, no longer convey its full scope.

□ 8.2   What are APIs and why are they important?

Computers, like audio systems, telephones and electrical appliances in general, need standard sockets that enable products to work together and, where relevant, to share common services. There may be more than one such standard on a worldwide basis, so that, for example, you need different telephone sockets and electrical plugs in the USA and the UK. However there are only a few such standards, so that it is not too difficult for vendors to cater for each one when developing products for global markets.

Computer applications similarly need to share common communication services, and to work with standard underlying operating systems and hardware designs. Unfortunately, the situation is much more complex than, say, the world of electrical appliances, with numerous overlapping and competing standards for linking software components together. As fast as vendors come together in an attempt to establish common ground for linking software pieces together, so it seems the situation changes as new demands arise. For example, the growth of applications in multimedia and virtual reality has brought demands for new standards that allow different media such as sound, video and graphics to be integrated into applications accessed by a common GUI (graphical user interface). Nevertheless, there are some ambitious schemes to bring order to the chaos of software development, one being Novell's AppWare, which is described in Section 8.8. Before describing the scope and range of APIs, however, it is worth looking at their history.

8.2.1 Brief history of APIs

The first computers had to be programmed in binary code, which required an intimate knowledge of the hardware design. Then came assembler, which aided the task of programmers by wrapping up common sequences of operations in single commands, although these were still specific to each machine. Subsequently, in the 1960s, the third generation of software development came to fruition – high-level languages such as FORTRAN and COBOL, which simplified the programming process further by providing more 'English like' commands such as read and write. High-level languages also introduced some degree of independence from the underlying hardware, as the languages were supported by different computer manufacturers, even though each type of computer still had its own operating system and hence each implementation of an application required machine-specific components to address the operating system for input/output and data storage tasks. The writing of applications still therefore required a knowledge of the specific hardware environment on which they were to run.

It was not until the birth of the personal computer that the first operating systems independent of the hardware they run on became available. By this time the early versions of UNIX were on the market but it was not until the 1980s that UNIX began to enjoy commercial success as a hardware-independent operating system. On PCs, however, this process started not with UNIX but with a now long-forgotten operating system called CP/M.

Gary Kildall, who developed CP/M, realized in 1976 that it was very tedious having to rewrite the operating system to accommodate each new hardware development, whether this was a new type of CPU or a new floppy disk controller. Therefore he split CP/M into two parts, with one containing all the code that needed to be changed to make the operating system work on a new hardware platform. In this instance, a new hardware platform might be the same computer with a new component inside.

The machine-independent part, which contained the essence of the operating system distinguishing it from alternative operating systems, could then be moved or 'ported' to any computer for which a machine-dependent part had been written. Furthermore, the machine-dependent part did not need to be restricted to just one operating system – it could provide an underlying hardware-specific platform that could be used by other operating systems.

This machine-dependent part of the operating system was christened BIOS (basic input/output system), because it provided the means by which an operating system could communicate with the hardware via low-level binary commands. The BIOS was an API in the sense that it provided a link between the operating system and the hardware it was controlling. As explained in Chapter 1, NetBIOS was an extension of BIOS allowing operating systems to communicate with an underlying network. It was an API in the sense that it allowed operating systems, initially DOS but later others, including many NOSs, to communicate with an underlying network. However, NetBIOS was also a primitive NOS itself in that it provided basic functions needed for computers to interoperate via a network; for example, it allowed each computer to be given a name for use by others in addressing data packets to it. Although the functions provided by NetBIOS were, and are, rudimentary, APIs providing more sophisticated functions emerged, such as Microsoft's Named Pipes. Also, as we now know, NOSs evolved that provided efficient server-based filing and print services. The origins of NetBIOS highlight the close relationship between the NOS and current APIs that enable desktop applications to interact with services such as relational database management systems that are accessed via LANs.

APIs also emerged from third generation programming languages such as COBOL. At the time these languages evolved, applications were becoming larger and yet the amount of main computer memory to run them was still severely limited; for example, a typical mainframe computer of the mid 1970s only allowed programs to occupy 64 Kbytes of main memory, which is about 20 per cent of that consumed by typical PC word-processing packages today, and just over 1 per cent of that provided by many PCs. The solution was to break applications down into components that could be run separately. By slicing applications up into smaller units, called subprograms or subroutines, applications could be squeezed into available memory, and were also easier to debug and maintain. However, computers had to provide facilities for subprograms to interact, and for one to call on the services of others. Such facilities were called procedure calls, and these were APIs in that they allowed one piece of software to interact with another. Frequently used subprograms became standardized and were available in libraries that could be called upon whenever required, saving programmers from duplicating code that had already been written.

The use of subprograms also heralded the era of client/server computing. This concept is not so new, having been employed by programmers in the 1960s when one program, the client, called on the services of another standard software component, the server. The difference now is that these processes can involve not just different software components operating within the same computer but also different computers interconnected by a network. Furthermore, just as NetBIOS evolved from BIOS, so the remote procedure call (RPC) evolved from the procedure call. RPCs are discussed further in Section 8.7.

Yet another direction from which APIs emerged was the effort to turn UNIX into a universal operating system that would run on all major hardware platforms. The objective was that applications written to run over UNIX would be independent of the underlying hardware and could be ported readily from one computer to another. UNIX was to do for applications what BIOS does for operating systems.

Out of this UNIX dvelopment emerged the notion that the application, as well as the hardware, could be made independent of the operating system. Each computer could then run the operating system best suited to it and its users without affecting the applications. This initiative was taken up by the Posix standards committees. Now a number of operating systems previously considered proprietary, such as IBM's MVS and Digital Equipment's VMS, comply with early Posix standards, which gives them some ability to run applications developed initially to run under other Posix-compliant operating systems. The Posix standards are in effect a set of APIs that enable applications to access services such as file management provided by operating systems in a standard way. Much of the Posix work has since been taken over by the X/Open group, in the Spec 1170 standards.

Other developments that have spawned APIs since the age of networking began are the arrival of graphical user interfaces (GUIs) and relational database management systems (RDMSs) for LAN servers. GUIs require APIs to access and execute the services they present to users. RDMSs require APIs for client applications to effect queries and updates in a standard way without having to know specific details of how that RDMS has organized the data.

More recently, the birth of multimedia applications and the move towards open systems have greatly increased the scope and variety of APIs. Now there are dozens of categories of API corresponding to every function and resource that can be accessed by an application. Nevertheless, like many other computer technologies, APIs may soon fall into the history bin. A concept called object oriented programming is emerging to replace them. The idea is that chunks of code performing a specific function, such as accessing a database, are presented to programmers as objects that can be mixed and matched to create complete applications without having to play around with APIs to accomplish the task. This concept of 'Lego software', where the pieces snap together, corresponds to the aim of the open systems movement in hardware – to enable computers from different vendors to work together without the need for customized black boxes in between.

Object orientation will still, however, require APIs to link the objects together; the difference is that the API functions will be built into the software components, avoiding the need for programmers to grapple with them. Full object orientation is still some way off but meanwhile there have been attempts to create some order in the increasingly complex world of software development for multivendor environments. The most significant development in the context of this book is Novell's AppWare, since it addresses the needs of network computing. The relationship between AppWare and APIs is explained in Section 8.8.

□ 8.3 Main categories of API

Categorizing APIs is a dangerous pastime as it is bound to end in omission, so we will not attempt to do so. Table 8.1 lists just the main ones, distinguished by what they are connecting together.

Within these broad categories are numerous subdivisions; for example, APIs exist that link network management systems together, such as IBM's Netview/PC, which is one type of application-to-application API. Other links, for instance with printers, are strictly speaking interfaces rather than APIs, as they define a set of parameters rather than software that has to be written, although this distinction is a hairline one.

8.3.1 Application to operating system

This is the most readily understood type of API. It is fundamental to making applications independent of the operating systems they run on. Indeed, APIs of this type are the foundation of portable applications, the best known group being those defined within X/Open's Spec 1170 specifications, previously known as XPG. These provide application developers with a set of APIs to plug their products into. Conformance with such APIs guarantees that the application will run on computers supporting versions of UNIX, and in future other operating systems, which themselves support these APIs. This X/Open group of APIs is subsuming work done by other standards bodies such as Posix, in an attempt to unite the computer industry behind a common set of standards for linking applications to operating systems. The role of the different standards groups is described in Appendix 10.

8.3.2 Operating system to underlying hardware drivers

This class of API also plays an important role in open computing because it allows a given operating system to run on different vendors' hardware. By the same token, it provides hardware vendors with a common standard to ensure that their systems can support a given operating system, and in turn the applications written for that operating system.

Table 8.1 Main categories of API.

Application – operating system
Operating system – underlying hardware drivers
Operating system – underlying network
GUI – local/client operating system
Client operating system – server operating system
Application – database
Application – application
Operating system – remote network

The best-known example is the BIOS used by successive generations of IBM-compatible PCs, which linked the DOS operating system with the underlying processor and input/output functions of the system. Another well-known one is Sun Microsystems' openly published Sparc specification, which allows clones to be made of Sun workstations. A more recently introduced example is Novell's NetWare systems interface (NSI), which defines how hardware drivers should interact with NetWare. Essentially, Novell cooperates with hardware vendors to port NetWare to its systems by writing appropriate hardware drivers that conform to NSI. Novell's work on processor-independent NetWare is described more fully in Chapter 10.

8.3.3 Operating system to underlying network

This class of APIs provides the basic data transport framework of a network, allowing operating systems to transmit data on behalf of the applications they are supporting. NetBIOS was the first well-known example and became a *de facto* standard for interoperability between different NOSs. Novell supports NetBIOS as well as TCP/IP but, when Novell's own proprietary IPX protocols provide the transport, NETX.COM is the API linking these with the desktop operating system, such as DOS.

8.3.4 GUI to local/client operating system

This class of API essentially maps the features of a particular desktop screen environment to the commands provided by the underlying desktop operating systems. This is a vital function because it allows an organization to select the GUI it wants and perhaps standardize on a particular one without being constrained in choice of operating system; it also allows software developers to give each customer a choice of GUI for using their products without having to write specific software for each option. However, there is still considerable work involved in configuring the GUI perfectly to the product and this is where development environments such as Novell's AppWare come in, providing tools that enable applications to work with different GUIs. More about AppWare is given in Section 8.8.

8.3.5 Client operating system to server operating system

This is closely related to the group of APIs for linking operating systems to the underlying network, as described in Section 8.33, since links between operating systems running on different systems also require the ability to communicate with the underlying network. The distinction is that there also has to be a higher-layer protocol to enable the two operating systems to understand each other; Novell, for example, has the NetWare Client API which provides the mechanism for software running in clients to issue instructions to a NetWare server via NetWare core protocol (NCP).

8.3.6 Application to database

This provides a standard mechanism for applications to query and update a database, without having to know details of how the data is organized. There are three contending APIs that enjoy widespread industry support, plus other proprietary ones from the relational database vendors themselves. An example of the latter is Oracle Glue for Oracle's relational database management system.

The three contending 'open' APIs are: Microsoft's ODBC (open database connectivity); IDAPI (integrated database application programming interface); and the SQL/CLI standard. All three conform to the common SQL*Net interface defined by the SQL Access Group, a consortium of vendors setting open database standards. However, differences in implementation mean that the three cannot interoperate with each other, so that an application written to the IDAPI API cannot run against a database that supports only ODBC. Nevertheless, some of the leading database vendors support all three standards. Of the three, IDAPI is the most sophisticated – whereas ODBC and SQL/CLI were designed only for SQL-based databases, IDAPI allows data to be accessed from non-SQL sources of data. Within IDAPI this is done through a navigational interface called NAV/CLI (navigational call level interface), which describes how to locate data in non-SQL sources. IDAPI is promoted by Borland International, IBM, WordPerfect and Novell itself. SQL/CLI was proposed by the SQL Access Group and X/Open, so it is the only one of the three with a completely vendor-independent flavour. In future the key NAV/CLI component of IDAPI may well be embraced within SQL/CLI, which would then become the obvious database connectivity API to adopt.

8.3.7 Application to application: what are RPCs?

APIs in this group are often called RPCs (remote procedure calls) and enable one application to call on the services of another. This is similar to the application-to-database APIs, except that there we are considering a relationship between a client application, which perhaps requires some data, and a server application managing the database on behalf of all users. RPCs, on the other hand, allow two client applications to cooperate; for example, an application calculating bonuses for sales staff might need to access another application running on a different computer to find out how much each sales person has sold. An RPC could be used to transmit the request.

RPCs are really an extension of facilities provided by high-level computing languages for a program to make a call to a subprogram providing a particular function or service. The difference is that an RPC allows the subprogram to be an independent application running on a remote computer, linked by a network to the application making the call.

Broadly, RPCs support three types of interaction between applications. One is where the primary application calls on a second one to perform a task, and waits for it to finish and the result to be returned before proceeding. Client/server computing will often be of this type, because the client will wait for the server to finish a task before carrying on. The second type is where the primary application calls on another to perform an operation but then continues without waiting for this to be completed. At a future time, the application called on to perform the operation then informs the primary task that it has finished and, if required, passes over the result it has obtained.

The third type of cooperative processing is the loosest arrangement, and probably not so relevant for users of smaller LANs. It involves one application calling on another to perform some tasks but not requiring a result and not being affected if the tasks are not completed. Network management sometimes involves this loose type of cooperative processing, when two or more management systems exchange information but do not necessarily expect anything in return.

8.3.8 Operating system to remote network

This enables a computer or LAN controlled by a given operating system to access a remote or dissimilar network. A good example of this type of application is Novell's NetWare for SAA, which allows a NetWare LAN to access an IBM network. To do this, the NOS must support network APIs that enable it to communicate with remote systems across the foreign network at the data transport level. NetWare for SAA has to support IBM-specific APIs, such as APPC (advanced program-to-program communication) for example. In a sense, therefore, this is a variant of the operating system-to-network category of API described in Section 8.3.3. However, it is listed separately because it is always a gateway function involving access to a network controlled by a different operating system.

Also in this category are APIs that enable telephone systems to be integrated into computer networks for applications in multimedia and computer integrated telephony (CIT). An example is the TSAPI (telephony services application programming interface) developed by the Novell Open Telephony Association (NOTA), which enables existing PBXs to be integrated with software on NetWare servers for applications such as telesales where details pertaining to customers can be called automatically onto a screen to coincide with a telephone conversation.

□ 8.4   How NOSs relate to and support APIs

APIs provide standard links between different components of networks and the computers attached to them. The function of the NOS is to control access to shared resources on a network and increasingly to facilitate cooperation between applications. Given that the NOS has to operate in multivendor networks not under the control of a single IT supplier, it can only fulfil this role with the help of APIs to provide links between the different components.

Without APIs, the NOS would need to provide its own code for every link, for example between a DOS client and a database server. The NOS software would quickly become too large to run on any known server and would also be inflexible as it would need a new release or option to cope with each new software or hardware product that came along. Increasingly, leading NOSs such as NetWare aim to provide a software environment that enables distributed applications to be developed as readily as possible, as is discussed further in Chapters 9 and 10. To do this they provide software tools that exploit facilities provided by the NOS itself and by standard APIs that are supported by all relevant vendors. An example is Novell's NetWare TIRPC, which is designed to free programmers from needing to know details of underlying APIs that provide access to the network transport protocols. In a sense this is an API of APIs, since it provides a common point of access to services that may be provided by a number of APIs operating at a slightly lower level. Such an API is available as a NetWare software developer's kit (SDK) which, as the name implies, is aimed at programmers building applications to run across NetWare networks.

TIRPC is an application-to-application API of the sort described in Section 8.3.7; it allows an application running on one computer to make function calls across a network to programs that run on another computer.

APIs for accessing databases are also of great relevance to NOSs, except on small peer-to-peer networks. As the NOS controls the server on which a database often runs, good integration between the two is essential for efficient operation. Furthermore, in the fast growing open networking arena there is a need for client applications to be able to access a variety of different databases. Standard APIs are therefore needed to allow client applications to work with a variety of databases without requiring programs to be written for each different requirement.

SQL (structured query language) was developed as a standard way of issuing queries to databases, and this is supported by many databases and by software that accesses them. However, SQL operates at a low level, being itself a form of programming language. Different combinations of SQL statements are required to access each type of database and so considerable effort is required to develop the SQL software needed to match a particular application or desktop operating environment with a chosen database.

General-purpose database APIs were developed to simplify the task of writing the code to access relational databases. Ideally there would be just one such API based on the SQL standard supported by all parties involved, including vendors of relational databases, NOSs, graphical user interfaces (GUIs) and desktop applications. However, commercial rivalries generally stifle any such outbreak of common sense at birth and thus, as described in Section 8.3.6, there are three contending APIs for linking applications to databases. The point of relevance here is that APIs such as IDAPI are supported as SDKs (software developers' kits) within the NOS environment and it is therefore possible to develop NOS applications, for example NetWare loadable modules in the case of Novell networks, that interoperate with any relational database, and in some cases non-relational sources of data, via the API. Some NOS vendors have gone further by fully integrating their software with the database themselves, selling the resulting package as a single bundle; such an example is OracleWare, comprising Oracle's database and office automation software combined with NetWare.

□ 8.5 How APIs relate to other key components of the network, such as data transport protocols

APIs are software toolkits for building applications on top of existing operating systems and NOSs, usually, but not necessarily, distributed across a network. They can also be viewed as building blocks for applications on top of some established networking platform and as such they provide the means to connect the various components of a network together. Figure 8.1 illustrates this schematically, depicting the role of APIs in linking together the various software components of a network, including data transport, database and applications. The role of the NOS is in controlling the process of interaction when applications have been written and in providing some of the APIs themselves. Indeed, Novell has gone further in developing AppWare, which is a complete software environment for building distributed applications, not necessarily restricted to NetWare LANs. We shall look at AppWare in Section 8.8.

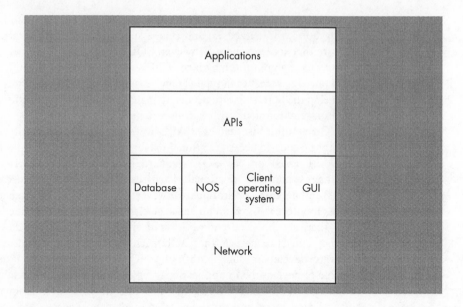

Figure 8.1 Rough schematic view of API's role in the network.

At a lower level of interaction, APIs link applications or operating systems via the underlying network transport protocols, without being concerned with the detailed mechanisms of the software. When APIs first surfaced during the 1980s, they were defined as a software layer linking a program with a communication protocol. Originally they were developed for specific operating systems and communication protocols, their role then being to enable applications running under that operating system to communicate across a network running the specified protocol. Taking this definition, NetBIOS was sometimes defined as an API, for it enabled applications running under DOS to communicate via transport protocols developed by Sytek, which co-developed NetBIOS with IBM. However, APIs were obviously of limited use if they were restricted to single operating systems and protocols. NetBIOS has since been adapted for use with other protocol stacks, such as TCP/IP, and is now also supported by operating systems such as OS/2 and even NetWare.

More sophisticated APIs in this category have since emerged, an example being IBM's APPC (advanced program to program communication), which enables PCs and LANs to communicate with systems across an IBM SNA network. APPC has been used by NOS vendors such as Novell to allow PC applications to access IBM host systems via the LAN.

□ 8.6　Is SQL an API?

SQL (structured query language) is not an API but rather an English-like language based on key words for accessing, defining, manipulating and controlling data in relational databases. Developed by IBM and the American National Standards Institute (ANSI), SQL is supported by all leading vendors of relational databases, providing a standard language for writing the portions of applications that access and control data. SQL does not of itself provide the tools for coordinating communication between an application and a database or within a network of databases – that is the role of APIs such as IDAPI, which in turn make use of SQL commands to manipulate databases.

□ 8.7　What is middleware?

Middleware, you may be surprised to read, has already been covered in this book – it is just that we have not mentioned the name yet, in an attempt to keep jargon to a minimum. However, as the book evolved, use of the word has soared to the extent that we could not afford to ignore it lest we be accused of serious omission. Middleware, logically enough, is the layer of software between client applications and server databases; as such, we have covered it in Section 8.4. It can be defined as the enabling technology for delivering a database service to applications in client/server networks.

□ 8.8　How does Novell's AppWare fit into all this?

AppWare can be regarded as an API of APIs. APIs proliferated during the early 1990s, serving in turn the growing number of different operating systems and network transport services. AppWare provides a single super API designed to provide conformance across all the different components that an application needs to link with. The objective is that an application written to the AppWare API will link up automatically with all the underlying APIs that AppWare supports.

AppWare encompasses a layer of software that resides between the applications and the underlying APIs of the networking platform that they run on. To do this, AppWare has to support all the relevant APIs, and it also depends on support from key players in the software field to ensure that their products work with the AppWare environment. Novell has been successful in courting some of the big software companies such as Borland and Oracle, although developers and users are unlikely to be seduced by another API on its own, even if it does subsume all other APIs. It would still be necessary to write the code to implement this API in each application and, besides, how many other such super APIs might emerge worthy of consideration? Microsoft certainly is going to do all it can to stall progress of AppWare, and the well-established players in the open system arena, notably Sun, have given it a decidedly cool reception.

The extent of AppWare's fortunes will hinge therefore on the strength and appeal of the software tools that minimize the amount of active coding needed in the environment. The objective is to create a software assembly line where components are integrated effortlessly using readily available tools. Novell calls such components AppWare loadable modules (ALMs), which could include existing desktop applications adapted to support the AppWare API. These ALMs will plug into an upper layer of software, called the AppWare Bus because it is analogous to the hardware bus of a PC, except that in this case it manages the interaction between software rather than hardware components. The AppWare Bus allows ALMs to interact and also facilitates the development of ALMs by linking with appropriate software development tools. Then, beneath the AppWare Bus is the AppWare Foundation, which is the software that deals specifically with existing lower-level APIs. This structure is illustrated in Figure 8.2.

ALMs can be built using Novell's ALM software developers' kit, which takes an object-oriented approach, stratifying the structure of programs into objects and functions that operate on those objects. Novell likens objects to nouns and functions to verbs but this analogy is slightly misleading, because an ALM can have just one object but any number of functions; for example, an ALM for managing a window would comprise the window object itself and functions for opening, closing, rescaling and moving windows within the overall screen.

The AppWare approach is the way forward for software development in the network computing era but commercial rivalries and realities are ensuring that other environments survive as well.

□ 8.9 How does Microsoft's Win32 API fit in?

A major design improvement introduced by Microsoft in both Windows NT and subsequently Windows 95 was support for 32-bit applications, the object being that future applications should exploit the full 32-bit addressing supported by Intel processors from the 386 onwards. The Win32 API was developed

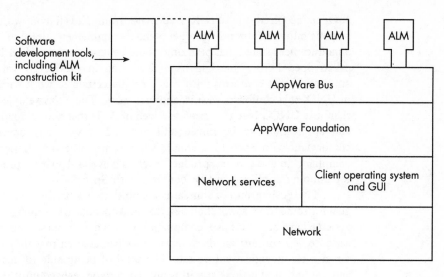

Software
development tools,
including ALM
construction kit

ALM   ALM   ALM   ALM

AppWare Bus

AppWare Foundation

Network services

Client operating system
and GUI

Network

Figure 8.2 Architecture of Novell's AppWare.

to provide software companies with an environment for building such 32-bit applications.

As well as facilitating the development of new applications, Win32 helps convert existing 16-bit programs to 32-bit mode to improve performance or to work effectively with new applications. Win32 is an example of an API linking an application to the underlying operating system, and as such is distinct from APIs like ODBC that are part of Microsoft's Windows Open Services Architecture (WOSA).

□ 8.10 What APIs are being developed or endorsed by standards groups such as Posix and X/Open?

Groups such as X/Open do not usually initiate standards; instead they sanctify existing standards that have come to be accepted by the industry, providing a common framework that is seen to be independent of vendors. When these groups do introduce what appears to be a new standard, closer inspection usually reveals that it is closely related to some existing proprietary or *de facto* standard.

The above is certainly true in the API sphere, where one of the most significant announcements came from X/Open in October 1993. At that time,

X/Open acquired the UNIX trademark from Novell and with it assumed responsibility for branding other vendors' implementations of UNIX. The announcement stated that branding would be based on a set of APIs collectively called Spec 1170. This had been developed in the UNIX world, and any application that conforms with it is virtually certain to work with any version of UNIX that conforms with it, and vice versa. The ultimate objective is wider than just UNIX, being to provide a web of APIs that allows operating systems and applications to be mixed and matched at will: any operating system conformant with Spec 1170 should support any other application that is also compliant. In this context, products such as Novell's AppWare provide the tools for building applications that conform with Spec 1170.

The Posix group of standards committees has been working towards this goal for some time, as we shall describe in Appendix 10. A number of operating systems have become Posix compliant but in the early stages this has been seen as more of a comfort factor to make users feel assured that they are not going down a technological cul de sac. The ideal of being able to match operating systems and applications at will is not likely to be realized until the late 1990s. More about this is given in Chapter 10.

☐ SUMMARY

In this chapter the various roles of APIs have been discussed along with their relationship with the NOS, paving the way for Chapter 9, which looks at the field of distributed applications and network computing from a loftier, more strategic perspective. APIs provide the tools and building blocks to achieve this, in cooperation with NOSs and operating systems in general, building on the physical network infrastructure.

What is network computing and what is the role of the NOS in this?

CHAPTER OBJECTIVES:

- To describe the benefits of network computing
- To explain how the NOS has evolved to become a key component in distributed applications
- To clear up confusion between different terms such as client/server, cooperative processing and distributed computing

☐ 9.1   Introduction

Put simply, the objective of network computing is to make all the data and applications needed by the employees of an organization to do their jobs available, wherever they are. This might embrace not just the office desktop but also homes and on-site locations, from which staff may need access to the network from mobile computers. The network itself should be as transparent as possible, appearing as if all applications and data reside in the computer where they are accessed.

Of course, many jigsaw pieces need to fit together correctly for this ideal to be anywhere near realized. Computers must be able to exchange data and messages, and at a higher level software components need to cooperate on larger tasks. Seen in this light, the heavily hyped concept of client/server computing is no more than a technology to help achieve this objective. The same is true of other paradigms like cooperative processing and distributed databases. The overall aim is to make the network function like a single distributed computer, with its various parts located as conveniently as possible for each part of the organization and its individual staff.

Network computing is therefore about much more than mere connectivity: it includes integration of applications and different network components, and the ability to present services and data to users via common graphical interfaces. For larger organizations it also involves convergence between voice, video, image and computing technologies. This all requires cooperation between different vendors on a scale unprecedented in the IT industry. In particular, it demands widespread agreement on network protocols, APIs and commonly available software tools for building applications that work across networks.

The role of the NOS has expanded to cope with new responsibilities in this area. Although it functions as a server or LAN operating system liaising with other operating systems, the major NOSs like NetWare 4.x also provide many other services, such as distributed directories and messaging, needed for an entire network to work as a single coherent entity.

During the first eight chapters of this book we have described the components of a modern network and the role of the NOS in marshalling these. The rest of this chapter brings all these threads together, taking a more strategic view of the NOS' role in networks, particularly larger ones. For small businesses with just one LAN, the goal of network computing is, in any case, easier to achieve and can be satisfied to a large extent by a single NOS, perhaps in conjunction with gateway software to access external public on-line services.

□ 9.2   What is network computing?

Network computing is concerned with making an organization's network operate like a single computer dedicated to each employee's needs. However, this does not mean giving everyone unlimited access to the organization's data. The need to protect sensitive information from unauthorized access and to prevent malicious or accidental loss or corruption of data requires the network to control and monitor the activities on it. Therefore, in our definition,

Table 9.1 Key requirements of network computing.

Common user access

Ability to find and access information quickly

Ability to control access to data and resources

Ability to make good use of processing resources on the network

'need' is defined by the employer, and the realization of this need is controlled by the network.

Table 9.1 lists the features of network computing. These could all, in principle, be achieved by a single large host computer accessed either by intelligent terminals capable of providing a graphical user interface or by desktop PCs. However, this is not a practical option for the reasons explained in Section 9.3.

☐ 9.3   Why network computing?

The movement to network computing is driven by an alliance of economics, marketing hype, technology directions and the reality of existing computer installations. This reality is that the increasing power of PCs and LANs has devolved applications to workgroups away from centralized host systems. This is allied to the economic argument that, by distributing applications geographically to the individuals or workgroups that need them, long-distance network traffic, which is expensive, is reduced and large expensive computer systems can be replaced by smaller cheaper ones. This leads on to the down-sizing argument – that it is cheaper to migrate applications from large centralized systems to a great number of smaller distributed ones. This argument is not always correct, because although computer processing power costs less when purchased in smaller units, the cost of managing and transmitting data across a distributed network is greater. However, whether correct or not, this is the way the industry is moving and the onus is therefore on managing distributed networks as effectively as possible.

Marketing hype then comes to the fore, as vendors offer to down-size existing applications onto smaller systems linked by a network. The same concept has been peddled under a number of attractive sounding slogans, such as 'right sizing' and 're-hosting'. The reality for many organizations is that the process of moving from a tightly controlled proprietary mainframe computing environment to a distributed networking one has been painful, and more costly than expected. NOS vendors such as Novell have been guilty of overselling LAN platforms for critical commercial applications but have at least imported key aspects of mainframe technology to their environments.

The technology incentives leading towards network computing come both in the shape of wide area networking developments and new software environments that make distributed applications easier to develop and manage. Data transmission technologies, such as frame relay, and ATM (asynchronous transfer mode), which bring LANs and WANs together, provide sufficient bandwidth at an affordable price for applications to communicate across enterprise networks. Software environments like Novell's AppWare are also making it easier to develop distributed applications across networks controlled by NetWare and other NOSs. In addition, there is the installed base argument: no large organization and very few medium-sized ones have all their applications and data concentrated in one place anymore – even if they have just one data centre, there will be numerous smaller systems that were originally installed for specific applications, for example in manufacturing, when there was no requirement to connect them to other computers. However, there is now a growing demand for wider access to data held on such systems, and in some cases for access to the processing capability as well. The aim is that computing tasks should seek the processors best able to handle them, and this will not necessarily be the largest or the one nearest to the user. The advantage of network computing is that it does not require ageing systems to be thrown away and a fresh start made. In principle, any existing system can join but in some cases the cost of connecting up ancient computers and applications will exceed the price of purchasing and installing newer and smaller servers. Hence the disadvantage of network computing is that the ideal is hard to achieve in practice.

This does not mean, however, that networks cannot continually improve and move closer to this ideal; for example, it is now possible to have global directories of information and catalogues describing where to find items contained in a variety of inconvenient sources, such as older proprietary systems that do not conform to new data access standards and even paper-based records. Also, it is increasingly possible to integrate video and voice into existing networks to build multimedia applications. Novell's NetWare Video 1.0, for example, allows multimedia applications to be developed on existing NetWare servers, accessed from Microsoft Windows. NetWare servers can store and replay audio and video sequences, and these can be integrated with text, digital images and coded data in a variety of applications, including training and sales promotion.

□ 9.4   What are the ingredients?

Table 9.2 lists the main raw ingredients needed for a network computing platform. On top of this there has to be the commitment to make it work and to manage the process properly, rather than just developing applications and the relevant links on an *ad hoc* basis.

Table 9.2 Main ingredients of a network computing platform.

Physical network

Computers

Operating systems and NOSs

Network management and security systems

Appropriate APIs

Applications

Relational database management systems

The components cited in Table 9.2 have all been described earlier in the book, except relational database management systems (RDMSs), which are described briefly here, and applications, which are really a separate subject. The relationship between applications and the NOS was touched on in Section 3.11. The key point as far as network computing is concerned is that applications need to cooperate closely to provide the functions of groupware within a workgroup. The NOS needs to be closely involved to coordinate the transmission of data between the processes and provide access to shared resources, such as the database, in an effective way.

Following a period of increasingly close cooperation between some NOS vendors and application software companies, the most significant development in the field came early in 1994 with Novell's acquisition of the major word-processing and groupware software vendor WordPerfect. This followed two earlier key acquisitions by Novell, of Digital Research to gain access to DOS, and of UNIX System Laboratories for UNIX. The result was that Novell can now provide complete software solutions for workgroups, including the applications and client operating system as well as the NOS. Microsoft was already able to do this when Novell took over WordPerfect, so Novell's move can be seen as defensive in the face of Microsoft's aggressive push into the workgroup scene during 1993 when the Windows for Workgroups NOS was bundled with the standard Windows desktop operating system.

Relational database management systems

To begin with, two definitions of database jargon: a query is a request for information, such as 'how many of our customers live in New York?'; a transaction, on the other hand, involves changes to the data, an example being a cash withdrawal from a bank account.

Relational databases have become the prevailing way of organizing data for most commercial applications. Data is arranged in tables, each of which contains a list of items that fulfil one particular relationship: a list of names and addresses could be one such table, while another might contain the same names and the ages of the people; a third might contain all the names in the list of people who own a car, and details of the car models. Queries can then be run against the database, such as: 'tell me the names of all people living in London between the ages of 20 and 30 who own a car made by Volvo' Entries in the first table would be examined, retaining the names of those with a London address, and the second table would then be read, pulling out those aged between 20 and 30. The names from the second table would be cross-referenced with those from the first to determine those that fit both categories. The process would be repeated with the third table to find the subset that also owns a Volvo.

Without an RDMS, this process could involve constant fetching of records from the database across a network to the client application to examine whether they match the specified criteria. The RDMS can perform queries in the machine running the database, so that only the records actually needed by the client application are transmitted across the network. The RDMS also handles the editing of data, when new records are added or existing ones are modified or deleted. This task involves ensuring that the database remains consistent when changes are made. Different tables may be related, so that any update affecting one would require changes in all. In the example just given, the deletion of a name could involve changes to all three tables. The RDMS has to know all the relationships between data in different tables, so that it can ensure that all relevant tables are updated as a result of actions taken by a client application.

In large networks, data on the file server controlled by the NOS will usually be stored in a relational database, therefore the NOS needs to relate to the RDMS in order to obtain data on behalf of a client application. This process can be done more efficiently if the NOS is well integrated with the RDMS so that the two function as a single coherent database server platform.

In a true network computing environment, databases distributed across different computers may need to cooperate on given queries or transactions. This leads to new problems, because data residing in different places needs to be updated consistently. So why not hold all data in just one central location where it can be looked after properly, and where problems of consistency between different systems do not arise? One reason is that having all data held centrally would involve a large amount of traffic on the network and would not fully utilize the distributed LANs that most organizations now have.

The alternative approach is to disperse data to bring it as close as possible to the applications that use it most, with local RDMSs implemented in dedicated servers for particular workgroups. The ideal is a fully distributed database that performs for programmers and users alike as a single RDMS running on just one machine. This would allow the performance of networks to be tuned by shunting data around to different locations without affecting applications and without programmers being aware of it.

However, to achieve this, the problem of maintaining consistent data must be overcome. Single transactions often generate updates on multiple databases linked by a network, so it is important to ensure that either all of the relevant updates are carried out or none of them. Various techniques have been developed to tackle this, although none solve it completely – ideals are by their nature unattainable.

Most prominent of these techniques is the two-phase commit protocol, which ensures that all databases maintain a record of their previous state during a transaction so that they can roll back if some event occurs that prevents the transaction being completed. Under this technique, a program called the coordinator takes charge of the operation. Suppose a transaction updates a database at three sites; the first of the two phases then involves the coordinator instructing all three RDMSs to prepare either to commit to the updated data or roll back to the state they were in before the transaction. Each RDMS keeps a record of its previous state and attempts to write the update into a log in preparation for executing it in the database. If this write is successful, the RDMS replies 'OK' to the coordinator, or else 'not OK'. In the second phase, the coordinator receives the three replies and if they are all 'OK' it informs each RDMS to commit to the update already recorded in the log. If any one reply is 'not OK', it instructs all the RDMSs to roll back. It is up to each RDMS to ensure it has sufficient backup procedures to minimize the risk of losing the log entries in the time interval between replying 'OK' and being asked to commit to the update. With proper implementation, therefore, two-phase commit provides virtually total consistency but there is the price to be paid of a heavy processing overhead on the system coordinating the transaction.

Alternatives to two-phase commit have been developed, among the most successful being Sybase's Replication Server. Sybase believes that two-phase commit is too vulnerable to failures of individual machines on a network, as it only works if all systems on which participating databases are being implemented are on-line. Sybase's Replication Server allows the network to continue in the event of a machine failing, by allowing each site to control the primary version of its data, with synchronization controlled by the Replication Server. Then if a system fails, others can continue working, with the Replication Server keeping a log of transactions and automatically resynchronizing the whole network when the failed system is restored. Hence Sybase overcomes the problems involved in updating a number of distributed databases simultaneously by allowing updates to take place over an extended timescale that varies with the application. The only vulnerable part is then the Replication Server itself, which should be implemented on a highly resilient machine.

The NOS needs to be aware of the various distributed database methods in order to cooperate smoothly with the RDMSs to control the servers involved effectively – it will often be involved in the data transmissions required to perform the distributed updates. Not surprisingly, therefore, NOS vendors have been working closely with leading database vendors. Novell, for example, cooperated with Oracle in the development of OracleWare, a shrink-wrapped product combining NetWare with Oracle's RDMS, and Microsoft has enjoyed a close relationship with Sybase to tie the latter's SQL Server RDMS with the former's NT Server NOS. The main remaining task of this chapter is to summarize the role of the NOS in helping to bind multiple servers and LANs together.

□ 9.5 What is the role of the NOS in network computing?

The traditional role of the NOS is confined to single LANs or workgroups, in controlling communication between client and server computers, and in managing shared LAN file systems. However, the arrival of NetWare 4.x and NT Server heralded the move by NOS vendors to compete for control of larger networks, providing the facilities needed for applications distributed across multiple LANs. Table 9.3 lists the facilities that top-end NOSs now provide to support network computing across multiple interconnected LANs, as opposed to within a single LAN. For smaller networks, not all these facilities will be needed; however, in contrast, all are required for global networks serving multinational companies.

Note that the facilities listed in Table 9.3 are in addition to those expected of any standard NOS, in particular a good file system and print services. The facilities are all described elsewhere in the book.

NOS vendors have approached network computing in different ways, depending on their resources and position in the market. Novell and Microsoft have attempted to span the whole network from the desktop to top-end LAN servers, stopping only when they reached mainframes and other large host systems. They thus provide a complete range of network services, covering all the facilities listed in Table 9.3. Other NOS vendors cannot afford such universal coverage and aim only to fit into the overall jigsaw. Artisoft, for

Table 9.3 NOS facilities supporting multiple interconnected LANs.

Global directory and messaging services

Data migration facilities

Comprehensive network security features

Support for different human languages

Good management and ability to interact with other large-scale network management systems

Support for automatic distribution and upgrading of client software

Ability to route data between servers on different LANs efficiently

Ability to access different types of system such as IBM mainframes and UNIX hosts

Good management of server memory

Support for key APIs that enable applications to cooperate across a network

Ability to embrace image and video as well as conventional data for multimedia applications

Software tools to help developers build real networked applications example, developed LANtastic for NetWare, enabling users of its peer-to-peer LANs to integrate seamlessly with larger-scale NetWare networks. However, we saw in Chapter 5 that there remain problems in achieving adequate integration between some NOSs, in particular NetWare and NT Advanced Server. An objective of network computing is to allow organizations to adopt the most efficient system for each component of a network without affecting the whole.

Other peer-to-peer NOS vendors have kept their focus on the workgroup and the need to integrate well with external services but Banyan Systems continues as it always has, in addressing enterprise-wide networks, although without covering the whole spectrum. The company focuses on directory services, messaging and network management but lacks the sophisticated data management features of NetWare.

□ 9.6 Is client/server the same as network computing?

The answer to this question is 'no', although you might be forgiven for thinking they are the same, judging by the pronouncements of some vendors. However, strictly speaking, client/server is one approach to distributing applications between two computers: one computer runs the client part, which is typically but not necessarily a desktop process for a single user, while another runs the server part of the application, generally a generic function shared by a number of users, such as database management. Client/server computing, sometimes described as the client/server model, is described more fully in Appendix 11. The point to stress here is that it is a term for methods that allow applications to be distributed in such a way that one computer acts as a server running processes on behalf of a number of clients. Usually the relationship between client and server is not one-to-one, since a server may be accessed by a variety of clients. Furthermore, given that servers are controlled by multi-tasking NOSs such as NetWare, one server can be working for more than one client at a time. In addition, a client may have access to multiple servers and again this can happen simultaneously. For example, an executive information system may need information about the performance of sales staff from one server and information about total sales of particular products from another. These two tasks could take place at the same time, so that the results need to be combined quickly to yield statistics linking individual sales people to numbers of each product sold.

However, there are other methods of distributing applications between computers on a one-to-one basis. Remote procedure calls (RPCs) can be used for communication between applications in various ways, as described in Section 8.3.7. Often this will be some client/server arrangement, with one application performing a task for another but it can also involve loose cooperation between two tasks, which is the third of the three types of use for RPCs described in Section 8.3.7.

Client/server computing can thus be seen as just a part of network computing, albeit an important one. Not all applications are based on the client/server model; for example, a large network might be controlled by several overlapping management systems, which exchange information loosely but each enjoy equal status in the network.

☐ SUMMARY

Network computing is really a collective term embracing the whole information technology infrastructure of an organization. This includes not just the physical network but also the software components needed to support distributed applications; it also embraces all the supportive applications, such as network management and security. The client/server model is an enabling part of this overall infrastructure, as is the NOS. Like the components within it, the network computing fabric is constantly evolving. In Chapter 10 we attempt to predict the main changes to come before the next millennium, and highlight how the NOS will evolve in step with these.

How is the NOS likely to evolve?

CHAPTER OBJECTIVES:

- To establish what will be the key emerging technologies in high-speed wide area networking, LAN/WAN integration, multimedia, user interfaces and object-oriented programming
- To set out how the NOS is changing to support these new technologies
- To explain what relevance each of these technologies has for organizations of different types and sizes
- To chart the likely future evolution of the NOS

☐ 10.1   Introduction

In Chapter 4 we established that selecting a NOS involves more than just an assessment of the product's more apparent technical merits, it also requires consideration of the product's staying power in the field and the commitment of the vendor to emerging technologies. Now we shall look in more detail at what the emerging technologies are, how operating systems in general are changing and what NOS vendors are doing to meet the new challenges.

The NOS itself has already evolved far from its origins as a LAN file system controlling a single type of server, which was usually an enhanced Intel-based PC. At the high end, the focus has shifted from the server to the network as a whole, and the leading NOSs are already becoming independent of the underlying processor so that they can be implemented on different hardware platforms. They are also offering a growing range of services for controlling and managing the network and are beginning to provide the platform not just for running applications across a network but also for developing them.

At the low end, the main trend is towards tighter integration with the desktop environment, so that applications such as groupware can provide seamless links between members of a workgroup without users having to be directly concerned with any communication process. In Section 10.5 we shall take this discussion a little further with a look at the likely course of future NOS development. The remaining sections of this chapter examine other developments in communications technology and network structures that the NOS will have to accommodate.

☐ 10.2 Summarizing what organizations and users want

Table 10.1 lists some key properties that organizations would like from their network, embracing the needs both of end users and software developers.

The NOS cannot satisfy any of these needs on its own but can make some contribution to all of them. Most of these objectives require good network navigation, so that remote data, applications and resources can be located. Leading NOSs do this by providing global directory services and also, at a lower level, by supporting appropriate internetworking hardware such as routers and bridges.

The question of communication between user and computer is not traditionally the preserve of NOSs but is becoming so as the distinctions between desktop and network software blur. Novell's Personal NetWare and Microsoft's Windows 3.11 both address the workgroup LAN embracing the desktop and NOS. Future versions of these will introduce object-oriented technology that will help build applications that are easier and faster to use; object-oriented technology and its implications are explained in Section 10.3.

The NOS itself does not address the physical process of the user interface, but will have to support whatever techniques, such as speech recognition, are used. Also, in multimedia applications the NOS must be capable of supporting the use of different types of data object and their transmission around the network. Possible data objects include video clips, sound bites, photographs, graphs, drawings and text; all of these must be capable of being stored and brought together when appropriate in multimedia applications. Novell made its

Table 10.1 Desirable properties of a network.

Ability for users to communicate with their computer and manipulate information more easily, for example inputting by direct speech or handwriting

Ability to access information quickly and easily, irrespective of where it resides on the network, and to present it in a digestible form

Ability to access applications irrespective of where they reside on the network

Ability to shift programs around the network to take advantage of particular processing or other resources – note that this implies portability of software between different computers

Ability to share information, applications and resources with predefined groups of users

Ability to control access to any resource from all parts of the network and specify which users can access which data or resources

Ability to develop applications in convenient building blocks (or objects) that can then be assembled in different combinations

Ability to support emerging multimedia applications that require greater bandwidth and integration between different technologies

first major move into multimedia in December 1993 with the launch of Net-Ware Video 1.0, described in Section 10.4.

The growth in multimedia applications will dramatically increase the amount of data transmitted across networks, so stimulating the development and implementation of higher-speed networking technologies, notably ATM (asynchronous transfer mode), which is a protocol capable of carrying data right across a network spanning both the LAN and the wide area telecommunications links. The ATM protocol is described in Appendix 2.

Leading NOS players have to ensure that they can cope with increased data rates and support greater network throughput. Novell made attempts with NetWare 4.x to improve support for high performance with its burst mode protocol and large packet facility (LIP), which are described in Section 10.4.

Further improvements will be needed if NOS services such as printing and file serving are to benefit from emerging faster technologies that are capable of transmitting data at speeds an order of magnitude or more greater than traditional LANs. NOS vendors are working with suppliers of high-speed technologies to develop adapter cards to connect workstations and servers to the new technologies.

As well as demanding greater bandwidth, multimedia applications require tighter integration between computing and telephony applications, which is also necessary for applications in computer–telephony integration. The efforts of NOS vendors on this front are touched on in Section 10.4.

☐ 10.3 What are the main technology directions in networking?

In this section we shall examine the chief strategic areas of network development, then in Section 10.4 we shall describe what the leading NOS vendors are developing in these areas.

The areas are summarized in Table 10.2. Note that there is some overlap between them; for example, a distributed directory service is a prerequisite for a distributed network operating system. Some of these developments are more mature and better understood than others. However overriding all of them is the indisputable fact that networks are becoming larger and substantially more complex, and this has led to a boom in network outsourcing, in which organizations hand over their networks to a third-party specialist company. The outsourcing company takes full responsibility for the network, including procurement of systems and services, so saving the user from having to grapple with increasingly complex purchasing and management decisions.

A few organizations have gone further and outsourced their entire IT operation, including all in-house computer systems. In such cases the outsourcing provider is in principle responsible for decisions relating to all aspects of the IT platform, including network operating systems. The point of dialogue between the user and outsourcer is over the applications, which dictate how the underlying platform should develop.

Outsourcing of networking and IT in general is undoubtedly on the increase but, being a service rather than technology trend, it is not listed in Table 10.2. Let us now examine each key technology trend in more detail.

10.3.1 Faster transmission and switching technologies

The key trend in the LAN during the mid 1990s is towards the use of faster switching technologies providing users with quicker response from the network, both for standard on-line applications and access to large files of data. Over the WAN, the main trend is also towards fast switching, largely through the implementation of services based on the ATM (asynchronous transfer mode) protocol. ATM can also be used locally for traffic between LANs, and may in due course replace the LAN itself, providing a single homogeneous end-to-end switching technology. However, this will not happen for a few years and maybe not even then, since it is not clear if ATM will be suitable for all types of local data traffic.

Before discussing this subject further, we shall backtrack to the late 1980s when it looked as if the only way to make LANs faster was to replace the prevailing access and control technologies of Ethernet and token ring, which imposed a limit on how fast data packets could be transferred from computers

Table 10.2 Main technology directions in networking.

Faster transmission and switching technologies

Advanced object-based desktop operating systems

Distributed network management

Global network services

Distributed portable network operating systems

Multimedia applications

Client/server applications

---

to the network. The prime candidate was FDDI, which is described in Appendix 5.

FDDI gained some ground as a backbone technology for interconnecting local LANs and a version of it called CDDI (copper distributed data interface) has been developed for delivering FDDI at the full 100 Mbit s^{-1} to desktop computers via unshielded copper cable. Subsequently, both FDDI and CDDI were rather overtaken by technological events which extended the life of Ethernet and token ring, avoiding the need in many cases for new adapter cards in computers attached to the LAN and preserving existing investments in network software. One idea was to preserve the access methods of Ethernet and token ring, while improving the throughput by allowing more than one system on the network to transmit data packets simultaneously. Normally with both Ethernet and token ring, only one attached PC can transmit a packet at a time but by having a central switch with all systems attached to it in a star-shaped cabling configuration, all devices can in principle transmit data simultaneously, although this depends on the switch having sufficient capacity to sustain communication at full LAN speed between all devices simultaneously. However, it rarely happens in practice that every device on a LAN wants to transmit at full throttle at once, so that a switch with less than the required capacity will provide the required boost in performance. In effect, a switch gives each device, or small clusters of devices, a private Ethernet or token ring LAN linking it with other systems on the overall network.

The way Ethernet switching works is described in Section 6.3.1. Token ring switching is similar; indeed at the physical cabling level it is identical, as shown in Figure 10.1, although it is more complex to implement and as a result very few companies have done so – one such is Bitex, and another Chipcom with help from the godfather of token ring, IBM. Token ring switching requires careful timing by chips in the central switch to give attached devices the impression that a token is being circulated between them (the operation of token ring is described in Appendix 5).

Other high-speed LAN technologies have also emerged, notably Fast Ethernet, promoted heavily by a group of companies including 3 Com, and 100 VG Any LAN, promoted by IBM and Hewlett-Packard. Unlike LAN

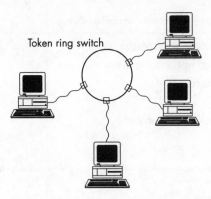

Token ring switch

Figure 10.1 Token ring switching. Attached devices or clusters of devices are arranged in star-shaped configuration around the switch. A token is broadcast from the switch to each device at staggered time intervals to give devices the impression that a token is circulating sequentially between them.

switching as just described, which still operates at the standard LAN speeds, these two methods increase the speed to $100 \, \text{Mbit s}^{-1}$.

Fast Ethernet uses the existing CSMA/CD access method but transmits packets more quickly once they are on the network, which in turn speeds up the rate at which each device can send packets.

100 VG Any LAN applies to both Ethernet and token ring and replaces the access methods of both these LANs with a single new technique called Demand Priority Protocol designed specially to handle the higher speeds. However, it retains the signalling methods of Ethernet and token ring and can run over the same cabling infrastructure.

Both Fast Ethernet and 100 VG-Anylan have their advantages and disadvantages. The latter, in supporting both Ethernet and token ring, provides a single upgrade path for users of either and runs on standard grade 3 unshielded cable, which many organizations have already installed. So 100 VG Any LAN may look a good move as a possible interim step towards abandoning Ethernet and token ring altogether in favour of a single high-speed switching technology at the local level, possibly ATM. 100 VG-Anylan also scores by having a more efficient access method for existing Ethernet applications but it does impose an economic handicap in needing new adapter cards for devices attached to the LAN. Advocates of 100 VG-Anylan, such as Hewlett-Packard, argue that new adapter cards will be needed anyway to migrate to faster transmission technologies because existing ones lack the processing capability. Champions of Fast Ethernet, such as 3 Com, maintain that if new adapter cards are essential, it is better to wait until ATM cards for PCs are available, as this will provide even greater performance and also link more seamlessly with wide area networks of the future. However, it is unlikely that standard PCs will need, or be able to exploit, the full power that ATM can bring until the turn of the century at least. Direct connection to ATM networks will only be required for workstations transmitting large amounts of data in a short time for some applications in multimedia and high-resolution graphics.

The immediate trend in transmission within the local area is thus towards high-speed switching of data packets within cabling hubs, with ATM then being used as a backbone technology although not generally for direct attachment of PCs. On large sites, backbone routers will be used to interconnect local LANs to wide area services, using a variety of protocols including IBM's SNA APPN, TCP/IP and frame relay.

ATM is set to predominate as a wide area switching technology, providing high-speed and scalable bandwidth for trunk data connections, but connection to the ATM network will often be made via other protocols, with frame relay being increasingly favoured. Frame relay was designed specifically to meet the needs of LANs interconnected over wide area services. It provides access to WAN services for the data packets transmitted across LANs, and avoids much of the overhead of error correction and flow control imposed by the other predominant WAN packet switched protocol, X.25.

Figure 10.2 illustrates how all these protocols fit together schematically in an end-to-end network. The figure starts with a workgroup of locally connected PCs, linked through to a backbone serving a whole campus, and then goes on to a WAN. In principle, as already noted, ATM could provide an end-to-end network service but in practice a typical network will continue to have a mixture of protocols including some of those listed in Figure 10.2, at least until the new millennium begins. The ATM protocol is described in Appendix 10, along with other high-speed protocols.

10.3.2 Advanced object-based desktop operating systems

This development is less imminent than most of the others described in this section for the majority of computer users, but software vendors are almost unanimous that it is the way forward. Indeed, operating systems of this type are already appearing on the market, such as Taligent developed by a consortium founded jointly by IBM and Apple and later joined by others such as Hewlett-Packard.

Novell and Microsoft are also both active in this field, the former with AppWare and the latter with its Chicago development which is a progression from MS-DOS and Windows. More about these is given in Section 10.4, and see also Section 8.8 for a general description of AppWare.

What are objects and what benefits will they bring?

The growth of network computing is one factor driving the movement toward object orientation, as it is sometimes termed. Currently, a typical large network links a wide variety of computers all conforming to different standards for both software development and user access to applications and data. Object-based

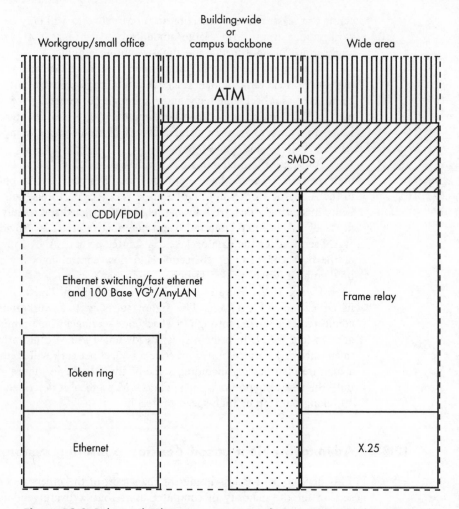

Figure 10.2 Relationship between existing and emerging networking protocols.

operating systems should provide benefits for both end users and software developers. For the former, the aim is to make applications and information easier to access and manipulate through common intuitive commands that build on current GUI (graphical user interface) standards. For software developers, object-oriented operating systems should be useful in providing a framework for existing software modules to be combined readily in new distributed applications.

The intended benefits of object-based operating systems are:

• easy access to information across networks;

• better integration of different media types in single applications;

- quicker delivery and maintenance of software;
- more intuitive way of using computers for real applications.

Objects can either be: units, or collections of information; software modules that perform a particular task; or combinations of both. Examples of the former are a drawing produced by a paintbrush program, a spreadsheet from the popular Excel package, a bite of digitized sound produced by a SoundBlaster card or a clip of digitized video. Given suitable hardware, any of these objects should be capable of being dropped into a multimedia document which can then be displayed appropriately; for example, a document describing a holiday home could be annotated with a graph describing climate in the area and a short video clip of the location. Currently, pulling all this together requires considerable manipulation but on an object-based system it should be as easy as merging two existing text documents. Examples of object software modules include various options for an office system, such as word processing, spreadsheets, diary, project scheduling and electronic mail; these can be combined as objects to develop a customized office environment for a particular workgroup without requiring additional software to link the objects together.

At a more advanced level, objects could also be combinations of data and software modules; for example, objects representing the components of a car could contain both a description of the shape and construction, and also functions that enable those components to be tested during assembly. These functions would need to link to overall testing modules, which could be combined to simplify the process of assessing that a particular design meets criteria for safety, performance, comfort, fuel economy, environmental factors and so on.

Much work remains to be done to make this more advanced scenario possible and it is important not to expect too much from the object movement – for many traditional applications, object-based technology will bring little advantage in the foreseeable future. However, for larger sites, it holds considerable promise in reducing software maintenance costs, which currently outstrip the cost of new application development in most cases. The expectation is that existing applications can be gradually extended by adding new modules in incremental steps, leaving the main body of software intact. At present, the addition of new software often involves substantial modifications to numerous existing programs.

10.3.3 Distributed network management

Currently, many large networks are managed by systems that do not fit well together, making it hard to obtain a consistent overall view. The role of emerging standards in facilitating better interaction between managers of different network elements is described in Section 7.5. It should become easier to interconnect different network element managers as objects, although this is unlikely to happen in the immediate future. A more realistic hope is that it will become easier to provide limited links between existing network management systems so that they can at least feed basic information about the status of the components they are responsible for to an umbrella management system. It will then be possible to provide an overall network map that can be interrogated at progressively more detailed levels to yield information right down to the status of local workgroup servers, printers and even client desktop systems.

Another welcome development would be management systems that enable organizations to obtain information about the status of lines provided by a telecommunications carrier. Currently, if for example a private trunk circuit fails, no information about the expected time for that link to be repaired is available to the user organization's network management system. However, joint projects between leading carriers and computer companies are looking to providing such information; for instance, British Telecom has been working with IBM on linking the two companies' network management systems. Then BT's Concert system can provide information on the status of public circuits to users of IBM's Netview network management system.

10.3.4 Global network services

Considerable progress has already been made in this field, such as from Banyan Systems and Novell, which both provide a global directory service. Nevertheless, further progress is required with several aspects of this, particularly in addressing the needs of mobile staff. Here the basic requirement is the ability to access the network from anywhere in the world without jeopardizing the security of key applications and data. This needs two essential features: firstly, that the network be able to identify users irrespective of how and where they gain access; secondly, it must be possible to identify where each user has come from. The latter feature may be needed to guard sensitive information from possible unauthorized access, which is easier to obtain from some locations than others. It may be desirable to prevent legitimate users from accessing certain information or network resources when they are dialling over public circuits, while allowing them access from their offices. In other words, ability to roam the network may depend not just on users' identities but also on their locations. A related facility is single logon, enabling users to access all network resources for which they have authorization through a single sign-on procedure. The aim is to give users a single identifier and password for the whole network.

These facilities are not necessarily provided by the NOS and may be independent applications, but security functions in particular do rely on the operating systems that control key resources. LAN servers have become key resources as they now hold critical applications and data and are, of course, controlled by the NOS. Yet, despite an obvious growing role in global network security, most NOSs still lag behind traditional host operating environments, such as IBM's MVS, in this field.

Another type of global service where further progress is inevitable is the automatic distribution and maintenance of the NOS software. On large networks comprising hundreds of servers, it is difficult to maintain consistency and compatibility between different software releases for a given NOS. The ability to down-load software across a network to specified servers with automatic testing of the new configuration would be an advantage; such procedures are already being carried out for other types of critical network software, for example in multiprotocol routers.

10.3.5   Distributed portable network operating systems

By 'portable' we mean NOSs that run on different hardware platforms and by 'distributed' the additional ability for a number of systems running the NOS to work together. This provides the platform for distributed applications.

Traditionally, most NOSs have been tied to Intel-based PC servers, from which they have been enhanced to provide access to other operating environments such as Digital Equipment's VMS. Most small-scale peer-to-peer NOSs still run only on standard PCs; however both NetWare and Windows NT can now run on a number of platforms, enabling them to form the basis of a complete networked environment. More details are given in Section 10.4.

To be classified as distributed, a NOS must support intelligent interaction between different servers, with the ability to make them all appear to client applications as a single server. Figure 10.3 shows a network with a NOS running on three servers that all appear to the user as a single super server. The key link element is a distributed directory which enables requests for data, applications or network services to be passed efficiently between servers.

10.3.6   Multimedia applications

Multimedia means different things to different people, ranging from the mere use of a SoundBlaster card to inject a few spoken words into documents to full blown virtual reality complete with three-dimensional holographic projections. However, essentially it requires integration into single applications of at least two different media types chosen from the following: coded data, graphics, drawings, document images, still photographs, video and audio. In principle it could also embrace taste and tactile sensations. All of these can be held as digital data on the same storage media, and the requirements are for suitable hardware for the applications to run on, and for software to integrate the different elements into coherent applications. For NOSs the main need is to provide facilities that enable servers to handle the different types of data as easily and efficiently as possible. The leading NOS vendors are doing this, as we see in Section 10.4.

(a)

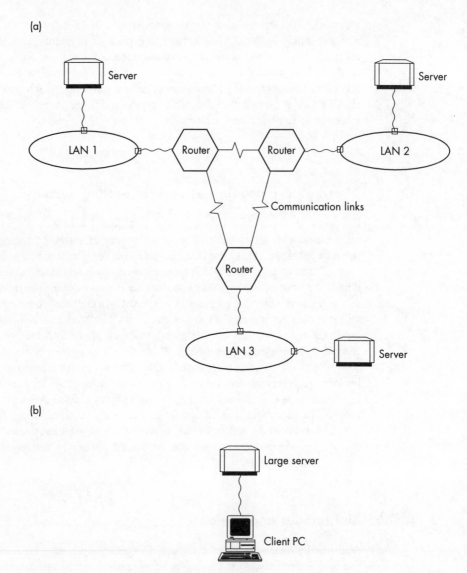

(b)

Figure 10.3 Network of three servers linked by a directory service: (a) physical network; (b) logical network – that is, how it appears to users and client workstations.

10.3.7 Client/server applications

This may appear to be the most mature of the seven areas described in this section but there is considerable work to be done to make the client/server platform as reliable and robust as traditional host-based systems. The problem is that a client/server application can involve cooperation between computer systems and software components that use different protocols and are under the control of different operating systems.

Some organizations still prefer host-based systems linked to dumb terminals for specific applications, because the environment is easier to control and cheaper to maintain. However, not many in the industry would deny that the client/server approach based on intelligent desktop systems interacting with shared servers is the way forward, because it is more flexible and better able to support growth and emerging technologies; it is also potentially more resilient because it is not dependent on any single component, provided it has been designed correctly.

NOSs are playing a key role in making client/server environments more appropriate for large-scale commercial applications by providing tools that support software development on their platforms, and facilities to help manage the increasingly complex networks on which such applications run.

□ 10.4 What are the NOS vendors doing to support these technologies?

Table 10.2 listed the key areas of development for NOSs. We shall now review briefly some of the work NOS vendors are doing in each of these areas.

10.4.1 Faster transmission and switching technologies

The focus of NOS vendors here is on enabling servers to cope with the increased throughput of data resulting from these new technologies, and embracing the new network components within their management systems. For the latter, leading NOS vendors have been working with makers of routers and hubs that will implement new switching technologies to ensure the emerging networks can still be managed from the NOS. Microsoft, for example, has cooperated with leading hub and router vendors to enable its desktop management system (formerly called Hermes) to interoperate with the software used to control these networking devices.

Figure 10.4 shows the possible role of a NOS in a future high-speed local network based on ATM, whose operation is described in Section 10.3.1. An important point is that whereas all existing LAN technologies, such as Ethernet and token ring, require all devices to transmit data onto the network at the same speed, ATM supports variable speed. Thus servers, for example, which because they perform tasks on behalf of a number of clients transmit and receive data packets at a higher rate than the clients, can be given a greater bandwidth in an ATM network.

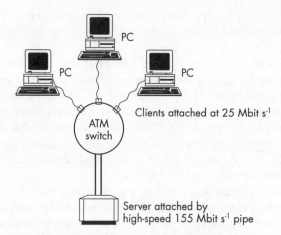

PC

PC   PC

Clients attached at 25 Mbit s⁻¹

ATM
switch

Server attached by
high-speed 155 Mbit s⁻¹ pipe

Figure 10.4 Client/server ATM network.

So on the network in Figure 10.4 clients are each given 25 Mps bandwidth. However, the server is attached to the local hub at $155\,\text{Mbit s}^{-1}$ (one of a number of speeds allowed by the ATM standard), which means that it must respond to requests much more quickly than on a standard $10\,\text{Mbit s}^{-1}$ Ethernet network. The NOS must also be able to accept management messages coming from the hub using the SNMP protocol (described in Chapter 7) so that it can provide overall control of the whole network. It is worth stressing that the core NOS software itself does not need altering to support high-speed networking technologies; the change needs to be made to the device driver software which shields the NOS from the underlying transmission technologies. At this level, NOS vendors have been working with providers of adapter cards for ATM to ensure that the NOS software supports these cards and can cope with the increased speeds.

The requirement for improved server performance to keep pace with faster networks is met partly by increasingly powerful hardware. However, although in theory the NOS need not be changed, it does have to provide fast file access to allow data to be obtained sufficiently quickly. NOS vendors are continually improving their products along these lines. An example of such an improvement is Novell's burst mode protocol, which was an option in NetWare 3.11 but integral to NetWare 4.x. Running in conjunction with the IPX transport protocol, this increases the amount of data that can be transmitted at any one time without being acknowledged by the receiving station, which is often a client PC. Previously, each packet required an acknowledgement and was retransmitted if this was not received, slowing down network performance. With burst mode, the sending and receiving stations can negotiate how many packets are transmitted in a single burst. The principle is illustrated in Figure 10.5 which compares burst mode with the old single mode. The figure also shows a burst of packets being received incorrectly, after which the

(a)

Single mode:

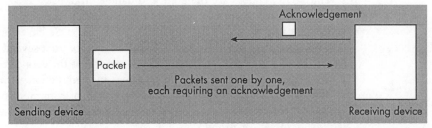

Burst mode:

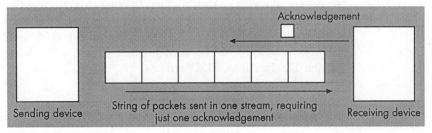

(b)

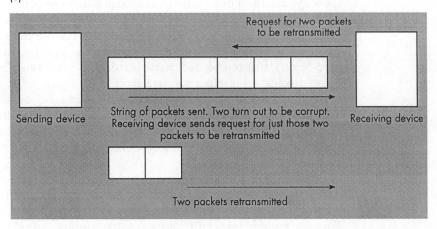

Figure 10.5 Novell's burst mode protocol: (a) burst mode compared with old single mode; (b) how burst mode handles packets that are corrupted during transmission.

receiving station requests only the packets that were corrupted to be re-sent.

Two other key developments on performance that are supported by several NOS vendors are the ability to handle large packets so that more data can be sent and received in a single transmission, and support for parallel processing in the server. For some time, leading NOSs have supported multi-tasking, which enables the server to handle requests from several users at once, but if there is just one disk drive, only one request for data can be handled at a time. By supporting multiple disk drives in conjunction with conventional multi-tasking, a NOS can access data on behalf of a number of users simultaneously; this improves response, especially if the bandwidth of the network is also increased in proportion.

A further point is that NOSs available on different hardware platforms may not perform equally well on each one – the NOS may be better adapted to one type of hardware than another. In order to improve performance, leading NOS vendors are cooperating with key computer makers to ensure their software is optimized to make best use of the hardware. Microsoft, for example, has worked closely with Digital Equipment to ensure that Windows NT works well on DEC's Alpha RISC systems.

10.4.2 Advanced object-based desktop operating systems

In this field only the big NOS players, in particular Novell, Microsoft and IBM, can afford the necessary investment; other NOS vendors are having to fall in line with standards and products developed by the main manufacturers. Novell's AppWare, described in some detail in Section 8.8, is one of the most ambitious and comprehensive efforts in the field, with a grand design that sounds like a blueprint for the future of IT. The overall objective is to crystallize all the tools and facilities needed for distributed applications into discrete components, called objects, that can be readily assembled. This poses two problems: firstly, a huge amount of enabling software must exist, which works smoothly and invisibly, and this is by itself a major development task; secondly, there may in the end be so many objects that the job of building large applications is only marginally less difficult than it was. Even so, technologies such as AppWare at least promise to make the chore of maintaining complex software easier and less costly.

Microsoft is also making major strides in this area, for example with its OLE (object linking and embedding) technology, which is in reality an open standard available to any software developer writing applications for Microsoft's Windows environment. OLE focuses on documents, providing features for dynamic sharing of objects so that changes in one document are automatically reflected in others that share the same object. It preserves local formatting, so that a spreadsheet chart, for instance, can be copied into a word-processing document while retaining its original tabular structure, thus avoiding the user having to rearrange the chart's numbers, which was necessary with earlier techniques for sharing data such as Microsoft's own DDE (dynamic data exchange).

OLE provides the framework for Microsoft's more recent developments, such as Windows 95, the successor to MS-DOS and Windows 3.11, which was developed in the project code named Chicago. Now is a timely moment to delve a little deeper into Windows 95, which was about to be launched when this book was published.

Windows 95

Microsoft's new desktop operating system, called Windows 95, starting with version 0, is substantially different in structure from Windows 3.11. Yet to users of existing Windows 3.11 applications it appears to be almost identical, except that it provides some additional features, including better reliability and slightly improved performance. While providing a framework for emerging desktop applications in multimedia that will benefit from new object-based technologies, it has been designed to be completely compatible with existing MS-DOS and Windows-based applications. Because so many existing MS-DOS and Windows applications run on Intel 386-based PCs, Windows 95 had to work efficiently on these computers, even though most desktop systems sold up to the time of the launch run on at least 486 chips. A further design objective was therefore to achieve performance at least as good as Windows 3.1 on a 4 Mbyte 386 system running the same tasks with the same applications.

Yet such applications will not benefit from some of the new features of Windows 95, although Microsoft has managed to exploit some of the 32-bit facilities when running old 16-bit applications in a process called thunking. The key new features of Windows 95 that were not present in Windows 3.11 are:

- new file system, ending dependence on MS-DOS for file access and manipulation;
- new graphics;
- incorporation of networking support derived from LAN Manager;
- support for 32-bit application and the Win32 API described in Chapter 8;
- improved reliability for all applications;
- compatibility with legacy Windows and MS-DOS applications at equal or greater levels of performance than users were getting.

The most obvious advance in Windows 95 is the completely redesigned file management system, finally severing the link with MS-DOS in Microsoft's strategic low-end operating system, as Windows NT had already done at the high end. Successive releases of Windows had already weaned themselves from MS-DOS for new tasks, but still relied on it for file management and access on local disks.

All file management applications now run in protected mode using 32-bit code, which improves performance and reliability. Using 32-bit rather than 16-bit code means that data can be processed and moved around in larger chunks. The implications of protected mode are described in Appendix 8.

Another major enhancement in Windows 95 is the virtual machine manager (VMM), which is the heart of the operating system as it takes care of low-level memory management and scheduling which determines overall performance. VMM enables a Windows 95 to run multiple programs, including old MS-DOS applications, concurrently. Furthermore, new 32-bit applications each receive their private address space in the CPU. This means applications appear to have the whole CPU to themselves even when others are running at the same time, which means that they do not interfere with each other or conflict in their demand for resources.

However, above all, Windows 95 is a full network operating system, coming with the old Windows for Workgroups functions built in. Although it can be purchased as a single-user system, this is really a special case and the product can subsequently be expanded to serve a workgroup by installing additional copies but without the need for an upgrade.

Finally, Windows 95 is more object oriented in that it supports stronger links between documents and files shared within workgroups. Using Microsoft's object linking and embedding (OLE) technology described in Chapter 8, documents can be shared between different applications while preserving formatting information.

10.4.3 Distributed network management

In this field, NOS vendors need to be able to link their own management systems with packages that control other elements of a network, including wide area links and network components such as hubs and routers, in addition to computers. Management of large networks involves cooperation between many different elements including the NOS manager, which can all only work together by adherence to common standards. These standards, in particular SNMP, are described in Chapter 7. The point to stress here is that adherence to standards, although necessary, is not sufficient in itself to deliver flexible management systems capable of coping with global networks. It is also necessary for NOS vendors to cooperate with other key players in the network management arena to provide integrated systems capable of spanning the whole network. The leading NOS vendors are in fact doing this; Microsoft, for example, has been working with Hewlett-Packard to integrate their respective management systems and create a distributed management system embracing desktop systems as well as all elements of the network. A version of HP's OpenView management system for the Windows NT platform was launched in 1994.

There is also a trend towards integration of network management with systems management. Until the early 1990s, these were regarded as largely separate domains but are now coming together to provide coherent end-to-end management of the whole IT enterprise. Microsoft is well placed in this field, having developed the Hermes system management software which has been adopted by a number of other network management players, including Hewlett-Packard and the UK company Network Managers.

10.4.4   Distributed portable network operating systems

With the exception of UNIX, most operating systems were originally developed for a single hardware platform. However, the situation with NOSs is somewhat complicated by the fact that some were originally built on top of standard computer operating systems. Banyan Systems' Vines, for example, was built on UNIX. It therefore enjoyed the portability of UNIX, having the ability to run on a wide range of computers. Microsoft's LAN Manager was originally based on OS/2 and so could run on all computers on which OS/2 had been implemented, which originally was chiefly standard Intel-based servers and PCs, although it was subsequently ported to UNIX, and then its sequel, Windows NT Server, was made available on a wide variety of platforms, competing with UNIX as a hardware-independent distributed operating system.

In contrast, Novell's NetWare was built from the bottom up as a network operating system, originally for PC-based servers, although more recently Novell has started migrating NetWare to other platforms in its PIN (processor independent NetWare) project. To develop PIN, Novell cooperated with the relevant hardware vendors to migrate or 'port' NetWare to those vendors' computers. In the initial stages after PIN was announced in 1993, Novell was working with three system vendors – Hewlett-Packard, Sun Microsystems and Digital Equipment – bringing NetWare 4.x on to Hewlett-Packard's PA-RISC systems, Digital's Alpha AXP and Sun's Sparc systems. Novell also hopes to attract other partners with the aim eventually of making NetWare 4.x available on all major hardware platforms, including IBM mainframes.

However, this is not the whole story, as typical NetWare environments comprise more than just the core code, with usually a number of NLMs (NetWare loadable modules). In future, users may want to migrate their existing NetWare applications to a new platform if this appears cost-effective but naturally they will be inhibited from doing this if the task of moving all the NLMs appears onerous. In practice, the task will not be great for NLMs that do not make direct calls to the operating system and which do not involve hardware-specific features. In these cases, the NLM can be moved to the new hardware just by recompiling, although hardware-specific NLMs will require some additional programming. Guidelines to help with NLM migration are available from Novell and its PIN partners.

The other significant development under this heading is the integration of the NOS with traditional PC operating systems. This was seen both with Microsoft's Windows for Workgroups, bringing Windows and LAN Manager together, and with Personal NetWare, uniting Novell's DR-DOS, which is an MS-DOS derivative, with the stripped-down version of NetWare originally called NetWare Lite. The developments described in this section pave the way for future fully distributed network operating systems, as discussed further in Section 10.5.

10.4.5 Multimedia applications

Here NOSs have a major role in storing, managing and controlling access to the data, especially when the multimedia applications are based on PC LANs. Microsoft's main emphasis has been in making multimedia applications readily available from its Windows environment, leading to the Microsoft Video for Windows desktop multimedia software. Microsoft has exploited its expertise in this field by developing operating systems for video games machines, such as Sega Enterprises' Saturn 32-bit system.

Novell, on the other hand, has placed more emphasis on use of the server to store and play back video and audio sequences. Novell demonstrated its serious intent in the field with the acquisition in July 1993 of the multimedia specialist company Fluent Inc., which became Novell's multimedia product division. The first product resulting from this acquisition followed swiftly in December 1993 in the shape of NetWare Video 1.0, which is an NLM allowing digital video and synchronized audio to be stored, managed and played back from NetWare 4.x servers; the product incorporates techniques to ensure that video and audio sequences are not disturbed by sudden surges in network traffic. Video and audio data streams are separated, and the rate of transmission is dynamically varied in an attempt to maintain a constant data rate. Nevertheless, for applications requiring immaculate quality, Novell recommends using a dedicated video server and then configuring the network in a star so that each device has a guaranteed bandwidth; this ensures that video data is transmitted at the correct speed.

This example highlights the fact that the trend towards switching hubs and star-shaped network topologies fits well with the arrival of multimedia applications. These developments are allowing existing applications in telecommunications and broadcasting to be integrated with traditional computer applications via the NOS. In fact, Novell has been a driving force in telephony/computing integration through the NOTA (Novell Open Telephony Association) formed in March 1994, whose members include leading telecommunications companies like Alcatel, AT&T, Ericsson and GPT, which will implement NOTA's TSAPI (telephony services application programming interface) into their products. TSAPI provides a standard software interface for PBXs to be linked with NetWare networks for CIT (computer integrated telephony) applications. Desktop applications that conform with TSAPI will be able to access client/server CIT applications; these include mixed-media mailboxes in which messages can be sent to a single mailbox by fax, electronic mail or voice, and possibly annotated with still images or accompanied by video sequences.

10.4.6 Client/server applications

The NOS provides the basis for client/server applications through its control of servers and the data they hold. The main developments have been the extension of the client/server concept to large networks embracing multiple servers and other types of host system. The ideal is that a client application should be able to exploit data or other resources anywhere in the network. The role of the NOS here is to ensure that all servers on the system appear to client applications as just one server. Global directory services enable this to happen with respect to servers controlled by the NOS; for other host systems, the NOS can provide gateway facilities. However, for full integration it is necessary that a version of the NOS should run in the host environment to ensure that seamless access to host data can be provided for client applications.

The leading NOS vendors are aware that in order to provide platforms for client/server applications that are sufficiently robust to run serious commercial applications, they need to cooperate with companies with products covering other parts of the picture. This includes makers of PCs, servers and also key networking systems such as routers and hubs. Along these lines is Microsoft's technology and marketing agreement with Cisco, the world's leading router manufacturer. This involves integration of Cisco's remote access routers with Windows NT Server to provide a complete client/server platform competing directly with traditional host-based systems, particularly IBM mainframes, thus allowing Microsoft to exploit Cisco's expertise in transporting IBM SNA data alongside other types of traffic over networks of LANs inter-connected by multiprotocol routers. Microsoft hopes to persuade SNA cus-tomers to move their applications to a client/server environment based on Windows NT. As an interim step, Microsoft is promoting its own SNA running on the NT operating system to provide access to the existing mainframes from PCs attached to the client/server network. The thrust of Microsoft's strategy is illustrated in Figure 10.6, which shows two networks: a traditional IBM one with PCs accessing a mainframe; and Microsoft's proposed interim step with access to the mainframe gained via its NT server. Meanwhile, according to Microsoft's view of the world, the applications will be migrated from the mainframe to one or more Windows NT servers. The link with the mainframe will have finally been severed. The only drawback is that many large organi-zations still need the data storage and management facilities provided by mainframes, and a good number were not convinced that the early versions of Windows NT were as robust as their familiar mainframe operating environ-ments, such as IBM's MVS.

☐ 10.5 How operating systems and particularly NOSs will evolve

Two trends are shaping the development of operating systems during the 1990s: the first is the move away from large centralized host computers towards dis-tributed systems of different sizes communicating and interacting across a network; the second is a move towards what can loosely be called application portability, to give organizations the freedom to choose the most cost-effective hardware on which to run their software. Such portability can be achieved in two ways. One is to make applications independent of the underlying operating system which provides the link with the hardware and resources needed for it to execute. The other is to make the operating system itself independent of the hardware. In the latter case, an application may be tied to a particular operating system but could still be ported to different hardware because the operating system itself is not tied to any underlying hardware.

Operating systems have evolved in line with these developments. The move towards distributed applications based on the client/server model is leading to the integration of different operating systems. NetWare, for example, can now run alongside DEC's VMS operating system providing NetWare clients with access to applications, data and resources located in a DEC network. Another example is IBM reworking its OS/400 operating system, originally developed for its mid range AS/400 host systems, to make it run effectively on LAN servers. The aim is to produce a complete distributed operating system embracing both the LAN and, if required, back-end application and corporate data servers.

Operating system companies are also addressing the portability issue from both the angles just described. They are implementing standards developed by groups such as Posix and X/Open to provide application portability across different operating systems. As described in Chapter 8, a key group of standards is X/Open's Spec 1170, which provide application developers with a set of APIs to plug their products into. Conformance with these APIs guarantees that the application will run on computers supporting versions of UNIX, and in future other operating systems which themselves support these APIs.

Operating systems are also being ported to different platforms. At the same time, recent microprocessors, such as the PowerPC chip developed by IBM and Motorola, are capable of running several operating systems simultaneously. This will mean that users will be able not only to replace their hardware without changing the applications but also to implement a different operating system if this is deemed necessary to increase performance or provide additional functions. This is important because it is the operating system as much as the hardware itself that determines how well a computer will perform.

In parallel with this trend towards hardware-independent operating systems, NOS vendors are distributing their products more effectively across different systems. The aim is to make the computers of a network work together more effectively as a coherent whole rather than the partial sum of disjointed parts. Microsoft's Windows NT, for example, is a scalable platform capable of expanding from a single-user operating system to a distributed networked system, although it has yet to embrace large host systems. Similarly, Novell's combination of UnixWare and NetWare provides an upgrade path from a single-user system to a large network. Meanwhile Microsoft, Novell and IBM, the three leading players in large-scale network operating systems, are moving towards single coherent product ranges that will allow progressive growth from a single PC to a large network. The principle is that you start with a single-user

(a)

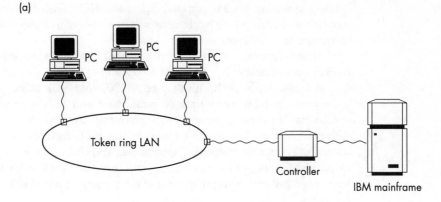

(b)

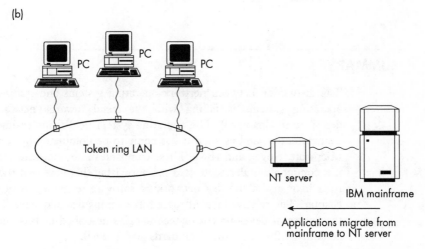

(c)

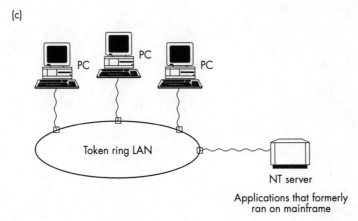

Figure 10.6 Microsoft's strategy for weaning users away from IBM mainframe: (a) PCs accessing IBM mainframe directly; (b) PCs accessing IBM mainframe via NT server; (c) *fait accompli*!

desktop operating system and add first basic NOS functions and then more sophisticated facilities for larger networks by means of modules, without having to change to a different software range.

There remains the question of how well different operating systems will co-exist on a network. It is true that all leading operating systems will conform to standards, such as X/Open's Spec 1170, that will allow portability of applications but for some time to come there will be a poor level of inter-operability between different NOS platforms such as NetWare and NT Advanced Server. This may well prevent organizations from choosing the best operating system for particular applications and instead they may be tempted to standardize on single operating platforms such as Windows NT in the knowledge that this will run on most of their systems and avoid interoperability problems.

☐ SUMMARY

The distinction between network operating systems and traditional computer operating systems is fading with the trend towards network computing, described in Chapter 9. The operating system field is increasingly regarded as a single entity, and as such it has come to be dominated by three companies: Microsoft, Novell and IBM. These companies also dominate the NOS field as it is commonly understood. It is not surprising therefore that they have pivotal roles in many of the key networking software technologies described in this chapter. The relative fates of these three companies may have little bearing on the course of development of technologies described in this chapter, but will certainly influence which standards will prevail.

Case study: Bass plc

CHAPTER OBJECTIVES:

- To set out the strategy of a major NOS user and describe some of the problems and issues that have been encountered so far
- To describe how issues raised in the book, such as network management, have been tackled by a major NOS user

☐ CS.1   Introduction

The Bass group plc installed a distributed network of LANs during 1993 that illustrates many of the key points covered in this book – these include network management, interoperability between LANs and existing host computer systems, installation of networking components such as routers, staff training and, above all, selection of the NOS.

In the present case, Novell won a tender to supply the NetWare 3.11 NOS (later upgraded to 3.12) but, as with many other large sites, there were indications that Microsoft could make inroads with NT Server, as Bass was already a heavy user of Windows applications. Also, like many other large organizations, Bass has decided so far not to upgrade from NetWare 3.12 to NetWare 4.0, deeming that the drawbacks of such a move could outweigh the benefits.

□ CS.2 Setting the scene

Bass had, over the previous five years, installed a large IBM SNA network linking over 200 IBM AS/400 mid-range systems at divisional level for central processing. These AS/400s were also used at lower levels within the divisions, such as distribution depots and social clubs, for a variety of core commercial applications, and there were also some Unisys mainframes running both legacy applications and the Taverns Central Retail System. The Group wanted to introduce networked PCs as the standard desktop interface to the computing service, initially with the introduction of a full office and mail infrastructure but progressing to the development of a new generation of client/server systems. The chosen strategy involved the selection of key products and suppliers based primarily on market leadership, while retaining the AS/400s for the core transaction processing and data maintenance.

However, first the group had to decide what sort of network it wanted in order to know what kind of suppliers to seek. The decision was taken to install PC LANs for new client/server applications in local workgroups, while retaining the AS/400s for departmental and corporate applications and indeed migrating the Unisys programs to them. The group also wanted to consolidate all systems around a common network in order to provide universal access to information throughout the organization, rather than running two separate networks with one interconnecting the AS/400s and the other the new LANs.

As explained in Chapter 6, routers are usually chosen to interconnect LANs across a large geographically dispersed organization, and this was the path chosen by Bass. Now six key components of the whole IT infrastructure could be identified: mid-range host systems, routers, cabling hubs, LAN servers, desktop workstations and operating systems, including the NOS. As desktop servers and workstations are usually based on industry-standard technology in the shape of processors from either Intel or AMD, there was no need to commit to a particular supplier for those, but for the other components it made sense to standardize on one supplier in order to simplify the management tasks and have just a single point of contact for support. In four of the five remaining areas the group chose a leading supplier: Cisco for routers, Microsoft's Windows for the desktop operating system, Novell for the NOS and IBM for further AS/400s, of which the group had 213 by mid 1994, for departmental and host applications. Only in the case of cabling hubs did Bass plump for a company that did not lead its field, but even this choice, UB Networks (formerly Ungermann–Bass), was a pioneer of hub technology. In fact, UB might well have led the hub market had its marketing been as good as its technical innovation.

□ CS.3 Reasons for the choices made (especially that of NetWare)

The Group's Director of Planning and Control, Allan Paterson, insisted that these suppliers were not chosen solely because they were each the biggest in their fields. However such choices are inevitably related to market dominance; for example, IBM's AS/400 was selected partly because it had the largest base of available off-the-shelf applications, which of course follows from its dominant position in the mid-range business system market, and Cisco because it provided products suitable both for core routing at the heart of a large network and also smaller systems for accessing the core network from smaller branch sites. In practice, these facilities could only be made available by large established suppliers.

Novell was chosen because, at that time, NetWare was the only NOS possessing the required additional functions, such as the ability to access IBM AS/400 applications from the LAN. As explained in Chapter 6, Novell markets a product called NetWare for SAA which enables client workstations attached to a NetWare server to access IBM applications from the Windows environments with which they are familiar. Furthermore, NetWare for SAA allows IBM applications to be accessed across the network, via Novell's IPX transport protocol, as far as the IBM systems. By avoiding the need to carry SNA protocols across the wide area network in addition to IPX, routers have one less protocol to handle, so reducing processing overheads.

In 1992, the decision was made to make a major investment in networked LANs as part of a project to develop an enterprise-wide office infrastructure. At that time, the Group already possessed some LANs, using a variety of NOS solutions, principally Microsoft LAN Manager, IBM LAN Server and Novell NetWare. But at that time there was some uncertainty over the future of IBM LAN Server as IBM had only recently split from Microsoft over the development of that NOS (see Chapter 2). In addition, Microsoft's LAN Manager, which was then almost the same as LAN Server, was rejected because it did not match NetWare's all-round stability and facilities, according to Bass

Head of Network Development, John Pook, which suggests that IBM LAN Server was also rejected for technical reasons.

The fact that the group was already committed to Windows was not considered to be a strong motive for choosing Microsoft for the NOS as well. Windows interoperates reasonably well with NetWare and there is plenty of expertise available to make them work together – indeed, Windows/NetWare interoperability is a popular subject at conferences and seminars.

Bass's Alan Paterson commented that the key drivers in the selection of Novell were: '(a) the slightly larger installed base than the other products, and (b) clear market leadership at that time backed up by a positive vision.'

□ CS.4 Will NT Server make inroads?

More recently, the group has started evaluating Microsoft's NT Server to investigate whether it is complementary or an alternative to NetWare. Paterson admitted that the NT Server would have been a serious contender had it been available when the decision on the strategic NOS supplier was made. As it was, he expected that the NT Server would be increasingly used within the organization, although the group remained committed to NetWare for the immediate future.

However, Novell would no doubt feel more secure about this account if Bass sealed its commitment by migrating to NetWare 4.0, which has additional facilities for large distributed networks of the sort possessed by Bass (see Chapter 2). Although Bass is an obvious candidate for NetWare 4.0, its use has so far been rejected because Paterson does not think it offers any obvious benefits to the company. Nevertheless there are two potential benefits: (1) global signon, the ability for users to log on with a single command to all applications anywhere on the network for which they are authorized, although NetWare 4.0 on its own would not provide that facility, according to Paterson; (2) a global directory naming service, which enables users to locate applications on any NetWare server on the network. The latter will be of interest to Bass when the group starts distributing applications across multiple servers, which would require a directory to enable the NOS on each server to locate a particular piece of software. Currently, the main requirement for remote communication from NetWare servers is to access AS/400 applications, which is covered adequately by NetWare for SAA running under NetWare 3.12.

☐ CS.5   Network management strategy

Novell might also be disappointed that Bass has decided not to use its network management software to complement the core NOS. Early in 1994 the group was considering its network management strategy but decided that Novell's NMS (NetWare management system) was too expensive and immature, not yet providing sufficient coverage or integration of the whole LAN, including applications running within the server.

At the time of writing (late 1994), Bass was reviewing its network management strategy with the objective of enabling a single station to determine what was going on right across the network, down to the level of server and even client applications in remote LANs. Bass currently possessed reasonable network management facilities at the local level but no facilities for remote monitoring and control of LAN servers. By providing greater remote control, costs could be saved by reducing the amount of on-site management needed.

Bass already had good local physical management of LANs via UB Network's Net Director, used to manage the UB hubs. This enables devices within the hubs and attached to them to be monitored and configured but provides no access at the application level. Hewlett-Packard's OpenView platform is used to provide remote visibility across the wide area but again this is only at the network level and does not penetrate into LANs beyond the routers used to interconnect them. So what Bass is seeking is a product to integrate the management components already in place, incorporating server management, and to extend the visibility down to applications to provide a more comprehensive view of the overall network activity. One possibility would be to take system management products from Hewlett-Packard, as these would blend in naturally as an extension to the existing Openview applications.

☐ CS.6   What is the group doing about security?

The Bass security strategy can be summed up as prevention of unauthorized access to data and applications but not at the expense of jeopardizing the overall goal of making information more widely and easily available. Paterson admitted that attitudes have changed in the last 10 years as the value of providing managers with the best information possible as soon as they need it has become more apparent. Information was formerly regarded as a valuable asset that needed protection, and was assigned only to individuals who would control access to it. Now information is viewed as the fuel that drives good decisions and so should be available to whoever needs it within the organization, even if this increases the risk of unauthorized access.

Nevertheless, the group is well aware that security breaches can be very damaging, both to data and systems themselves, and in more extreme cases to overall business confidence. It minimizes the risk of external hacking by dial-back security, which makes it almost impossible for anyone to enter the network from a telephone number not known to the system.

Closely related to security is the drive towards single signon, and here the group is providing access to a random password generator. This improves security by giving users random passwords so that they do not use those, such as the name of a spouse, that can be readily guessed by potential hackers. Clearly, if users are given wider access throughout the network through a single point of entry, it is doubly important to ensure this entry point is well guarded.

Bass now favours the creed of empowerment, which means giving end users more rights over access to data and applications distributed across the network.

□ CS.7 Have there been problems with NetWare?

Paterson believes Bass would still choose NetWare if the decision were to be taken in 1994, which suggests that the product has on the whole lived up to the high expectations the company had of it. In general, only minor problems have been experienced at a technical level but the group was at one point unhappy with Novell's perceived lack of experience in dealing with large corporate clients, which became apparent when Novell introduced the upgrade from NetWare version 3.11 to 3.12. Having a large network distributed across many sites, Bass was obviously concerned that the upgrade should not have any implications for wide area connections. Paterson complained that Novell released the new version and made 3.11 obsolete without consultation with large customers such as Bass. Also, despite assurances from Novell that 3.12 was totally compatible with 3.11 so that in theory no configuration changes needed to be made, differences did in fact exist in the way some protocols were handled. In particular, there were techniques for boosting performance over the WAN, but the network needed to be re-tuned to take advantage of them. Better advance warning of the changes and the implications for large networks should have been provided, perhaps in the form of advance technical bulletins for customers.

Historically, Novell marketed its products through distribution channels and, according to Paterson, was slower than some software companies, notably Microsoft, in realizing that it needed to build direct relationships with large corporate clients. However, he does concede that Novell is now learning how to build good corporate relationships so that it can evolve from being a supplier of shrink-wrapped products to a provider of enterprise networking solutions.

☐ CS.8 Has the Bass Group's move away from the mainframe to client/server solutions saved money?

It is often difficult or impossible to determine whether or by how much a particular IT strategy has saved money. The group has definitely reduced costs but at the same time the penetration of IT within the organization has increased dramatically, which is a key part of the strategy. The result has been that investments in new hardware and application development have offset the savings. In fact, the total IT budget has remained constant even though the number of users has increased. Whether this would still have happened if the mainframes had been retained could be debated, but in any case there were other reasons, such as empowerment, for favouring client/server apart from saving money.

☐ CS.9 How has Bass managed to keep its staff aware of the rapid developments in the network and the kinds of application running on it?

Bass has a distributed management structure in which individual operating units are responsible, as far as possible, for their own destiny. This also applies to IT, so that each division is expected to develop the skills it needs to support its users and applications. However, it is not cost-effective to maintain all the in-house skills needed to cover all aspects of the fast-moving networking business, and it certainly does not make sense to duplicate rare, and therefore expensive, skills across many sites. Bass has tackled this dilemma by making use of dealers and suppliers where possible, and then maintaining a small elite central team of support staff to which users can turn either as a last resort or to help with specific projects. So when it comes to NetWare, the group relies on dealers to provide a first line of technical support in many cases.

At the same time, the group is establishing a small core of people within what it sees as a centre of excellence who will be fully qualified NetWare engineers, having gone through Novell's CNE (Certified NetWare Engineer) programme, as described in Chapter 4. Such accreditation is as much to give the centre of excellence credibility throughout the organization as to provide the skills it needs. The objective is to have a first-class team that can help solve problems that arise when implementing new networked applications in the divisions. There have, for example, been several projects designed to establish dial-up links for sites such as betting shops and bingo clubs to access existing AS/400 applications. These applications often require sessions to be kept permanently open even when nothing is happening, which requires spoofing to emulate the polling signals in order to give the central application the impression that the session is still open. The implementation of spoofing requires specific expertise, which the division may not have but which can be provided by the centre of excellence from people who have already solved similar problems elsewhere in the group.

□ CS.10 Has the age of network computing arrived for Bass?

Until quite recently, the IT strategies of the Bass Group and most other large organizations were shaped by the traditional suppliers of centralized main-frames, often IBM. This has now totally changed. As the incumbent mainframe supplier, Unisys has changed its relationship with Bass to a more service, systems integration oriented role. And as IBM has lost control over the desktop architecture, so the shift of power has moved to the suppliers of software at the heart of the emerging client/server LAN-based applications. In early 1994 this implied two companies: Microsoft because it controls the desktop and Novell because it controls the LANs. Other companies, such as Hewlett-Packard through its influence in network management and IBM through its large presence with the AS/400, have played a role, but Paterson is unequivocal in his declaration that Novell and Microsoft are the principal players. This fact indicates that the age of network computing has arrived. The group's IT empire no longer has a single nerve centre and the intelligence has become distributed across numerous sites. This is helping to achieve the group's ideal – 'information anywhere to anyone at any time.'

Appendix 1: Key internetworking technologies

The use of bridging and routing for interconnecting LANs to create a network of multiple LAN segments or to provide a link between geographically remote LANs is described in Chapter 6. This appendix looks at some of the variants and options within these two basic techniques. The evolution of bridging into LAN switching is also described in the bridging section.

☐ (1)   Bridging

In their basic form, bridges simply provide a filter between two LANs interconnected by point-to-point links as described in Chapter 6. On large networks, bridges were overtaken by routers but then made a reappearance in the guise of LAN switches, more particularly for Ethernet LANs but also for token ring.

Before the LAN switching era, bridging was enhanced for both Ethernet and token ring LANs to make it more suitable for large networks. For Ethernet LANs the spanning tree algorithm was developed to enable alternative routing to be provided between pairs of LAN segments without forming a closed loop. With Ethernet, being a broadcast technology in which data packets are transmitted across the whole segment, it is important to avoid forming any closed loops that would enable data to circulate endlessly. Clearly, if two Ethernet LAN segments are connected by two bridges to provide an alternative route should one of the bridges fail, a closed loop is formed, which is not allowed. Spanning tree solves the problem by keeping one of the bridges closed in normal use, so there is no closed loop, and bringing the standby bridge into operation if the primary one fails. However, this means that only one bridge is in use at any one time. The spanning tree algorithm was subsequently improved by several proprietary techniques, such as the Retix adaptive routing method, which allowed both bridges to be used if they are working, while preventing data from circulating more than once round the network so preserving a logical closed loop.

Token ring LANs do not present this problem because the network is closed anyway and data is not broadcast to all devices simultaneously, but instead circulates from node to node. The main requirement for token ring bridging is to facilitate the creation of large networks while maintaining acceptable performance and adhering to timing restrictions. The source routing technique was developed by IBM to accomplish this. In a network of LANs interconnected by source routing bridges, the source, that is a device such as a PC sending data packets onto the network, ordains what route each data packet will take. The source inserts precise details of the route into each packet, and each bridge on the way reads this routing information and either filters or forwards accordingly. Detailed discussion of spanning tree and source routing can be found in other books in the Data Communications and Networks series (such as Hunter, *Local Area Networks: Making the Right Choices*, 1993, Wokingham, Addison-Wesley).

Bridging has always outperformed routing in terms of raw performance but lacked flexibility and control. It subsequently evolved into the LAN switch which became popular for segmenting networks down into small workgroups or even individual workstations to maintain performance.

The story of LAN switching began with the use of bridges to subdivide a large LAN into smaller segments, restricting local traffic within each segment to make the available bandwidth go further. Routers were subsequently introduced to many networks to perform this function in addition to providing more sophisticated control over transmission of data. However, as networks became increasingly loaded they had to be divided into ever smaller segments just to maintain performance. This became costly and inefficient to do using routers, which were not designed for networks containing very large numbers of segments.

Meanwhile Ethernet bridges had evolved into Ethernet switches. Essentially a LAN switch is a multiport bridge interconnecting a number of LANs greater than two. Superficially this makes it like a router, the difference being that it operates on layer two protocols just like a bridge does, which makes it faster but means that it cannot distinguish between layer three protocols such as IPX and IP. This, in turn, means that it cannot be used to filter layer three protocols as a router can; it does, though, enable an Ethernet switch to operate within a network in which just one layer three protocol is used.

An Ethernet switch examines layer two packets and filters them if they are destined for the segment from which they came; if not, the switch forwards the packet to the segment containing the node to which it is addressed. This is just like bridging, except that the switch is capable of forwarding packets to any one of a number of segments rather than just one. Devices that need high throughput, typically servers, can be given a segment all to themselves, which means they can occupy a whole 10 Mbit s⁻¹ of Ethernet bandwidth.

Token ring switching works on a similar principle but is less common for two reasons: firstly, it is more complex and therefore more expensive to implement; and secondly it is less necessary because the performance of token ring networks degrades less drastically in heavy traffic.

☐ (2) Routing

The basic function of a router is to determine which path a data packet will take between LANs. This function requires a specific protocol for routers to exchange essential information about the availability of routes in the network, changes in configuration and also the nature of packets being transmitted so that they are handled correctly. Such information enables each router to calculate routes effectively and ensure that each packet is delivered intact to the destination point, which is usually a LAN segment.

Routing protocols are of two types: distance vector and link state. The former, the most common in earlier routers, involves exchange of information between routers that are adjacent in the network. Each node then digests the information and then transmits it to its neighbours; in this way information propagates throughout the network. Examples of distance vector routing protocols are IPX RIP (routing information protocol) used with Novell's IPX protocol stack, IP RIP and Cisco's IGRP (internet gateway routing protocol) for the TCP/IP stack, and RTMP for the AppleTalk stack.

Routers using link state protocols, on the other hand, broadcast information about themselves and immediate neighbours to all other routers within a predefined area. This sounds as if it is going to generate more traffic than distance vector methods because it is sending the information to more than just the immediate neighbours. However, most link state methods are more selective about the information they transmit, only making a broadcast when there is a change to report. Distance vector methods transmit a lot of repetitive information at regular intervals.

Examples of link state routing protocols are OSPF (open shortest path first) for the TCP/IP protocol stack, IS-IS for the OSI stack, and NLSP (NetWare link services protocol) for NetWare networks. Link state protocols are more suitable in large networks, whereas distance vector ones are often preferred for small networks, and also for the smaller peripheral parts of large ones. Indeed, link state and distance vector protocols can co-exist in the same network and often do, with many routers supporting both.

Appendix 2: Major network protocol stacks

All protocol stacks resemble the seven-layer OSI interconnection model described in Appendix 3; indeed, the common ones also have seven layers. There has been almost universal agreement over the bottom two layers, at least for local communication within LANs. It is in layers three to seven that the major protocol stacks differ: apart from OSI itself, the principal ones are TCP/IP, IBM's SNA and SNA APPN, and Novell's IPX.

There are also a number of protocols used just for transmission over wide area networks which complement or cooperate with the ones just mentioned. The difference is that WAN protocols generally operate just in layers two and three, as their only function is to provide network interconnection between source and destination local networks. The physical link over the WAN, specified in layer one of the OSI model, is provided by the telecommunications carrier or whoever is providing the service.

Older WAN protocols such as X.25 operated in layer three, but more recent ones, such as frame relay, work in layer two, providing a more seamless end-to-end service without the traditional boundary between LAN and WAN – at least, that is the theory.

TCP/IP

The TCP/IP standards are sometimes confused with those of OSI since their structure is very similar. In fact, in the bottom two layers they are identical, as TCP/IP uses OSI standards such as Ethernet and token ring LANs. The two standards differ from layer three upwards but there are signs of convergence in the top three layers where OSI standards are starting to predominate. TCP/IP is completely different from OSI in layers three and four which define how to establish end-to-end connections between systems attached to different LANs. It is in these middle layers, for transporting data across a network, where TCP/IP protocols are widely used. The higher-layer TCP/IP standards are sometimes used but, on many networks, TCP/IP standards are found only in layers three and four. The upper layers may comprise OSI standards or proprietary ones. So when people talk about TCP/IP, they often mean just the third and fourth layers of that protocol set, for here TCP/IP has become so firmly established that it is quite likely to become part of the OSI group of standards in future.

TCP/IP protocols defined

There are two reasons why TCP/IP standards are widely used in layers three and four to support the interconnection of LANs: the standards were developed earlier than those of OSI; and they were designed specifically for internetworking, that is connecting LANs together. The protocols were developed largely for this purpose by the US Internet Engineering Task Force.

Architecture of TCP/IP

TCP/IP, strictly speaking, only addresses layers three and four of the OSI model – the internetworking and transport layers, and usually runs over Ethernet or token ring LANs, which fill layers one and two. The IP part, corresponding to OSI layer three, controls connections between LANs and the WAN connecting them, and routing through the WAN. The TCP is the transport protocol, responsible for providing end-to-end data transmission between applications; it coordinates the flow of data to ensure that devices are not swamped with data they cannot handle.

TCP/IP has been extended to provide facilities in the upper application layers. These correspond to the top three OSI layers:

- Telnet, which allows PCs to log in remotely to host systems running TCP/IP protocols, by emulating, that is supporting, appropriate screen and keyboard functions;
- FTP (file transfer protocol) which allows users to transfer files across TCP/IP networks;
- SMTP (simple mail transfer protocol) is an electronic mail utility. The word simple is apt, and SMTP has been widely criticized for failing to provide adequate email facilities; as a result, there have been moves to embrace the OSI X.400 messaging standards within TCP/IP;
- SNMP (simple network management protocol) for managing TCP/IP networks, which is described in Chapter 7.

Future of TCP/IP

The future path of TCP/IP has become clear now that major network users around the world are insisting that it must continue to be supported. The main part of TCP/IP, that is layers three and four, will probably be subsumed into OSI as options. On the other hand some, OSI protocols, such as X.400, may actually replace existing TCP/IP higher-layer options. Currently, the X/Open group is developing software to bridge TCP/IP with OSI protocols; it therefore looks as if the two standards sets will converge, without users having to go through a painful conversion process.

SNA

The original structure of SNA is shown in the middle part of Figure A2.1. As can be seen, it is very similar to OSI, the main difference being that SNA layers four and five together are equivalent to OSI layer five, while OSI layers three and four are together equivalent to SNA layer three. The differences largely follow from historical factors. SNA was originally developed for centralized hierarchical networks in which all communication was controlled by one or a few large mainframe computers. These large computers were accessed by dumb terminals via point-to-point connections. This meant that there was no need for great sophistication in the lower network layers because in a sense there was not much of a network. However, in the early days of networking, telecommunication links were far less reliable than now, so a great deal of SNA was

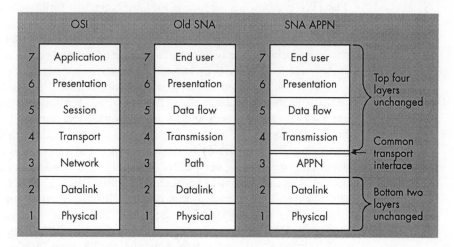

Figure A2.1 Structure of SNA.

concerned with error control and recovery, to protect users and applications from the effects of poor communication links.

The onset of LANs caused little change initially. IBM's preferred solution to interconnect LANs was via bridges which communicated essentially over point-to-point connections. To enable more complex networks of interconnected bridged LANs to be established, IBM developed the source routing protocols that are described in Appendix 1. These became part of the SNA model but, despite pressure from IBM, were never accepted by ISO as part of the OSI model.

Realizing that the LAN industry was moving away from bridging towards routing over wide area networks, IBM decided to refit SNA to give it a more distributed structure. New protocols called APPN (advanced peer-to-peer networking) that support intelligent routing were developed and brought into SNA. The difference between the new version, called SNA/APPN, and the old SNA is shown in Figure A2.1. The common transport interface introduced between layers three and four of the SNA model is designed to make SNA protocols more interchangeable with OSI and TCP/IP protocols. The interface supports mixing and matching of SNA protocols with others in the layers immediately above and below it.

SNA/APPN has been designed to suit the requirements of both LANs and the wide area networks connecting them, as well as catering for remaining traditional networks supporting dumb terminals.

IPX

The IPX protocol set was developed by Novell to facilitate communication between PCs and file servers across a NetWare LAN. IPX was subsequently used also to route data over a network of interconnected NetWare LANs. On a large network, IPX may be one of a number of protocols being routed between LANs over local circuits or remotely over telecommunications links.

IPX evolved from XNS (Xerox network systems), developed by Xerox, and is still used on another NOS, Banyan Vines. NetWare networks therefore use a very similar protocol set to Vines networks, which makes it possible with some adjustments to interoperate the two directly. Like other proprietary protocols, IPX (and XNS) is consistent with the OSI model but IPX was developed specifically for LAN operation, and therefore contains more functions in the bottom layers than does OSI. The IPX protocols work very efficiently on LANs, having been designed for that purpose, providing faster response than TCP/IP or OSI protocols. TCP/IP, on the other hand, is efficient for inter-LAN traffic, as opposed to communication within each LAN. Figure A2.2 compares the fundamental structure of IPX with the OSI model.

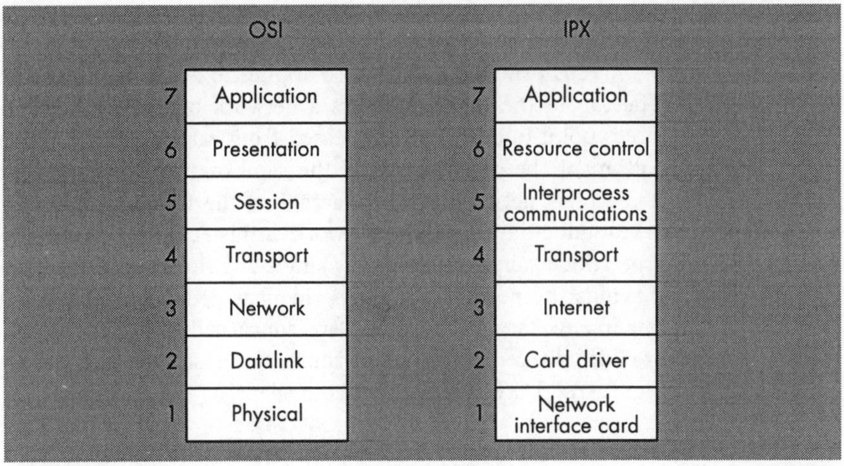

OSI		IPX	
7	Application	7	Application
6	Presentation	6	Resource control
5	Session	5	Interprocess communications
4	Transport	4	Transport
3	Network	3	Internet
2	Datalink	2	Card driver
1	Physical	1	Network interface card

Figure A2.2 Comparing IPX with OSI.

WAN standards

Both SNA and TCP/IP are end-to-end protocols with the ability to embrace both LANs and WANs. SNA, being a proprietary protocol, is used only within private networks while TCP/IP, as well as being used for private networks, provides the transport for the massive global internet network which is open to both organizations and individuals.

There are, however, protocols suitable just for WANs. Earlier ones, such as X.25, operated in layer three of the OSI model, providing a wide area network service with flow control and error checking, but more recent protocols, such as frame relay, provide higher performance by operating in layer two just like LAN protocols, taking advantage of the fact that modern digital telecommunications links are now highly reliable. As a result they do not need error-checking facilities which impose a processing overhead.

This is especially relevant for LANs because frame relay is ideally suited to transmitting LAN traffic over a wide area network – it is really a sequel to X.25. Like X.25, frame relay provides an interface to a switched wide area network handling data in packets, but it is more efficient than X.25 and supports much higher speeds, particularly for interconnecting LANs. It provides a basic communications service in layer two of the protocol stack, beneath network layer protocols such as the IP part of TCP/IP. Many routers can access a frame relay network, enabling LANs to be interconnected at high speeds over a separate wide area network. In this case the frame relay network provides what appears to each router as a point-to-point connection, although in fact there is a switched network between the routers.

This principle, which also applies to X.25, is illustrated in Figure A2.3. The top of the diagram shows a network of three routers interconnected by direct point-to-point circuits leased from a telecommunications operator. The bottom of the diagram shows the same network interconnected via a public frame relay network. One advantage of the frame relay network is that, being based on a large public network infrastructure, it should provide greater protection against failure of any single circuit; it could also save money, because it avoids the need to pay for permanent dedicated links between each pair of routers. As far as the routers are concerned, the frame relay network simply provides direct point-to-point connections, so that the two networks shown in Figure A2.3 are functionally equivalent.

ATM (asynchronous transfer mode)

ATM is emerging as an end-to-end protocol providing high-speed transport embracing both the LAN and the WAN. Indeed a major appeal of the technology is its promise to end the current distinction between LANs and WANs. In the shorter term, however, it will be introduced alongside existing protocols such as Ethernet and token ring at the LAN level, and frame relay over the WAN. Its role will be to provide a fast pipe for data over which existing protocols will be encapsulated; this means cutting up existing data packets into the fixed-length cells required by ATM and then reconstituting them at the other end of the link.

The original idea of ATM was to provide a single multiplexing and switching service for all forms of electronic traffic, so that a given physical path could carry video, voice and audio simultaneously in the same underlying packet format. ATM provides a very high switching rate for packets of fixed size called cells; these are 53 bytes long comprising a 5-byte header and 48 bytes of data, which is sometimes called the payload.

ATM cells will be transmitted at $155\,\mathrm{Mbit\,s}^{-1}$ over the WAN or $622\,\mathrm{Mbit\,s}^{-1}$ over public synchronous digital hierarchy (SDH) services. However, until such services are available later this decade, the only option is to establish private ATM networks over high-speed point-to-point connections; ATM can thus in principle be run at whatever speed the user chooses. Another key point is that ATM networks will allow bandwidth to be allocated flexibly to different applications so that account can be taken of variations in demand during the day. Video and audio connections can be given guaranteed performance, while less urgent data applications can be restricted when access to more important network services is needed.

Before the advent of full public wide area ATM services in the late 1990s,

(a)

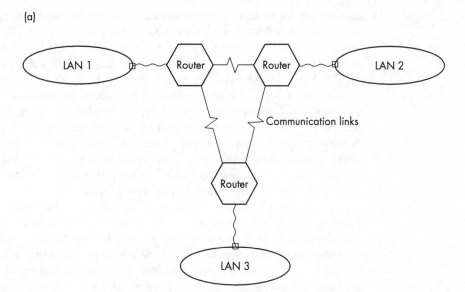

(b)

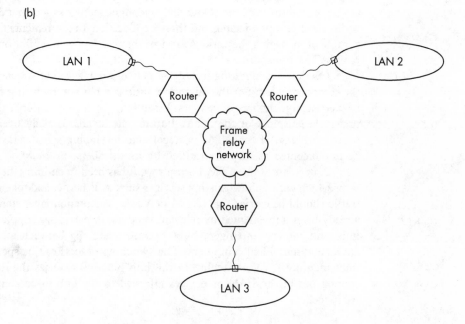

Figure A2.3 How frame relay network provides the equivalent of point-to-point connections between LANs: (a) three routes interconnected by point-to-point links; (b) same LANs connected to a public frame relay network, which provides the same functionality.

carriers are introducing interim services at somewhat lower speeds, notably frame relay and SMDS (switched multimegabit data service). SMDS, which carriers such as BT are starting to offer, is in a sense a hybrid of existing LAN technology and the ATM cell switching technique. Like LANs, it transmits variable-length packets and allows the network to be shared, which achieves economies of scale. However, SMDS runs over an underlying transport mechanism of fixed cells and this imposes an overhead as the variable packets need to be broken into fixed cells, limiting future potential for very high speeds. A range of speeds between 2 and 34 Mbit s^{-1} is being offered, so SMDS can in many cases allow LANs to be interconnected at full speed. SMDS also has the potential to reach the 155 Mbit s^{-1} that will be supported by underlying SDH networks but this will probably be its limit.

Although ATM was originally envisaged as a wide area protocol, its potential as a universal medium for all forms of electronic traffic has obvious appeal within local networks as well. In an ideal world, ATM would provide an end-to-end service like the telephone network, comprising a hierarchy of switches. In fact, the objective was that ATM would become the telephone network and every other kind of network as well. However, there are two problems: the first is how to migrate to this Utopia from the current messy state where computer networks laid out in various topologies carry data formatted in numerous different protocols; the second is that global ATM networks are not as straightforward as traditional telephone networks – demand for bandwidth is far less predictable and there are additional requirements for software capable of managing the various services that carriers would offer on top of the basic ATM transport.

Carriers are investing heavily in network management software to tackle the second problem but the migration issue is a big one requiring cooperation between a large number of vendors. Essentially, such cooperation is taking place under the auspices of the ATM Forum, the standards body overseeing the overall progress of the ATM protocol and developing specifications that can be implemented as they are ratified by its members.

A key part of the ATM Forum's work has been in defining the adaptation layer which defines how existing services such as Ethernet and token ring LAN traffic should be carried over ATM networks. Adaptation layer standards have already been implemented by relevant vendors, in particular suppliers of LAN hubs and routers. Intelligent hubs provide switching between attached local LANs and individual computers. The switching process can be speeded up by implementing ATM switching in the hub but this requires the data packets coming out of the LAN or devices attached to the hub to be converted into ATM cells.

Appendix 3: OSI seven-layer model

For applications to cooperate across a network, there needs to be a hierarchy of ingredients ranging from a physical communications link at the bottom to some agreed structure for the information being transmitted at the top. As computer networks began to evolve during the late 1960s, it soon became clear that anarchy would prevail unless some effort was made to establish a common framework for the various tasks involved in communication.

The first such framework was IBM's SNA network architecture, introduced in 1974. The basic form of SNA served as the basis for the OSI protocols that emerged gradually during the 1980s and early 1990s. The difference was that while SNA was purely for networks comprising systems either manufactured by IBM or compatible with IBM standards, OSI was designed for open networks comprising computers from a wide variety of vendors.

This inevitably meant that OSI standards took longer to evolve, as they were set by committees representing all the major vendors. In the lower two layers of communication, which deal with LANs, OSI standards are now well established, not just in multivendor but also in SNA networks. However, at the higher levels, where greater complexity is involved, OSI standards have been slower to mature and to be implemented in products. In some cases the standards have been so slow to arrive that other *de facto* standards have already won widespread support. A good example is the TCP/IP protocol stack, which is widely used on LANs and described in Appendix 2. In some cases the equivalent OSI protocols are then modified so that networks based on the established *de facto* standards can migrate smoothly towards them. At the same time, the *de facto* standards sometimes move gradually towards the equivalent OSI ones, so that the two sets gradually converge.

This is happening in the case of network management, where the SNMP protocols developed originally for TCP/IP networks are moving closer to CMIP protocol.

Basic structure of OSI model

The motive for having seven layers rather than one is that it breaks the overall task of building a network down into manageable components. The network as a whole is then easier to install, maintain and enhance; for example, a change may just affect one or two layers of the OSI model and to implement it then requires amendments only to the layers affected rather than the whole network.

Each layer performs a specific set of tasks required for computers to inter-operate across a network, and communicates only with the layers immediately above and below. Each layer, except the top one, provides a service to the layer immediately above, and each except the bottom layer requires the service of the one immediately below. The whole networking process then comprises a set of seven interrelated groups of tasks.

The overall model is summarized in Figure A3.1. The seven layers fall into two groups: the upper application layers and the lower internetworking layers. The upper three layers ensure that two computer systems understand each other, so they can work together; they deal with the structure and pre-sentation of data, and coordination between the systems that are interworking. However, they are not concerned about how data gets from one system to another, this being the function of the lowest three layers.

The bottom three layers then handle the transmission of data packets across the network, and are not concerned about what the contents of the packets are. The top three layers deal with the contents of packets to ensure that all systems interpret them in the same way, and they also control the flow of data between the end systems.

So far we have described only six layers: we have left out the middle one,

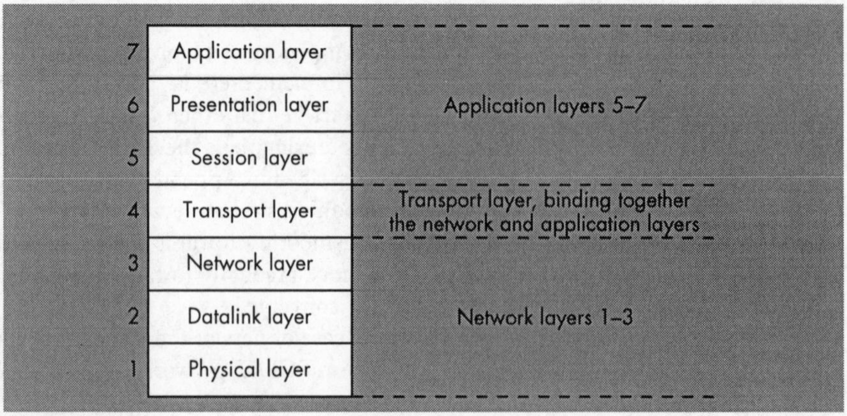

7	Application layer	Application layers 5–7
6	Presentation layer	
5	Session layer	
4	Transport layer	Transport layer, binding together the network and application layers
3	Network layer	Network layers 1–3
2	Datalink layer	
1	Physical layer	

Figure A3.1 Structure of OSI model.

the transport layer, which binds together the upper and lower layers, ensuring that it is physically possible to transmit data over the network. Should there be an error or the network be overloaded, layer three, the highest of the lower layers, informs layer four, the transport layer, that it is not possible to transmit data at that time. The transport layer in turn informs layer five, which may lead to a session being suspended with users perhaps receiving an error message that the network is temporarily unavailable.

It is possible to implement OSI without seven layers. In this case the function of a missing layer is fulfilled by joining together the layers above and below it; for example, it is possible to operate without a transport layer, in which case layer three communicates directly with layer five to handle transmission of data across the network.

The upper layers

Layer seven, the application layer, delivers the complete OSI service to user applications so that they can interoperate: one example is support for file transfer, which is required by many applications and provided by the OSI FTAM standard (file transfer access method); another is OSI-TP, required to coordinate the sequence of events for transaction-processing systems that are distributed across different processors on an OSI network.

Among the best-known layer-seven standards is X.400 for message transfer between office and electronic mail systems, although the ISO name for this is actually Motis (Message oriented text interchange system). X.400 was developed by the CCITT, but is now aligned with Motis. The overlapping role of standards bodies, such as ISO and CCITT, is described in Appendix 10.

Layer six, the presentation layer, ensures that data is delivered in an agreed format to the application layer – any conversion required between different data representations takes place in this layer. An example is conversion between two different character codes, such as ASCII to EBCDIC (extended binary coded decimal interchange code); ASCII characters are represented by different combinations of binary bits than those used for EBCDIC characters, and the translation between the two codes is done in the presentation layer.

Layer five, the session layer, controls the dialogue between two applications on different computers; for example, when a PC user is accessing an IBM mainframe via a LAN, a session will be set up and controlled within layer five. This ensures that applications are kept informed of any problems, and defines what kind of session it will be; for example, it might involve just on-screen interaction, or file transfer, or both simultaneously. The actual process of transmitting data from the PC via the LAN to the mainframe and back again is handled by the bottom four layers, which therefore provide a transport service to the session layer.

Layer four, the transport layer, is responsible for providing a path between applications and ensuring that data is delivered correctly along that path. Layer four normally performs error recovery, although some of this may be done in layer three.

Layer three, the internetworking layer, is responsible for finding a route across the network, and in some cases for error recovery, although the exact facilities depend on the type of network provided. A simple network comprising a few LANs linked by bridges would not need a layer three at all, because there is no routing to be done and error recovery is handled in other layers. On a more complex wide area network, however, layer three performs a vital role in providing resilient routing capable of avoiding single points of failure, and in guaranteeing error-free delivery of data.

Layer two, the datalink layer, is responsible for ensuring that data is faithfully transmitted across the physical medium itself between devices attached to it. Such devices may be PCs attached to a LAN or routers on a wide area network, the function being to ensure that data is not corrupted during its transmission between any two such devices across the physical link between them, which may be fixed, such as a fibre optic or copper cable, or a wireless link. This layer also corrects errors that occur on the medium but cannot cater for problems arising in higher protocol layers. LANs such as Ethernet and token ring operate here.

For LANs, layer two is divided into two sublayers. The lower of these two sublayers is the media access control layer (MAC), which deals with access to the actual physical medium. The upper sublayer is the logical link control (LLC), which controls the flow of data between devices on the LAN and ensures that data is reassembled correctly when it leaves the physical medium. All ISO LANs, including both token ring and Ethernet, are based on a common LLC sublayer. They differ only in the MAC layer, which defines how they access the physical medium – CSMA/CD being the access method for Ethernet and token passing for token ring.

Layer one, the physical layer, specifies the medium itself and the physical method used to access it. It is not concerned with how data gets across the link, therefore this layer may define first the cable itself, and then characteristics of the signal, such as the maximum length allowed without repeaters. The medium might be unshielded twisted pair (utp) copper cable, for example, in which case layer one describes the electrical characteristics of the signal and at what distances it should be regenerated. Layer one also defines the sockets for attaching devices to the medium. An example of a layer one standard is the 10BaseT for running Ethernet LANs traffic over utp cable.

Appendix 4: Basic LAN cabling structures, such as 10BaseT

LAN cabling structures have in a sense evolved in the opposite direction from computer applications as a whole. Whereas applications are becoming more decentralized with the move towards client/server computing, cabling systems have become centralized with network nodes physically connected to wiring hubs. As originally conceived, both Ethernet and token ring LANs required distributed wiring without a centre. In the case of Ethernet, nodes connecting devices such as PCs were connected in a tree-and-branch arrangement, sometimes called a bus, while with token ring they were connected in a physical ring. FDDI (fibre distributed data interface) also required nodes to be connected in a ring.

However, it became clear that the logical structure of a ring or bus could be preserved on top of different physical wiring schemes that were more resilient and easier to manage. The principle can be understood by comparison with the map of an underground rail network, where it is not necessary for the positions of stations to correspond exactly with their real geographical positions. All that really matters is that the stations have the correct relative positions to each other so that it is possible to work out routes through the network.

Cabling systems for both Ethernet and token ring have moved towards star-shaped structures in which devices are attached to central hubs, so making cable networks easier to maintain and providing a more flexible system for adding new nodes and moving existing ones. Structured cabling schemes such as AT&T's Systimax system embraced this way of cabling LANs to provide implementers with a well-founded basis for building reliable cable networks. This new way of cabling combined with the ability to run Ethernet over unshielded twisted pair cable also led to the 10BaseT standard, specifying how the Ethernet protocol can run over a star-shaped cable network. In the case of token ring and FDDI, no new physical wiring standard was needed to collapse the ring into a central hub.

LAN segments serving individual workgroups attached to small hubs then began to be interconnected via larger hubs or backbone routers. Local traffic could thus be confined to each workgroup using bridges or LAN switches but still greater flexibility became possible with the advent of more intelligent hubs that allowed devices to be filtered off from the local hub to which they were attached and reassigned to a different hub. Thus was born the virtual workgroup – a workgroup could now comprise people from different departments attached to different hubs, yet with traffic within it filtered off from other workgroups. To achieve this, the backbone hub had to be able to switch between local devices as well as between each LAN segment attached to it.

The other important point to note about LAN cabling is the rapid increase in the amount of bandwidth that can be provided over a given grade of cable. In the late 1980s Ethernet still required coaxial cable, and it was a significant breakthrough when it became possible to use unshielded cable in 10BaseT. Yet it rapidly became possible to run first 16 Mbit s^{-1} token ring and then 100 Mbit s^{-1} Fast Ethernet over unshielded cable. This led to the birth of the 100BaseT standard. Then in 1994 it became possible to support ATM at 155 Mbit s^{-1} over unshielded cable for limited distances.

Appendix 5: LAN topologies

The LAN topology describes the logical configuration of the network, or how it appears to the devices attached to it. We shall not describe how LANs work in detail, but point out how the traditional LAN topologies of Ethernet and token ring have been preserved while improving LAN performance in various ways. We shall consider Ethernet and token ring in turn, and then look at a more recently developed high-speed LAN technology, 100VG-Anylan.

Ethernet

Ethernet has evolved greatly since its humble origins in the early 1980s, as a technology in which data packets were broadcast from devices along a 500 metre length of thick coaxial cable, which could be extended to a maximum of 2500 metres through use of repeaters that regenerated the signal. The idea was that a packet would reach all devices almost simultaneously and then disappear off the end of the network. Devices either reject the packet or, if the destination address matches their own, accept it. The CSMA/CD method is used to gain access to transmit a packet when the network is free.

Ethernet has evolved to run over ever thinner cable and its performance has also been improved by dividing a network down into smaller segments within each of which local traffic is confined. In fact, with modern Ethernet switches each device can be given its own segment so that it has access to the whole 10 Mbit s^{-1} bandwidth without having to contend for access with other devices. This means that all devices can transmit their packets at the full speed allowed by Ethernet without having to wait for other devices to transmit theirs. The advantage of this approach is that existing Ethernet adapter cards can be retained, along with software already written to run over Ethernet LANs.

Another improvement then occurred to network system designers – over limited distances with nodes linked to local cabling hubs, there was no reason why transmission speeds greater than 10 Mbit s^{-1} could not be achieved using the existing CSMA/CD access mechanism by increasing the frequency with which signals were transmitted. In fact, a tenfold increase in speed was achieved with a new standard called 100BaseT for running Ethernet at 100 Mbit s^{-1}. This required new hubs and network interface cards (NICs) but existing Ethernet software would still work. Such an approach has appealed to some organizations as a way of improving performance further without major investment in a new transmission technology such as ATM.

Token ring

Similar performance improvements were possible with token ring but the economics were different. There was already a version of the token ring protocol designed to operate at 100 Mbit s^{-1} – FDDI (fibre distributed data interface), which was initially promoted as a backbone technology running over optical fibre for large campus networks. Subsequently a version of the FDDI standard, called CDDI (copper distributed data interface), was developed to run over unshielded twisted pair cable.

There was little point in speeding up the basic token ring protocol beyond 16 Mbit s^{-1} given that FDDI was already in place as a mature technology (unlike other 100 Mbit s^{-1} LAN protocols) and reducing in price. However, as with Ethernet the potential existed for improving performance by use of LAN switching to segment existing networks into smaller units. Token ring switching is technically more complex than Ethernet switching and therefore more expensive to implement in silicon. Hence it is less common but has been implemented by a few specialist vendors in the field such as Madge Networks.

100VG-Anylan

This protocol was initially designed as a way of migrating from Ethernet to higher speeds without some of the limitations inherent in the CSMA/CD access mechanism; it was then extended to provide an upgrade path from token ring as well. Like 100BaseT it operates at 100 Mbit s^{-1}, but can be used over greater distances of up to 4000 metres, compared with 300 metres for 100BaseT; this makes it more suitable for larger networks. It is also deterministic, which means that it provides predictable performance, which makes it suitable for transmitting data such as video that cannot tolerate variable delays.

There are two principal aspects of 100VG-Anylan: quartet signalling and the demand priority protocol (DPP). Quartet signalling involves transmission of data at $100\,\mathrm{Mbit\,s^{-1}}$ in four equal $25\,\mathrm{Mbit\,s^{-1}}$ portions over each of the four wires of a standard unshielded twisted pair cable. DPP replaces the CSMA/CD method of Ethernet and the token passing method of token ring. Instead of devices waiting until they can transmit without colliding with other devices' packets, they request permission from the hub to transmit. The hub then acts as a switch, directing the packet to its destination without any other node seeing it.

100VG-Anylan requires new hubs and adapters, and also new software drivers in devices attached to the network to handle the new DPP protocol. However, it does work over existing cabling used either for 10BaseT Ethernet or token ring.

Beyond these technologies, ATM is waiting in the wings, as described in Appendix 2.

Appendix 6: DOS file and directory structure

The DOS operating system serves as the basis for many NOSs, particularly low-end peer-to-peer ones. Even sophisticated NOSs such as NetWare were initially derived from DOS and have related structures.

In DOS, data is stored in different categories of file with names consisting of up to eight alphanumeric characters followed by optional suffixes of up to three characters after a point. The suffixes are essential, however, to identify certain types of DOS file; for example, .EXE files are executable program files while .COM files are command files. Other data files can therefore use any other extension to help identify them. Files are then organized in directories which are tables of contents listing their name, size and date they were last modified.

Directories can be arranged in hierarchies to subdivide files into more precise categories: they are physically arranged on the storage media in volumes, as described in Appendix 9.

Appendix 7: Network interface cards

Devices called transceivers were required to connect PCs to the early LANs based on coaxial cable. An additional piece of cable was needed to connect each PC to its transceiver.

Now that LANs increasingly run on twisted pair cable, PCs and servers are connected directly to the cable network via network interface cards (NICs). Indeed any device that connects directly to the network requires an NIC, or a device that performs an equivalent function. Network hubs, for example, may have modules that connect them to the network, which perform the same function as NICs but also handle additional processing needed to support various hub functions like network management.

In general, though, NICs are PC cards that slot into an expansion slot in the back of the PC or server, attached directly to the motherboard. Externally, the NIC is usually connected directly to the network, except in the case of a coaxial or fibre optic network, where instead a separate piece of cable joining the NIC to a connection box on the main LAN cable would be provided.

To send data, the NIC must first convert it from the form in which it is represented in the PC to that required for transmission on the LAN – only then can it actually transmit the data onto the LAN. The order of events is reversed when receiving data.

The NIC needs to be compatible with the data packet structure used for the LAN. As Ethernet and token ring require data to be structured in different ways, various different NICs are needed.

Performance considerations of NICs

The NIC can affect performance in two ways: firstly, it imposes a slight delay in transmitting data onto the network; secondly, by utilizing the CPU of the

PC or server, it can slow down applications using the network. However, the structure of NICs has evolved to tackle both these problems.

In the first place, the delay was reduced by integrating RAM chips into the NIC board as data buffers. This ensures that the NIC can cope with surges of data from either side without requiring a halt in communication. Should it receive more data than it can handle on its transmission path between the network and the PC's CPU, it places the overflow in a RAM buffer, while continuing to transmit as fast as it can. When the rush is over, the NIC then reads the overflow back from the RAM and completes the transmission. The advantage is that, although the NIC is restricting the flow of traffic by virtue of the limited capacity of its transmission path, it cannot be overloaded and maintains the link between the PC and the server throughout a transmission even when it cannot immediately transfer all the data. This can be particularly important over Ethernet LANs where, as we saw in Chapter 2, overall performance is very dependent on the number of attempts to access the network.

However, although the RAM buffer ensures that the NIC utilizes its own transmission channel as efficiently as possible without a break in communications between a PC and the server, the transmission path itself can become a significant bottleneck; this largely depends on the width of the bus, which can be 8, 16 or 32 data bits. A data bit is a single binary digit of information. Many early NICs used buses that were 8 bits wide, which meant that 8 bits of information could be transmitted concurrently. Indeed, as the NIC cannot transmit data in chunks greater than the PC can handle, such a width was essential until the advent of PCs based on the 16-bit 80286 CPU. Now most NICs use 16-bit buses to take advantage of the 16-bit internal buses of modern PCs. In reality, modern PCs based on EISA (extended industry standard architecture) and MCA (microchannel architecture) have the potential to handle 32-bit internal buses, but still use 16-bit buses. Future PCs may use 32-bit buses, and then NICs will follow. In general, it is no longer worth considering 8-bit NICs for desktop PCs, as the cost saving is minimal, while throughput onto a LAN from a typical PC is reduced by about 40 per cent. However 32-bit cost significantly more than 16-bit NICs, and so are too expensive for most desktop PCs, except where high performance is essential. They are worth installing in the file server, though, as the extra cost when split between each user is relatively small, while the substantial performance gain is enjoyed by everyone.

Another limitation of earlier NICs was lack of a CPU of their own, which meant they had to utilize the CPU of the PC or server, or reducing the speed at which users' applications were processed. Now most NICs have their own CPU, implying they are computers in their own right, able to perform the data buffering and processing required for accessing a LAN without the assistance of the PC or server CPU.

Appendix 8: Role of expanded and extended memory in Intel PCs and microprocessor developments related to the NOS field

The DOS operating system was designed at a time when PCs had only a fraction of the processing power and memory of today's models. At the same time, microprocessors themselves were limited in sophistication and unsuitable for running multiple tasks simultaneously. This appendix summarizes the microprocessor developments that have enabled the PC platform to evolve to its current maturity capable of running powerful networked applications.

The raw power of the central processor itself is obviously important, with increases in clock speeds of at least 100-fold since the first IBM-compatible PCs arrived in 1982. However, even more important are the design improvements in the CPU and overall PC architecture that have made it possible to run more complex applications with greater reliability. Such improvements include protection for applications while they are running, to prevent the memory they are temporarily using from being overwritten until it is no longer required. Also of importance are increases in the capacity of memory chips and the speed of internal communication buses.

The main function of the NOS is still to process requests from users, which may involve searching for and returning data, accessing an external service or sending a job to a printer. To maintain or improve performance in the face of growing numbers of users and applications that throw more data onto the network, three things need to happen: CPUs have to become faster; memory chips need to be capable of holding more data; and the communications channel between CPU and memory chips needs to speed up.

The original 8088 and 8086 CPUs could handle only 1 Mbyte of memory, and DOS was designed only to address 640 Kbytes of this. This memory became known as 'real memory' because it was fully available to all DOS applications. However, as this limitation began to bite, a method of overcoming it was developed for a new wave of DOS applications. This was called expanded memory, originally developed by Lotus and Intel, and later supported by Microsoft. It allowed applications to make use of extra memory by swapping in 64 Kbyte chunks from additional RAM chips and required a piece of software called the expanded memory manager (EMM) to control the swapping process, making it seem as if there were just a total of 640 Kbytes as far as the DOS operating system was concerned but providing additional main storage for applications. However, only applications designed to work with the EMM could exploit this development, and furthermore, it was of limited use for NOS applications because of the need to work in 64 Kbyte chunks, which retarded performance.

As a result, more sophisticated NOSs, such as the later NetWare versions, were designed to operate only with extended memory, which worked similarly to expanded memory but without the need to page in additional memory in 64 Kbyte chunks. Extended memory became available on 80286 and higher numbered CPUs (note that while DOS was limited to 640 Kbytes, the restriction for NOSs such as NetWare not based on DOS was the fact that earlier 8086 and 8088 CPUs could not address more than 1 Mbyte in any case), which allowed NOS applications to spread themselves out in continuous chunks of memory; for example, NetWare 3.12 can address 4 Gbytes.

Another development of relevance for the NOS was the partition of the CPU into four different levels providing varying degrees of performance and protection from failure. Novell decided at one stage to run all server applications in ring 0, which provided maximum performance but minimum protection from failure through having the memory of one application overwritten by another during execution. This protection was not necessary when applications ran as single tasks, because there was then no other application to overwrite the memory. However, it has become a growing issue with increasingly large servers running multiple applications weaving in and out of the CPU. With NetWare 4.0, Novell decided to allow server applications, that is NLMs, to run with the maximum protection of ring 3, as explained in Chapter 2.

The other main field of processor development pertinent to the NOS was in chips or chip sets for linking PCs and servers with the LAN. NICs have improved in line with other aspects of networking technology, and this has been made possible partly by faster chips and partly by the use of increasingly wide hardware buses – first 8 bits, then 16 bits and more recently 32 bits. A 32-bit bus will allow data to be moved 32 bits, or 4 bytes, at a time, making it four times faster than an 8-bit bus operating at the same serial speed.

The NICs attach to the peripheral interconnect bus, which in turn has speeded up and increased in width. A more recent development has been the shrinking down of NICs onto single chips which can be installed directly onto the motherboard of the PC or server. These then connect directly into the internal communications bus.

NICs contribute to network performance not just according to how quickly they move data on and off the LAN but also by the degree to which they avoid utilizing the main CPU of the server or client PC.

Appendix 9: Key aspects of disk drive technology

Disk drives record data on two or more platters rotating at around 100 times a second. Data is stored on the platters in tracks of around 1/50th of a millimetre (1/1250th of an inch) apart. Each track is itself divided into a varying number of sectors, each of which holds chunks of data, normally 512 bytes.

Data is read from and written to the platters by heads that skim just above the surface. A crash occurs when a head strikes the surface, having become misaligned after prolonged use or because of a design fault.

The performance of a disk drive depends not just on physical hardware characteristics, such as the speed of the head, but also on the method used to encode the data. Several methods have been applied, such as modified frequency modulation, but a detailed description of these is beyond the scope of this appendix.

Performance also depends on the disk drive controller which mediates between the operating system and the disk drive itself. There are various standards for controllers, one of the most successful being SCSI (small computer system interface). This allows data to be transferred at up to 32 Mbytes s^{-1}, which is more than adequate for current servers and supports in principle any device, not just disk drives.

A key development for the NOS has been the disk co-processor board, which improves the performance of servers. Such boards contain their own CPU dedicated to managing disk reads and writes, freeing the main server CPU for other tasks. When the CPU receives a request for the disk drive, it will send it to the disk co-processor board, which then performs the task independently. Such boards can support multiple disk drives simultaneously, and provide the basis for techniques such as disk mirroring discussed in the main body of this book.

Appendix 10: Groups involved in OSI standards

There is a hierarchy of bodies involved in OSI standards. Many such standards were initially developed by national and European bodies, and in some cases by individual vendors, later to be adopted as international standards. There are three international standards bodies involved: the International Standards Organization (ISO), the International Electrotechnical Committee (IEC), and the International Consultative Committee for Telegraph and Telecommunications (CCITT). ISO originally formulated the OSI model but IEC became involved with some LAN standards.

In order to avoid conflict, ISO and IEC set up the ISO/IEC Joint Technical Committee (JTC1) to work together on OSI standards. CCITT developed some OSI standards that relate to communication over telecommunications links; examples include X.25, and the V series standards for dial-up communication via modems, as well as ISDN. JTC1 and CCITT work closely together to avoid conflict and to ensure that the development of OSI standards follows a consistent path. CCITT is responsible for defining standards in layers one to three over public national and international telecommunications networks, while JTC is responsible for standards in layers four to seven generally, and in layers one to three over private networks such as LANs.

ISO/IEC JTC1

This, the primary force behind OSI standards, particularly the more complex higher-layer ones, is a voluntary organization comprising various national standards bodies as voting members. JTC1 is split into various subgroups, each of which deals with a particular area – for example, SC6 deals with data communications.

CCITT

The principal members of the CCITT are national telecommunications carriers such as BT plc and AT&T. However, computer and networking companies are allowed to participate as non-voting members. There are three types of CCITT standard. The V series refers to data communications over traditional analogue dial-up telephone circuits; the X series refers to dedicated data network services; while the I and Q series relate to ISDN.

We shall now describe briefly the European and US standards bodies that feed input into ISO/IEC and CCITT.

□ 1.   European standards bodies

CEN/CENELEC

CEN and CENELEC are the European groups of national members of ISO and IEC, respectively.

CEPT

This is the European Conference of Posts and Telecommunications, an association of European telecommunications and network operators and so, to an extent, a subset of CCITT.

ETSI

This, the European Telecommunications Standards Institute, is the part of CEPT responsible for formulating standards.

EWOS

The European Workshop for Open Systems develops and promotes OSI functional standards, which we described earlier in the appendix.

SPAG

The Standards Promotion and Application Group was formed in 1983 by twelve European IT firms to develop and promote conformance testing to OSI standards. Its role is similar to COS in the USA.

ECMA

The European Computer Manufacturers Association represents European IT companies, and also some US ones that trade in Europe. ECMA is involved in the development of higher-layer OSI protocols.

□ 2.   US standards bodies

ANSI, the American National Standards Institute

ANSI coordinates the activities of various standards bodies in the USA, and provides a forum for promoting US standards on the international front. The most relevant US bodies developing ANSI standards are CBEMA (Computer Business Equipment Manufacturers Association), which developed the FDDI standard, and IEEE (Institute of Electrical and Electronic Engineers), which introduced the famous 802 series LAN standards; for example, Ethernet was known as IEEE 802.3 before being enshrined by ISO and given a different number, while token ring was IEEE 802.5.

NIST (National Institute for Standards and Technology)

Among many activities, NIST promotes OSI functional profiles, such as EWOS in Europe.

COS (Corporation for Open Systems)

This comprises the big US computer and networking companies, and promotes acceptance and conformance testing of OSI standards, as SPAG does in Europe.

Internet Engineering Task Force

This is responsible for developing the TCP/IP protocols.

X/Open

This is a group of vendors and users dedicated to creating and supporting the standards for complete IT environments, of which the network and OSI are just part. X/Open is particularly concerned with resolving differences between existing groups of standards; for example, it has been developing software to bridge TCP/IP and OSI protocols.

ATM Forum

This is the standards body overseeing the overall progress of the ATM protocol and developing specifications that can be implemented as they are ratified by its members. Unlike any other IT standards body, the ATM Forum has drawn members from a wide range of industries including telephony, broadcasting and computer games, all working together to develop the key communications standard for emerging multimedia applications.

A key part of the ATM Forum's work has been in defining the adaptation layer which defines how existing services such as Ethernet and token ring LAN traffic should be carried over ATM networks.

Appendix 11: What is client/server computing?

Client/server computing involves the break-up of an overall application into two, or sometimes more, component tasks. Contrary to popular perception it is not a new idiom, having been used in traditional mainframe applications since the 1960s. The difference now is that it is usually understood to mean cooperation between tasks running on more than one computer. Another change is that client applications are now more likely to be personalized, whereas in the past a large number of users would typically be sharing client software running on the same machine as the server processes. In either case, server tasks are those such as database management that are shared by a number of applications. Client tasks are ones that give an application its unique identity, an example being an electronic diary. In this case the server component might be a database holding details of each employee's appointments, while the client part would comprise software updating the diary and presenting the information to users on their desktop PCs.

Client/server applications, as currently implemented, usually place control fully in the hands of the client component, although the server part might impose certain restrictions such as rights of access to data.

There are various different shades of client/server application which fall loosely into one of three categories: host-driven; desktop-driven; and peer-to-peer (note the similarity with the NOS concept of peer-to-peer).

Host-driven client/server applications are existing host-based systems with a friendly face. The server part of the application is unchanged but the client part has been distributed to desktop PCs which gain access through familiar interfaces. This form of client/server model applies to existing legacy applications where a number of users have similar or identical requirements. The heart of the application still resides on the host system, with the role of PCs restricted to presenting information and providing access to data and services. The task of the NOS here is just to provide a gateway to the host system and control the lower-level communication.

Desktop-driven client/server applications place control firmly with client

PCs. The server component typically manages the data on behalf of client applications, which may be of many different kinds. The server has no control over the shape of the client applications, although it probably will have the ability to control access to the data. The server component may reside on a LAN, or it could be an existing host system relegated from its previous role as application provider. The NOS often has a key role either in controlling the server or liaising with a larger host system acting as a back-end repository of data.

The peer-to-peer model is confusing in that it is often presented as the opposite of client/server computing. The difference is, in fact, that whereas the other two models are based on dedicated servers, this is based on the idea of servers also operating as clients. Indeed, the peer-to-peer model is described in the NOS context in Chapter 3, which looks at low-cost NOSs. The purpose is for a client workstation to act as a file server for other clients.

Much alternative terminology is associated with client/server, such as cooperative processing, down-sizing, right sizing and open systems. These all boil down to the fact that client/server models are designed to allow different computers from a variety of vendors to cooperate on overall applications.

Index

X